I0869468

CREATING *the* SOUTH CAROLINIANA LIBRARY

CREATING *the* SOUTH CAROLINIANA LIBRARY

JOHN M. BRYAN

THE UNIVERSITY OF
SOUTH CAROLINA PRESS

Publication of this book is made possible in part by the University South Caroliniana Society and the University Libraries of the University of South Carolina

Published by the University of South Carolina Press
Columbia, South Carolina 29208
WWW.USCPRESS.COM

Designed by Nathan W. Moehlmann, Goosepen Studio & Press

Manufactured in South Korea

29 28 27 26 25 24 23 22 21 20 10 9 8 7 6 5 4 3 2 1

Library of Congress Cataloging-in-Publication Data
can be found at http://catalog.loc.gov/.

ISBN: 978-1-64336-064-5 (cloth)
ISBN: 978-1-64336-065-2 (ebook)

Frontispiece: Harry Dodge Jenkins,
University of South Carolina Library, watercolor, 1927.

To

Anna Davis King

(1914–2012)

An inspiring librarian

Contents

Foreword

In many ways, the history of the South Caroliniana Library mirrors the history of South Carolina. As John M. Bryan so adeptly demonstrates in this volume, the fortunes of the library at South Carolina College (later the University of South Carolina) follow closely the economic fortunes of the state. From its beginnings it benefited from a booming state economy, which was driven by profits accrued from the cultivation and sale of cash crops made possible by the toil of an enslaved African majority. With its affluence, South Carolina sought to create a state college that would educate the young men of its most prosperous planter families. Remarkably, even during this early period, the college's library accounted for as many volumes as much older and more prestigious institutions in the North.

As the college grew, so did its reputation. That the library's architect, Robert Mills, would for at least the next two centuries be recognized as the Palmetto State's (and one of the nation's) greatest architects, only enhanced the prestige of the college and the library that stood at the center of its intellectual life. This volume thoroughly documents the architectural development of the college's libraries, with special emphasis on Mills's building, which today houses the archival collections of the South Caroliniana Library. Bryan's affinity for, and thorough knowledge of, his subject is evident in the historical architectural drawings and vivid descriptions that detail the substance, look, and feel of the college's libraries.

With the outbreak of the Civil War, South Carolina College and its library, like the state, entered a period of decline. The conflict left South Carolina impoverished, and the state's college suffered the neglect that accompanies any period of financial penury in state government. Reconstruction would introduce, for a brief time, a state university open to any and all South Carolina men regardless of race, but the institution struggled to survive. The end of Reconstruction brought the institution's closure, and the reopening of the college with segregated admission policies did little to reinvigorate the moribund school. The national institutions, with which South Carolina College and its library had briefly competed, outdistanced their former challenger.

Since those decades of prosperity and subsequent penury, the library has remained at the intellectual center of the college's activities. Its twentieth-century growth and the subsequent creation of the South Caroliniana Library followed a common path taken by libraries across the nation, which sought to separate circulating materials from rare manuscript collections that focused on certain topics or geographic locations. The South Caroliniana Library's collections would include papers and volumes related to the state, and it would join the South Carolina Department of Archives and History and the South Carolina Historical Society as one of three great manuscript repositories devoted to telling South Carolina's story.

As external forces had shaped the fortunes of the South Carolina College library during and after the Civil War, they also impacted the University's later efforts to collect South Caroliniana. In 1930 the University of North Carolina established the Southern Historical Collection and appointed J. G. de Roulhac Hamilton as its first director. Hamilton spent decades traveling the South and purchasing manuscript collections, including a significant number of South Carolina letters and diaries. Not to be outdone by their rival, Duke University purchased other valuable South Carolina collections for its rare book and manuscript library. The establishment of the South Caroliniana Library would prove to be an important and urgent countermeasure to these and other efforts to spirit away the state's written and printed treasures.

As it struggled to succeed, and later prospered, the South Caroliniana Library was blessed with professional staff and supporters who would be the envy of institutions nationwide. Bryan's history stands out because he has taken time to personalize the institution's journey by telling the stories of those dedicated individuals who made critical and enduring contributions, from long-serving directors Robert L. Meriwether, Erwin L. Inabinett, Allen H. Stokes Jr., and current director Henry Fulmer, to inspired and dedicated staff members and volunteers. This volume documents the stories of those individuals who played a vital role in ensuring the success of this noteworthy institution.

The long history of the South Caroliniana Library is one of success in the face of substantial obstacles. From its earliest origins among the ranks of the largest academic libraries in the nation, to its current role as the architecturally significant home to the state's largest private manuscript collection dedicated to South Caroliniana, it remains at the center of the University's historical and intellectual endeavors.

W. Eric Emerson

Preface

Libraries provide "the bridge over which civilization travels from century to century and hemisphere to hemisphere."

Francis Lieber, quoted in Patrick Roughen, "Francis Lieber and the South Carolina College Library"

The columns of the South Caroliniana Library evoke a sense of heritage, continuity, and quietude. We think of the building as a local landmark. In reality, however, it is neither quiet nor local. It is a hive of activity, and it becomes more meaningful when we remember outside forces that have influenced every aspect of its evolution.

The Caroliniana building was designed by Robert Mills and built in 1840 as the first freestanding academic library in the United States. It served the college for a century. When the college became a university and, in 1940, built a larger library, the historic Mills building became the home of "Caroliniana"— material related to the history of the state.

Exploring the history of the old library, we encounter the visions and constraints of the nineteenth-century builders. We recall where the college library moved and why. Librarians play cameo roles too: James Divver, an Irish immigrant who landed in New Brunswick, and "his wanderings thence I cannot trace; he came to Newberry . . . with his bundle on a stick, and taught a common country school." He studied "classics" in Newberry and Laurens, entered the junior class at the South Carolina College, and was hired as librarian while still an undergraduate. Another librarian, Erastus Everson, was a Union veteran who ran afoul of the Ku Klux Klan and "carried seven bullets in his body." In 1875, anticipating the end of Reconstruction, Everson slipped away without giving notice. Everson's successor, R. T. Greener, is especially memorable as the first African American graduate of Harvard and the first African American professor at the South Carolina College, and for an eventful career that included a posting as U.S. consul in Vladivostok, Russia. Margaret H. Rion should be remembered too, for around 1906 she started gathering Caroliniana into one of the reading room alcoves as a separate collection.

The 1876 national centennial stimulated interest in American history. Historians at the time were beginning to emphasize the use of original documents, and during the late nineteenth and early twentieth centuries, public and private collections of historical materials grew rapidly. Depression-era federal programs accelerated and codified archival activities, and the development of the Caroliniana Library was part of a nationwide movement to preserve, organize, and use historical documents.

Prof. Robert Lee Meriwether (1890–1958) is remembered as the founding father of the Caroliniana. He envisioned an ongoing effort to gather all types of material related to the history of the state; in 1937 he organized the University South Caroliniana Society, which still actively supports the library.

The South Carolina College received its first manuscript, *The Carolinian Florist,* as a donation from Gov. John Drayton in 1807. Today, in addition to printed items, the Caroliniana contains approximately 7,000 manuscript collections totaling about 11,520,000 pages. These letters, business records, diaries, and the related oral history interviews and photographs are maintained in climate-controlled storage. This material is similar to the miscellaneous family papers and photographs that many of us intend to organize one day. Librarians at the Caroliniana believe this material is important, for the Caroliniana is dedicated to the idea that all history is ultimately personal.

Lulled by the tranquility of the reading room, we are apt to forget the collection is an organic, growing thing. Behind the scenes, staff members are always processing donations and preparing indexes. Others are addressing curatorial problems; repairing, filing, and storing fragile material; maintaining the shelves by checking the location of each item; noting the condition of bindings; "re-housing" (making acid-free wrappings for fragile items); adding bar codes; and helping on-site researchers. The staff also deals with correspondence and telephone requests, makes copies of historic material, copes with logistics (the collection is housed in four locations), maintains websites, digitizes collections, organizes exhibitions, prepares newsletters, and hosts sundry events.

Much of the work is done outside the historic Mills building. The oral historian conducts interviews, the field archivist seeks material, and friends of the library often alert the staff that something meaningful may be available. The Caroliniana Library is a busy place.

Finally architecture, like orchestral music, is a social art, for many people are involved in the creation and use of a building. Thinking about the library and its collections evokes what Lincoln called "the mystic chords of memory" that "swell" and summon "the better angels of our nature."

By putting South Carolinians literally in touch with history, the Caroliniana expands our lives.

Acknowledgments

The affliction lacks a proper name, but a lot of us have it
and most of us are not looking for a cure. It is the passion for libraries.

PAUL DICKSON, *The Library in America*

ANNIVERSARIES PROMPT REFLECTION, and Henry G. Fulmer, director of the Caroliniana, suggested this book as part of the library's 175th birthday celebration. I want to thank him; Kenneth L. Childs, president of the University South Caroliniana Society, and Thomas F. McNally, dean of university libraries at the University of South Carolina, for their support.

Many people contributed to the research and production. Derek Gruner, university architect, analyzed Robert Mills's sketches and prepared drawings to help readers see what Mills envisioned. Yancey R. Modesto, an architect who works with Derek, helped with computer graphics.

Current and former Caroliniana staff made the project a pleasure. Edward Blessing worked with me every day. Mike Berry, Beth Bilderback, Travis Bland, Brian Cuthrell, Todd Hoppock, Craig Keeney, Terry Liscomb, Nathan Saunders, Lorrey Stewart, Linda Stewart, and Don Turner located resources. Andrea L'Hommedieu, the oral historian, provided transcripts of interviews. Elizabeth West, university archivist, retrieved administrative records, and Nicholas Doyle, an undergraduate intern, found pivotal documents in the Meriwether papers. In addition to dealing with questions, Graham Duncan also coordinated the acquisition of illustrations. Conversations with Ron Bridwell, Andrew Chandler, Robin Copp, Fritz Hamer, Rachel Haynie, Jamie Hendrick, Tom Johnson, Charles H. Lesser, David Rembert, Patrick Scott, Allen Stokes, Harvey Teal, and Robert Wynn were always productive.

In preparation for the restoration of the Caroliniana, many records have been moved to the Thomas Cooper Library. I am grateful to the Thomas Cooper staff; their contributions appear on almost every page. Joseph Askins, Marilee Birchfield, Kate Boyd, Karen Brown, Alexandra Trim, Timothy Simmons, Elizabeth Sudduth, William E. Sudduth III, Sharon Verba, Stacy Winchester, and the computer magicians Lance Dupre and Randy Heard — all of them helped.

Whitman Page and Elaine E. Sandberg, reference librarians at the State Library, often helped me find things.

Beyond the libraries, Christian Cicimurri, curator of collections at the university's McKissick Museum, took me behind the scenes to see Thomas Cooper's collection of minerals, fossils, and handwritten labels; Stephen Tuttle and

Marion Chandler, South Carolina Department of Archives and History, made state records accessible. Douglas Evelyn, former Smithsonian Institution administrator and director of the *Papers of Robert Mills* project, was, as always, helpful; Skip Moskey of Washington, D.C., author and historian, located the 1837 advertisement for the library building, and Robert Stockton, a distinguished Charleston historian, made the Caroliniana–Towell Library connection. I would also like to thank Pat Callahan, editorial, design, and production director, and her colleagues at the University of South Carolina Press.

I am especially grateful to two friends: Hunter Clarkson, who made many of the new images, and Lynn Barron for proofreading the draft.

CHAPTER ONE

The COLLEGE LIBRARY *before the* LIBRARY BUILDING

A written word is the choicest of relics. It is something at once more intimate with us and more universal than any other work of art. It is the work of art nearest to life itself. It may be translated into every language, and not only be read but actually breathed from all human lips; — not be represented on canvas or in marble only, but be carved out of the breath of life itself.

HENRY DAVID THOREAU, *Walden*

JOHN DRAYTON (1766–1822) DONATED his illustrated, handwritten copy of *The Carolinian Florist* to the South Carolina College in 1807. As the first manuscript acquired by the college, it is the cornerstone of the current collection of more than 11.5 million sheets.

The Florist's skillfully rendered illustrations, Latin taxonomy, and references to European botanical literature suggest its author never knew turmoil, that he lived a life of leisure. This is not the case. His mother died when he was four years old, and his father, William Henry Drayton, died when young John was eleven. His father's brother, Charles Drayton, controlled the Drayton patrimony and effectively disinherited John and his younger sister, Mary. As a young man, John studied in England and France. He returned to Charleston, read law with Charles Cotesworth Pinckney, and sued his uncle Charles. John Drayton claimed his grandfather's will had been misconstrued. He lost the first lawsuit but sued again and won. He did not win Drayton Hall, the ancestral seat, but the financial settlement made him financially secure and enabled him to enter politics.[1]

Rutledge College, circa 1875. All illustrations courtesy of the Caroliniana Library unless otherwise noted.

As governor, John Drayton approved the act creating the South Carolina College on December 19, 1801. When the new college opened three years later, on January 10, 1805, with nine students, two faculty members, and one building, the library was on the second floor above the chapel in Rutledge College. Rutledge resembled Nassau Hall at the College of New Jersey (now Princeton), where most of the South Carolina College trustees had been students. They lived in the wings of Nassau Hall and used its library, "a spacious room" on the second floor, for it was "the usual practice" in the early decades of the nineteenth century to locate the library on the second floor of a three- or four-story multipurpose building. In addition to New Jersey and South Carolina, "this was done at Yale in 1763, Bowdoin in 1805, Wesleyan in 1824, and Brown in 1835."[2] The structural reason for this arrangement was that "these rooms were about the same size and served all of the college community."[3]

The South Carolina College was just getting underway when Edward Hooker, a young tutor from Connecticut, mentioned its library in his diary:

> The central parts [of Rutledge] are designed for the Chapel, Library, Philosophical Chamber, Recitation rooms, etc. — the wings are designed for scholars' mansion rooms. . . . The chapel occupies the two lower stories of the central building . . . and is in a beautiful style of workmanship both within and without. The Library room above is supported by four stately Tuscan columns, which

A North-West Prospect of Nassau Hall, engraving by William Tenant, circa 1764. Library of Congress.

> rise from the area of the chapel with considerable majesty, and give to the room an appearance of grandeur. The galleries are supported by a row of smaller pillars. The room is nearly or quite square.[4]

The library in Rutledge must have been a "spacious room," for when it was moved in 1817, the trustees noted the space could be remodeled to provide accommodations for ten students.[5]

The interior of Rutledge College burned in 1855, and nothing remains of the original library room or the four "stately Tuscan columns." The mixture of candles, oil lamps, fireplaces, wooden frame construction, and undergraduates made fire an ever-present danger on early American campuses. Libraries in multipurpose buildings—like Rutledge—burned at William and Mary in 1705 and 1859; the same thing happened at Harvard in 1764. Princeton's Nassau Hall was destroyed by fire in 1802 and again in 1859.[6]

Because of this danger, antebellum regulations at South Carolina College stipulated that "students are particularly enjoined to be careful about fire, especially when they are obliged to leave their rooms, or to carry it through the entries, or up the staircases, and shall be liable for all injuries done to their rooms by negligence."[7] Fear of fire would be a factor in the decision to build a free-standing library in which the librarian was "never to carry or suffer to be carried, into the Library, a lighted lamp or candle, except in cases of necessity."[8] Despite the loss of the original room (the space

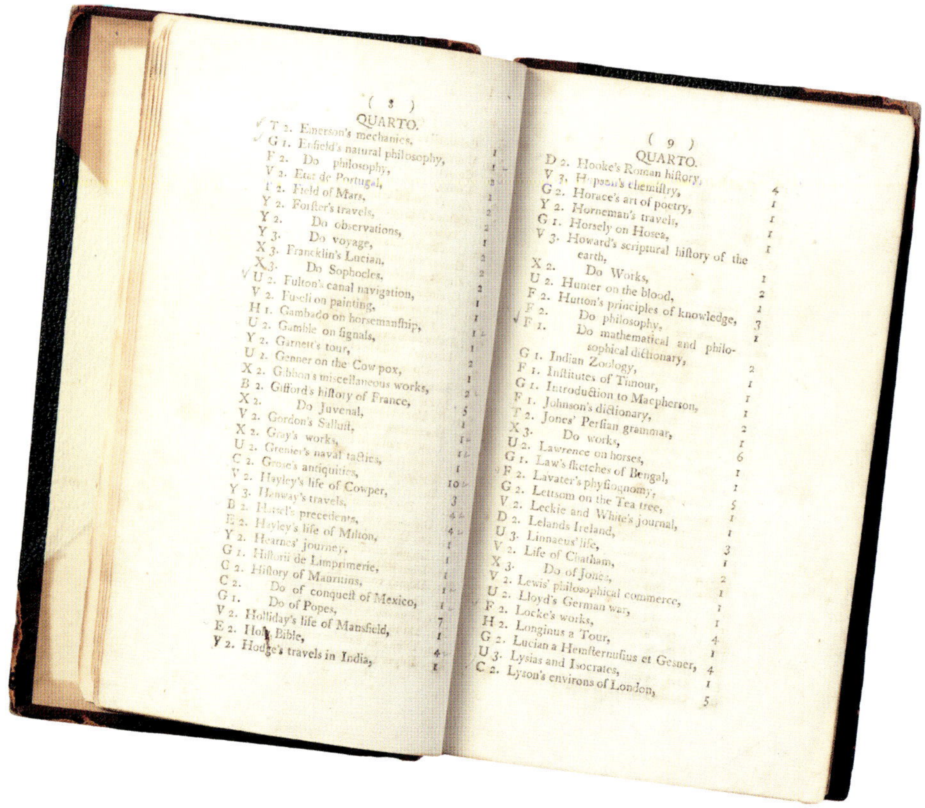

LEFT: South Carolina College Library catalog cover, 1807.
ABOVE: South Carolina College Library catalog, 1807.

was renovated a second time, circa 1918–1920, by George E. Lafaye, architect), various bits of information suggest what the first library in Rutledge was like.

The earliest catalog (1807) implies that the collection was organized by the size of the volumes, for the catalog is divided into four sections. The largest books are listed first under the heading "Folio"; there were 100 of these. Listed after the folios are 559 "Quarto" books, then 1,301 "Octavo" books and 183 "Duodecimo" books.[9] Within each division the titles and authors' names are abridged and arranged alphabetically. In addition each item is preceded by a single capital letter, which may refer to a specific shelf: thus students consulting the catalog would find under Duodecimo, "F.6 Crabb's *German grammar*"; under Octavo, "W.1 Adams' *Micrographia illustrata*"; and under Quarto, "G.1 Chandler's *History of the Inquisition.*"

Volumes from the early nineteenth-century South Carolina College Library. Irvin Department of Rare Books and Special Collections, University of South Carolina.

RIGHT: Elisha Hammond, silhouette photographed by H. C. Hall, Augusta, Georgia, circa 1900.

The first college librarian, Elisha Hammond (1774–1829), probably prepared the first catalog. He was born in Massachusetts, graduated from Dartmouth, and came south as a teacher. For several years Hammond was principal of the Mount Bethel Academy in Newberry County. He taught language and worked as librarian at the new college (1806–7) before returning to the Mount Bethel Academy.[10]

The initial selection of books was based upon recommendations made by the trustees, faculty, and various vendors. Miscellaneous, undated, loose receipts and lists of books show that during the early nineteenth century, the college librarian corresponded with book dealers in Charleston and Philadelphia; with Wiley and Putnam of New York and London; Charles de Behr, "Foreign and Classical Bookstore," also based in New York; Henry Stephens in London; and A. Vattemare, a European bookseller. Traveling faculty, including professors Henry J. Nott and Stephen Elliott, also bought books for the library.[11]

By mid-century an acquisition procedure had evolved and was codified: the faculty, trustees, and "literary visitors" recommended books to buy; the librarian submitted these

requests to the Trustees' Library Committee; and the committee returned approved requests to the librarian, who corresponded with vendors. The librarian typically also served as college treasurer and charged the costs of books either to specific departments or to the general fund.

Hammond, the librarian, labeled John Adolphus's *History of England,* published in London in 1802, as "S. Carolina College Library. No 1."[12] Its presence in the collection today is a testament to more than two centuries of stewardship. In addition to purchases, gifts have always enhanced the collection, and it is historically fitting that Gov. Drayton, who initiated the creation of the college, also made the earliest significant donation.

In 1807 he gave the new college his book-length manuscript, *The Carolinian Florist.* Like many manuscripts it offers multiple layers of meaning. First and foremost, it is a survey of plants in South Carolina: Drayton lists Latin and common names for more than a thousand species and often includes notes about blooms, seeds, habitat, and usefulness. Beyond its specific factual content, *The Florist* exemplifies the fascination with all aspects of natural history in the early Republic. Drayton knew his work was part of a larger whole, and he often refers to the work of other botanists—John Bartram, Benjamin Barton, Andre Michaux, and Thomas

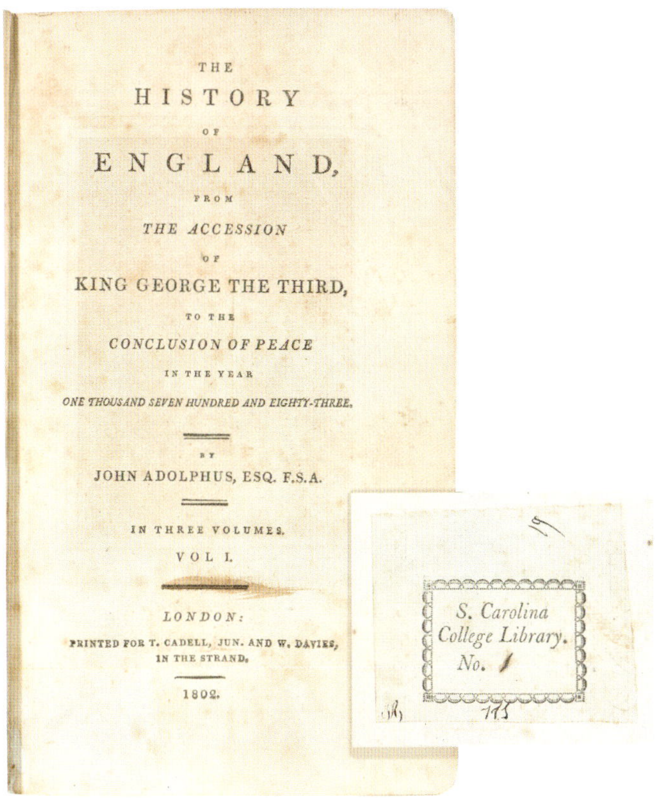

South Carolina College Library book no. 1: John Adolphus, *The History of England* (London: T. Cadell & W. Davies, 1802). Irvin Department of Rare Books and Special Collections.

Walter. At a personal level, the manuscript relates something about its author, his education and travel, his aspirations and aesthetic sensibility.

When he gave *The Florist,* Drayton wrote the trustees that botany was already "studied in some of our Colleges." He continued: "Come then, let us sometimes unbend the mind from more serious pursuits; and enjoy this calm, this delightful recreation. On the harmony of nature, its system is erected; its pursuits are mild; its discoveries pleasing. All of them tending to chase away enmities. To lead by calm reflection to that happy temper of mind, which makes even adversity not fearful, and which, when fortune favours, adds much to the pleasures we enjoy."[13]

Drayton's donation of *The Florist* was not a one-time gesture. His continued support of and vision for the college is manifest by subsequent donations of both classical and contemporary literature.[14]

The first set of rules, from 1807, helps scholars imagine how the library worked.

Of the Library

1. The Librarian shall give to the trustees of the College, a bond, with such security as they shall deem necessary, for the faithful performance of his trust.
2. No books shall be taken from the library, except buy [*sic*] the following persons, without special permission from the trustees, viz. the members of the senate and house of representatives, the trustees of the College, all such persons as have made a donation of the value of one hundred dollars to the library; the officers of instruction, resident graduates, and all the students.
3. The librarian shall open the library every Friday and Saturday, at such hours as the President shall direct, and

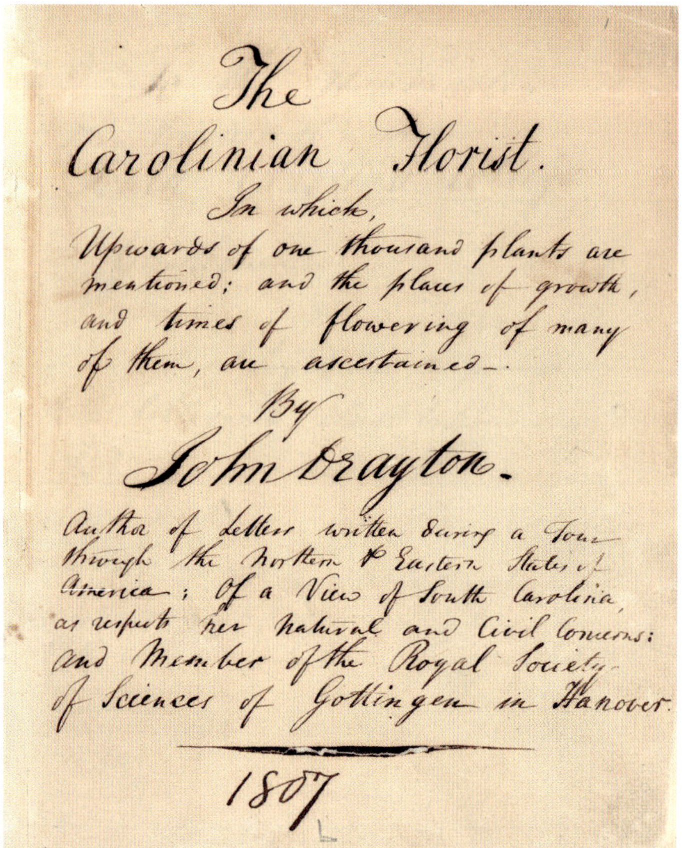
The Carolinian Florist.
In which,
Upwards of one thousand plants are mentioned; and the places of growth, and times of flowering of many of them, are ascertained—
By
John Drayton.
Author of Letters written during a Tour through the Northern & Eastern States of America; Of a View of South Carolina, as respects her natural and Civil Concerns: and Member of the Royal Society of Sciences of Gottingen in Hanover.
1807

John Drayton, *The Carolinian Florist,* 1807.

BELOW: *Amorpha fruticose.* John Drayton, *The Carolinian Florist,* plate 1.10.

shall deliver and receive books, agreeably to the following conditions and regulations:

4. The students shall come to the library in their respective classes, when sent for by the librarian; and no one shall enter the library beyond the librarian's table.
5. No book shall be taken from the library, until the student to whom it is delivered, shall have signed a receipt, specifying the number, size and title of the book; and this receipt shall be written by the librarian, in a book kept by him for that purpose.
6. No book shall be taken from the library, until it shall have been covered by the librarian with clean thick paper; and all the students are required to return the books to the library in the same good condition in which they were taken from it.
7. If any book taken from the library be lost or damaged, the delinquent shall replace it by a new one of equal value, within three months. If it be not replaced within that time, the librarian shall lodge an account with the treasurer of the College, against said delinquent, of double the price

of the said book, or set, if it belong to one; which account shall be charged in his next bill of tuition, and the money shall be applied to the use of the library.

8. No student shall be allowed, without special liberty from the President of the College, to take out or have in his possession at one time, more than one folio, which he may keep four weeks, or one quarto, which he may keep three weeks, or one octavo, which he may keep two weeks, or two duodecimos, which he may keep one week. Students who shall neglect to return books at the time required by the law, shall be liable to have their privilege of the use of the library suspended, at the discretion of the librarian.
9. No student shall lend to any person, or suffer to be carried from his room, any book belonging to the library, on penalty of a severe reprimand from the librarian; and if the offence be repeated, such student shall be denied access to the library.
10. The students are all required to observe the strictest decorum while receiving books from the library. Any student who shall violate this law, shall be deprived of the use of the library for one month.
11. All persons permitted to take books from the library, shall sign receipts for the same; and return them at such times as the trustees shall order.
12. No person shall be allowed to carry any book belonging to the library, out of the town of Columbia.
13. The librarian is strictly enjoined, never to carry or suffer to be carried into the library, a lighted lamp or candle, except in cases of necessity.
14. It shall be the duty of the librarian to keep the library neat and clean; and to see that all books taken from the library are returned, at least, three days before the vacation and before the commencement.
15. The librarian shall not lend the key to the library to any person, except a trustee of the College or one of the Faculty; nor shall he permit any student, in time of vacation, to take any books from the library, unless such student constantly resides in the College, and pursues his studies there.
16. Every student belonging to the College, shall pay to the treasurer of the College two dollars per year, to be charged in the bills of tuition, and to be appropriated to the use of the library.[15]

Until the middle of the nineteenth century, most college libraries were only open several hours each week, "principally for the withdrawal of books. Consultation of materials within the library was virtually forbidden, if not by statute, by lack of space, the lack of tables and chairs, and, in winter, the lack of heat."[16] For example, in 1850 the Bowdoin library was open for one hour three times a week; Middlebury, one hour per week; Brown, 10 A.M. until 2 P.M. each day; Yale, five hours daily; Columbia, twice a week from 1 to 3 P.M.; and Princeton, one hour twice a week.

The South Carolina College library had typically limited hours in the beginning, but by mid-century it was more accessible than its peers. The amended college bylaws of 1849 stipulated that the library must be open every day (except Sundays, Christmas, and the Fourth of July) from October 1 until July 15, accessible "such hours as the Library Committee shall appoint."[17] And in 1853 *Norton's Literary Gazette* described the South Carolina College library and noted that "during term the library is open every secular day from 9 A.M. to 10 o'clock P.M. During vacation, it is open every Wednesday, from 9 o'clock A.M. to 12 P.M."[18] Daily library hours in the mid-nineteenth century made South Carolina College exceptional.

It is worth remembering that the early library rules were no more restrictive than regulations that governed other aspects of undergraduate life; students who used the early South Carolina College library were compelled to "convene at sunrise in the morning, in the College chapel, to attend prayers; from thence they shall retire, either to attend recitations, or to pursue their studies, until they are summoned to breakfast; at nine o'clock, they shall return to their studies, and continue in their rooms until twelve, unless summoned to recitation; between twelve and two, they shall repair to dinner, when summoned; and at two, return to their rooms, and continue at study until five, unless summoned to recitation; at five o'clock they shall attend prayers in the chapel and be dismissed." Following afternoon chapel, at around 5:30, students were free until they "shall all return to their rooms at the ringing of the bell at seven O'clock in the evening, and continue at study until half an hour after nine o'clock, and shall retire to bed by ten o'clock."[19] The bylaws do not mention an evening meal, but they required students to eat in the Commons, each class sitting together in alphabetical order.[20]

In addition to being notable for its daily library hours, "the University of South Carolina was virtually unique in having the regular support of the state legislature. Before the institution opened its doors in 1805, the state legislature permitted the expenditure for books and apparatus of funds earlier allocated for salaries of the faculty. . . . About three thousand dollars was spent for library material before the college opened its doors."[21]

The initial appropriation for the new college provided $6,000 for the purchase of philosophical apparatus and of books for the formation of a library. Before the college opened in 1805, the legislature approved two more appropriations for the library, and beginning in 1813 the trustees designated the surplus of the tuition fund as a library acquisition fund, which during the period 1813–1845 amounted to $23,757. In addition to the tuition surplus, the library received another $5,000 from the General Assembly in 1823 and a similar appropriation in 1825. In 1838 legislation authorized an annual appropriation of $2,000 for the library, and in 1845 the comptroller general of the state reported that appropriations for the college library (1801–45) totaled $27,000. An historian of the college estimates the library received a total of approximately $90,000 from the state, the tuition fund, and other sources prior to 1853.[22]

The financial commitment to the collection did not extend to librarians' salaries. Library science did not exist as a profession in the early nineteenth century, and college librarians in antebellum South Carolina were typically younger faculty members who worked as librarians part time for a stipend of one hundred dollars per year.

James Divver (d. 1847), the librarian in 1823, serves as an example. An Irish immigrant, he landed in New Brunswick and "came to Newberry district in 1819, with his bundle on a stick, and taught a common country school until the fall of 1820." After studying "classics" in Newberry and Laurens, he entered the junior class at the South Carolina College. Divver was apparently hired as librarian before graduating in December 1824. He served briefly as college treasurer and as a tutor of mathematics, but "an unfortunate habit, too much indulged in, of using intoxicating drink, made it necessary for him to resign."[23]

Divver did not work in Rutledge, for in 1817 the library moved into a new, two-story Library and Science Building. (It never had another name.) The faculty apparently designed it, and their original plan called for an observatory on the roof. The Library and Science Building was built by Zachariah

South Carolina College, gouache circa 1820, by T. Uhlor.

Phillips at a cost of around $7,800. It was demolished in 1848, but a painting, a sketch, and the trustees' minutes make it possible to visualize this second home of the South Carolina College library.

The Library and Science Building was a red brick rectangular (seventy by fifty feet) structure with a hipped roof. The Uhlor painting suggests its facade facing the Horseshoe had a white belt course and panels above the first-floor windows. A sketch of the interior floor plans shows that in order to enter, one walked up a short flight of steps, for the first floor was elevated four feet above the ground. A central entry led into a hall, ten feet wide, running front to back on both floors. This hall must have contained the staircase. Standing inside the entry, visitors became aware of—and often smelled—Prof. Edward D. Smith's chemistry laboratory that occupied the left (east) side of the first floor. The library was on the second floor, directly above the laboratory; both rooms were approximately thirty by fifty feet, and both were well lighted, for they had windows on three sides. Shelving from Rutledge College was reinstalled in the new library room, and the shelves must have been tall, for in 1835, considering remodeling, trustees suggested "that all of the upper apartments of this edifice be thrown into one large Library room so that a more convenient arrangement of the books may be made. As it stands, most of the books are entirely out of reach without laborious climbing. But until the exact balance in their hands is understood,

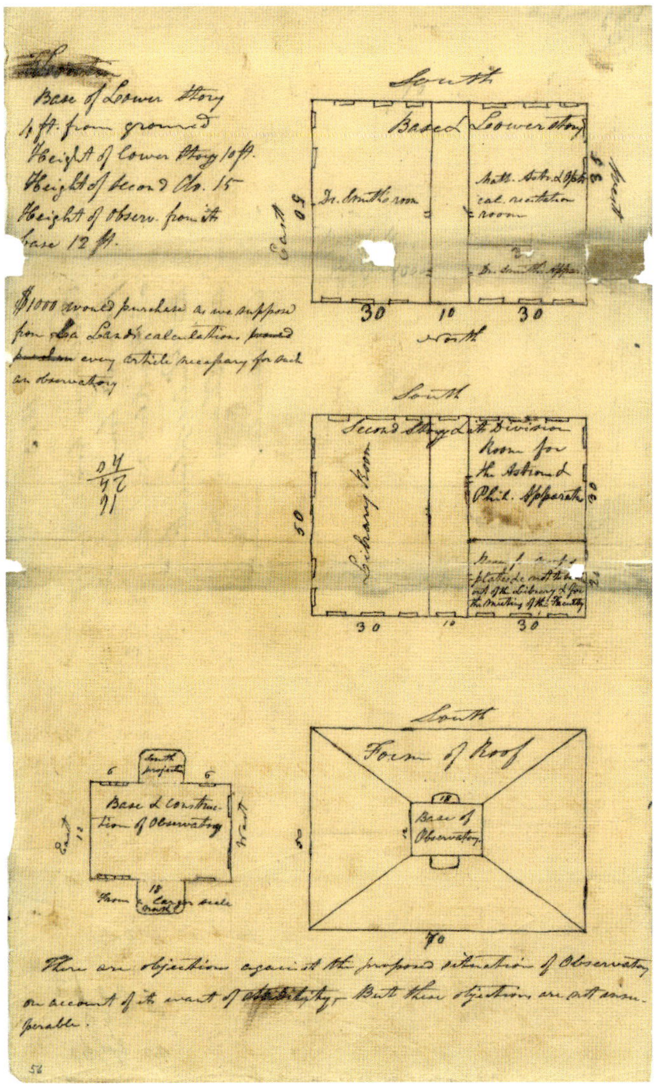

Library and Science Building of the South Carolina College, drawn by professors Christian Hanckel and Edward Darrell Smith, 1815. South Carolina Department of Archives and History.

they have not thought it prudent to make this alteration."[24] Nothing was done about remodeling or the shelves, and the library remained above the laboratory for the next twenty-three years.

Thomas Park, professor of languages, was serving as librarian in 1817. He supervised the move into the new building, and it must have been stressful, for at the end of the year, "upon hearing that his conduct as librarian was the subject of criticism at the State House and among the trustees he wrote them an indignant letter in which he resigned his position and informed the board that he had been serving as librarian for years at the miserable salary of $100 per year, and that the position gave him much responsibility and no authority, since each trustee had a key to the library." He had also received less salary than other professors for a considerable length of time, and his wife and children were in straitened circumstances: "I have had but one servant about my house this year and my family have taken in washing to prevent our expenses from exceeding our income."[25] As a result of Park's complaint, the librarian's stipend was increased to four hundred dollars per year. In 1847 it was increased to six hundred dollars.[26]

The Library and Science Building was still new when Johnathan Maxcy (1768–1820), the first president of the college, died. The college had flourished under his benign guidance. In 1820, 110 students were enrolled; to accommodate them, on either side of what would become the Horseshoe, buildings reflected this initial burst of growth. Opposite Rutledge, another Nassau Hall–type, multipurpose building, now DeSaussure College, had been completed in 1809. Two wells provided water. Students ate (presumably sitting in alphabetical order) in the new brick Steward's Hall. There was a house for the president, and two duplexes for married faculty. The Library and Science Building and the observatory — the latter was located behind the north range of the Horseshoe — were the final buildings constructed during Maxcy's administration.

The second president, Thomas Cooper (1759–1839), was unlike Maxcy in many ways. Maxcy had been an eloquent Baptist minister, trusted by parents, honored by the trustees, and respected by students. He was a genial, effective leader and was apparently content to watch the college grow. Cooper, on the other hand, was an atheist, intellectually restless, outspoken, and argumentative. He was sixty-one years old when he arrived in 1819, just months before Maxcy's death. Cooper had corresponded with Thomas Jefferson, James Madison, and Joseph Priestley, had published widely, and was the most distinguished faculty member when the first president died. The trustees asked him to serve as president pro tempore (1821), and the following year — by a vote of 10 to 9 — they offered him the presidency.

Thomas Cooper. Portrait by James DeVeaux, circa 1830.

Born in England, Cooper attended University College, Oxford, and studied chemistry but left without a degree, for he apparently refused to pledge fealty to the Church of England. His interest in the new science of geology led him to develop a notable collection of minerals and fossils and bolstered his argument against the biblical story of creation. He became involved in radical politics and supported the French Revolution before immigrating to America in 1794. In 1799 he was jailed under the Sedition Act for libel against President John Adams and, after being released, served briefly as a judge in Pennsylvania but was charged with "arbitrary conduct" and forced to resign. He then taught chemistry and political economy at Dickinson College (1811–14) and the University of Pennsylvania (1818–19). He hoped to obtain a position at the University of Virginia, but nothing materialized, so he accepted a one-year appointment as professor at the South Carolina College.

Thomas Cooper was controversial, and the earliest history of the college presents a thoughtful analysis of his strengths and weaknesses as a president.

> His understanding was strong and vigorous. . . . He had in largest measure the element of independence. . . . His style was bold, sententious, dogmatic, but clear, simple,

> and perspicuous. . . . Never, perhaps was there a better lecturer, a finer teacher. He had the enviable gift of telling well and impressively all that he knew. . . . With wonderful art he could weave a dinner with Priestley, a glass of wine with Robespierre, a supper with the Brissotians, or a race for the Convention against the Duke of Orleans into a lecture upon asbestos, soda, or magnesia. His reading and intercourse with men had furnished him with a fund of anecdote, and this he dealt out on all proper occasions with the best effect.

Or again: "His industry and enthusiasm were unsurpassed." Cooper modernized the curriculum. LaBorde praises him as a teacher and adds that "had he been content with a Professorship, he might have reposed in peace and quiet. In an evil hour he accepted the Presidency, and then his troubles began."[27]

Cooper had no interest in prudence or diplomacy. "No man was more tenacious, dogmatic, or had a bolder and more uncompromising spirit. . . . His life had been spent amid storms and tempests, and the howling of the wind and the muttering sound of the thunder were music to his ears. He could not sit still; he must plunge into the chaos and confusion. . . . He was a partisan with more than usual bitterness."

Cooper's interest in politics drew him into the debate about states' rights. As the nullification movement began gaining momentum, he declared in 1827 that "it is time to calculate the value of the Union." Northern newspapers pilloried him for broaching the subject of secession, but within the state this particular controversy enhanced his reputation, and it did not harm the college. Perhaps it is telling that in the 1849 *Library Catalogue* "Cooper's (Thos.) *Political Economy*. 1 vol. 8 vo" is listed immediately above *Copley's History of Slavery,* for in the decades prior to the Civil War, Cooper and his colleagues did much to provide and promote the rationale for secession, and beginning in the 1830s, outmigration of alumni carried their influence far beyond the borders of the state.[28]

Cooper's outspoken atheism was another matter. He was among the first American academicians to lecture about the new science of geology. He began collecting fossils and minerals as a young man in England and continued to collect when he came to America. Geology, he believed, proved that

Ichthyosaurus fossil. Thomas Cooper Collection, McKissick Museum of the University of South Carolina.

Coal. Thomas Cooper Collection, McKissick Museum.

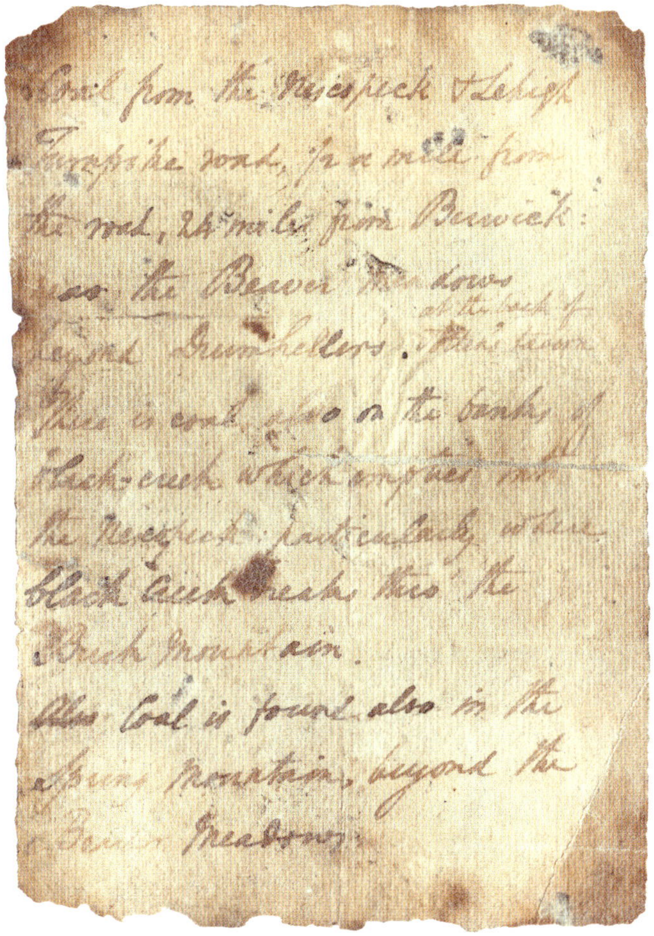

Coal from the Nescopeck & Lehigh
Turnpike road, 1/2 a mile from
the road, 24 miles from Berwick:
near the Beaver Meadows
beyond Drumhellers. at the back of [illegible]
There is coal also on the banks of
Black-creek which empties into
the Nescopeck particularly where
black creek breaks thro' the
Buck mountain.
Also Coal is found also in the
Spring mountain, beyond the
Beaver Meadows.

Coal label by Thomas Cooper. McKissick Museum.

the biblical account of creation was erroneous, and clergy throughout the state concluded he was "a dangerous heretic who was exerting an insidious and pernicious influence upon the minds of impressionable youth." Editorials castigated him throughout the 1820s, and in 1831 a legislative committee held hearings. Cooper's articulate, unapologetic defense saved his job temporarily, but his success enraged his critics. For two more years the trustees tried to tamp down the controversy, but public opinion continued to build against Cooper and, by association, the college.[29]

Enrollments declined. "The impact of the opposition Cooper had aroused began to be felt in 1833, when only eighty-six students enrolled, and in 1834 this number declined to fifty-two." Cooper resigned as president on November 27, 1833, but he was retained as a lecturer of chemistry. This demotion did not mollify his critics, and when "enrollment dropped to the pitiful total of twenty in the late fall of 1834 it became evident to all that a thorough reorganization was necessary." Reluctantly, the trustees requested and received the resignations of Cooper and, for good measure, the entire faculty on December 9, 1834.[30]

Many people admired Cooper's intellectual integrity; consequently, when he was forced to leave the college, he was hired by the legislature to collate and publish the laws of South Carolina, a task that occupied him until his death.

During the turbulent end of Cooper's administration, Edward W. Johnston was the librarian (c. 1834–35), and he prepared the second library catalog. Johnston printed it privately in 1836, for, perhaps caught in the wake of Cooper's troubles, he left the college and moved to Virginia. His catalog shows the collection had been reorganized and now included approximately four thousand books.

Thomas Cooper, lithograph by E. B. and E. C. Kellogg after William H. Brown, 1845.

In the catalog "Explanation," Johnston writes, "the arrangement adopted in the following catalogue, is that of the Baconian system of knowledge: the books . . . are placed in three great classes—of Memory, of Judgment, or of Imagination."[31] Johnston's 1836 South Carolina College catalog was prepared while the library was located in the Library and Science Building, so the "Baconian" organization was in use before the freestanding library was built.

Memory, as a category, meant topics related to history, biography, natural history; judgment included philosophy, metaphysics, ethics, mathematics, and theology; and imagination referred to the verbal and visual arts. Within each of the three major headings, the books are grouped under subheadings, again reflecting the "Baconian" system; for example, under the subheading "Greek Poets and their Translators," some sixty volumes are arranged alphabetically by author. Entries are more descriptive than those in the 1807 catalog: for example, "Dionysius Cato. *Disticha—Graeco-Latine, ab Arntzenio,* 8 vo, Amsterdam, 1754."

In closing Johnston laments that

> the calls of absolute necessity compelled the Librarian to determine to seek his literary fortunes elsewhere. . . . The entire contents of a large Library, most inconveniently arranged, were "cum multo pulvere, sed exign lucro," to be taken down, from very lofty shelves, to be catalogued, and to be replaced, by his own hands alone. The absence of many volumes from the collection, in hands from which they were vainly attempted to be recalled, and the continual flux and reflux incident to a Library in active use, rendered omissions inevitable, and led to the necessity of describing many tomes, their dates and contents, from memory alone. Almost the entire publication has been printed, too, while he was absent from Carolina. Bedford County, Virginia, July, 1836.[32]

The little that is known about Edward William Johnston is interesting. On September 25, 1836, shortly after leaving the college, he wrote to Langdon Cheves Jr. They must have fished together, for Johnston was effusive about

> a four-days expedition, on foot, with but a single companion, into the wildest recesses of the Virginia mountains! How you will glow, when I tell you of the 53 speckled trout caught in a day! How you will turn pale with envy, to hear how we climbed untrodden hills and plunged thro' torrents never visited before! And then, the scenery!—whatever, of picturesque, black forests and gigantic mountains and vast rocks, and wild clear streams falling into continual cascades, can offer by their most fantastic combination. My forte is certainly spirited description and stirring narrative: but, upon an occasion, like the present, where, if I shine, I am sure to make a friend unhappy, I know how to forbear.[33]

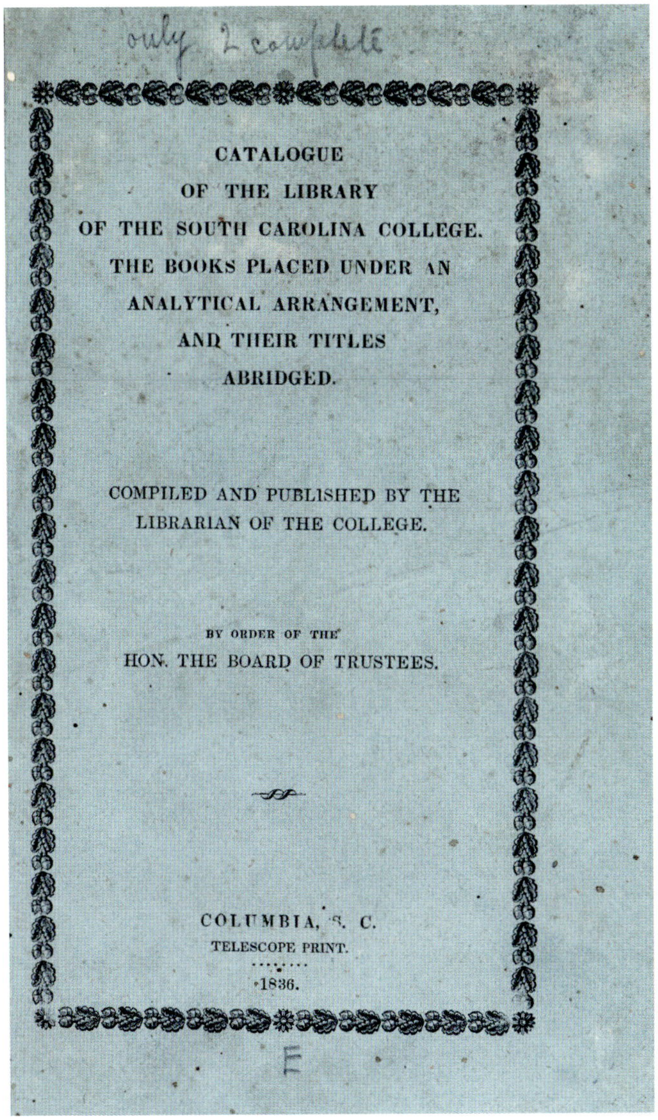

CATALOGUE
OF THE LIBRARY
OF THE SOUTH CAROLINA COLLEGE.
THE BOOKS PLACED UNDER AN
ANALYTICAL ARRANGEMENT,
AND THEIR TITLES
ABRIDGED.

COMPILED AND PUBLISHED BY THE
LIBRARIAN OF THE COLLEGE.

BY ORDER OF THE
HON. THE BOARD OF TRUSTEES.

COLUMBIA, S. C.
TELESCOPE PRINT.
1836.

South Carolina College catalog cover, 1836.

After describing the fishing trip, the librarian-sportsman outlined a plan to revive a defunct journal, the *Southern Review,* and wondered if Cheves could help him. He also noted, but did not describe, the possibility of a job in Washington, and said he had begun a biography of "Henry."[34] Apparently none of these projects came to fruition, for no trace has been found of Johnston for the next twenty-two years, but in 1858 he was hired to prepare a catalog for the St. Louis Mercantile Library, and the following year he became the Mercantile Library's librarian. He had to resign in 1862, for he refused to take an oath of allegiance to the Union.[35]

Architecturally speaking, Cooper's administration was a period of stasis and decline.[36] The only architectural evidence of his presidency is the substantial brick wall around much of the old campus. He suggested the wall to the trustees in 1832, ostensibly to constrain obstreperous undergraduates.

Cooper was embattled when the wall was built; consequently it evokes his futile attempt to fend off his critics, to keep the outside world at bay.

As enrollment leveled off and then declined, there was no need for new buildings. Maintenance was neglected too, and this set the stage for Cooper's successor, Robert Woodward Barnwell (1801–82). Barnwell's brief presidency, from December 1835 until November 1841, opened with a burst of growth and construction that would not be equaled for 120 years.[37]

On December 8, 1836, Barnwell's first formal, annual trustees' meeting, the Committee on Repairs reported that they "are entirely of the opinion that the present building used as a library is unfit for that purpose. Besides the imminent danger which must be daily incurred in having the chemical Laboratory, the Library and mechanical and Philosophical apparatus in the same house, the present building is entirely out of repair, the sleepers and partitions in the lower part of the house being entirely decayed and ready to fall, the roof leaks and the floors are rotten. The committee recommend that a new building, entirely separate from the other buildings be erected for the use of the library."[38]

Nothing was done about a new library building, but the issue was now on the agenda, and two years later Barnwell, joined by Stephen Elliott and D. J. McCord, addressed the trustees again. Their 1838 recommendation prompted the creation of the new building:

> as it seems to be the desire of the State to build up at this point an institution of learning that shall render her independent of other states in the education of her sons and in the maintenance of a literary character, it is necessary that an extensive Library should be created to which men of letters may resort with the certainty of finding whatever books their researches might require. Our library cannot at present answer this demand, for although it is a good one, as far as it goes and the books very choice and valuable, yet is it sadly deficient in almost every department of science or literature. It is impossible to pursue any branch of study thoroughly without having recourse to other collections, involving great inconvenience and expense. Rich intelligent and liberal as the state of South Carolina is, she ought not to remain another day without adopting some method of remedying this deficiency in the library of the college with the stock of books already in her possession, and annual appropriation of $3,000 by the legislature for the regular and systematic increase of the library added to the balances of the tuition fund as they may annually accrue would in a very few years, with an expenditure that would not be felt, give us a library amply sufficient for all the requirements of learning. Such an enlargement of the library would also act beneficially upon the college, as it would give her very soon, a pre-eminence over the collegiate institutions of our neighboring states and attract to her walls students from every quarter of the southern country. Your committee would therefore pray your Honorable Body to recommend to the Legislature such an annual appropriation and to request permission to add to it the balance of the tuition fund for the systematic increase of the library. . . .
>
> All of which is respectfully submitted
>
> R.W. Barnwell, ch. Stephen Elliott, Jr. D. J. McCord.[39]

The new library building was President Barnwell's crowning achievement. It is concrete evidence of the antebellum trustees' ambition for the college.

CHAPTER TWO

ROBERT MILLS *and the* COLLEGE LIBRARY

The greatest glory of a building is not in its stones, nor in its gold. Its glory is in its Age, and in that deep sense of voicefulness, of stern watching, of mysterious sympathy, nay, even of approval or condemnation, which we feel in its walls that have long been washed by the passing waves of humanity.

John Ruskin, *The Seven Lamps of Architecture*

To understand the creation of the college library building (c. 1837–40), it should be placed in the context of Robert Mills's career and his relationships with the college president, Robert Woodward Barnwell, and Gov. George McDuffie (1790–1851).

Prior to the library, Mills was involved in two projects for the college. In 1802 he submitted a proposal in the competition for the initial college building. He split the $350 prize with a "Mr. Clark," and this was the first time he was paid for architectural work. Twenty-five years later he designed the Maxcy Monument, a memorial to Jonathan Maxcy, first president of the college. This relatively small obelisk is notable as his earliest complex use of the Egyptian Revival style that he later used for the colossal Washington National Monument.[1]

The new library was his final work on campus. When it opened in the fall of 1840, it was the first freestanding academic library in the United States, and its reading room was an architecturally distinguished replica of the Library of Congress.[2] The library was Mills's last work in South Carolina, his native state.

Mills was born in Charleston on August 12, 1781, during the Revolution. Shortly after the war ended, a neighbor, James Hoban, won a design competition for the new President's Palace. Hoban moved to Washington. Mills followed and worked for him as an apprentice draftsman. There he met Thomas Jefferson, who encouraged him and furthered his education by allowing him to study architectural books and drawings. Jefferson also provided a letter of introduction to

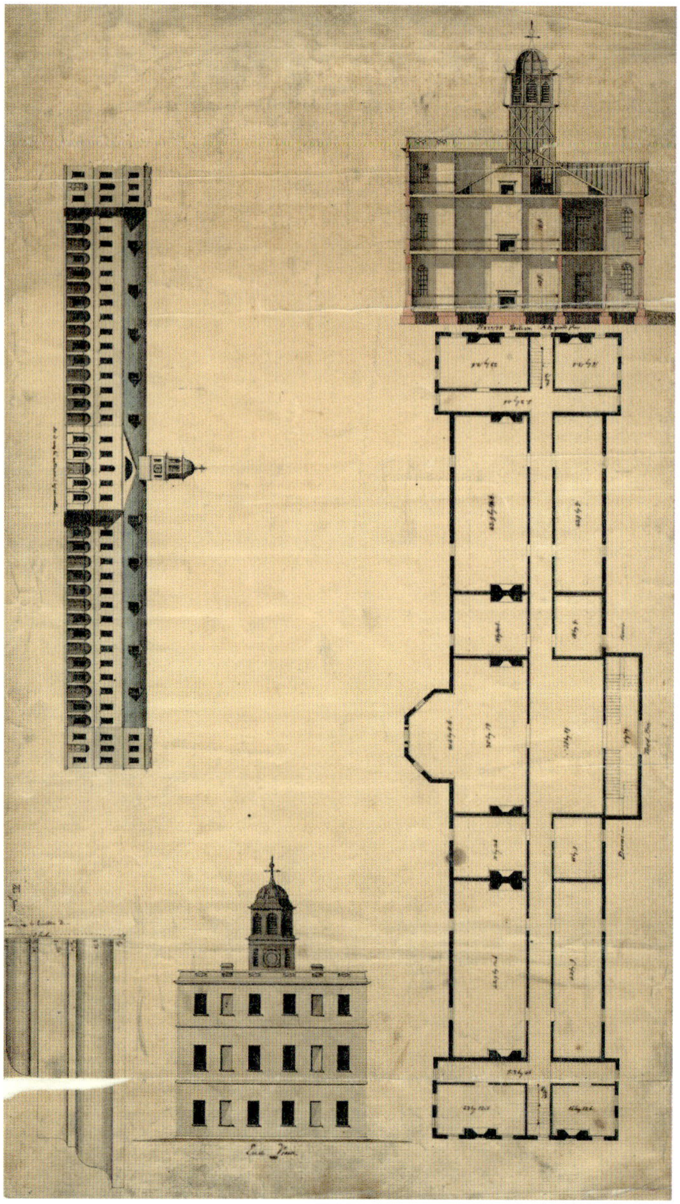

Robert Mills, proposed building for the South Carolina College, 1802. South Carolina Department of Archives and History.

Robert Mills, Maxcy Monument, 1827. Photograph by Hunter Clarkson, 2016.

South Caroliniana Library, south facade.
Photograph by Hunter Clarkson, 2016.

Benjamin Henry Latrobe, the best-trained architect in America. Mills worked for Latrobe for at least six years (c. 1802–8) before setting up his own architectural practice. For the next ten years, he worked primarily in Philadelphia and Baltimore.

In 1819 Mills returned to South Carolina, and as architect for the state Board of Public Works, he was responsible for the creation of courthouses, jails, and other public projects throughout the state. His position was subject to annual legislative approval, and in 1823 he was not reappointed; consequently, for the remainder of the decade, he worked on a building-by-building basis rather than as a salaried employee. Mills left South Carolina in 1830, and a decade later, while working in Washington, he proposed a library that would double as a ceremonial, arched entrance to the South Carolina College campus.

One of his early projects for the state foreshadowed his initial proposal for the library. In 1822 he had designed a gatehouse and barracks for the Charleston Powder Magazine complex, describing it as being "two stories high, and covering the grand gateway leading into the magazine court." Before this gatehouse barracks was demolished (c. 1940), a Charleston newspaper said it was "a most picturesque ruin of a building distinguished from all other structures around Charleston by two Roman arches through the center and an up and down stairs room in each wing. Obviously a gate yet the parapet gables and absence of battlements gave it the appearance of a home rather than a military structure."[3]

After losing his salaried position in 1823, Mills looked for ways to supplement his income. During this period he produced the *Atlas of South Carolina* (1825), the first systematic mapping of any state, and *The Statistics of South Carolina* (1826), an 808-page, county-by-county description of the history and resources of the state. He also sought work elsewhere, and South Carolinians who helped him obtain federal work influenced the creation of the college library.

In 1830, seeking federal employment, Mills sent a copy of the *Atlas* to President Andrew Jackson and asked Jackson to mention him to the secretary of war, Joel R. Poinsett. Both Poinsett and Jackson were South Carolinians. Poinsett, as a member of the state Board of Public Works, had supervised Mills's work in South Carolina.

Traveling north to tend to business in Baltimore, Mills stopped in Washington. He visited Sen. John C. Calhoun and met with George McDuffie, then a member of the House of Representatives from South Carolina. Three years earlier McDuffie had composed the inscription for the Maxcy Monument, and later, as governor of South Carolina (1834–36), he helped obtain appropriations for the college buildings.[4]

Meeting McDuffie in the House of Representatives, Mills gave him a proposal to improve acoustics in the House chamber, and knowing his wife, Eliza Barnwell Smith Mills, was worried about their financial future, he wrote to her describing what happened next:

> [I] went up into the gallery of the house to witness the course that this business would take. I saw Mr. McD. Deliver the papers to the Speaker & speak with him. I saw the Speaker open the roll, look at it, turn over to the plans, examine these and as an opportunity occurred while speakers occupied the floor he commenced from the beginning of the MMS and continued reading it regularly thro'. I thought this indicated an interest in the subject, and might result favorably.
>
> After reading a communication from the President & Secretary of war, and before the regular business of the

> house commenced, the speaker announced to the house that he had received a letter from Robt. Mills Architect communicating a plan for improving the Hall of representatives &c and wished to know the pleasure of the house concerning it. . . . Mr. McDuffie then rose and made a few remarks in relation to the plan which he said he had examined and it appeared to him to be the most feasible plan that had yet been offered. . . . The speaker then put the original motion before the house for printing and engraving the plans, and referring it to the Committee on Public buildings, when it was agreed to. As soon as the Speaker handed it to the Clerk of the house, I observed him examining it very minutely, then others got it from him & examined it, and so it passed thro' many hands. I then went down and requested Mr. McDuffie to procure me the paper that I might revise them for publication, as I had no idea that they would take this course, which he did.[5]

Mills's acoustic plan for the House of Representatives was approved; implementing it became his first significant job for the federal government. He and Eliza moved to Washington. She opened a school, and he quickly obtained more federal work.

When McDuffie presented Mills's plans, Robert Woodward Barnwell was a member of the U.S. House of Representatives.[6] Like McDuffie, Barnwell knew Mills's earlier work in South Carolina, for he was a lawyer and was in the South Carolina House of Representatives when Mills was creating courthouses and jails throughout the state. Ten years after McDuffie presented Mills's proposal to the U.S. House, Barnwell, who became president of South Carolina College in 1835, initiated the construction of the new library.

By birth and bearing, Barnwell was what Jefferson described as a natural aristocrat. He was tall, slender, and graceful, and for several generations his family had owned sea-island cotton plantations in Beaufort and Colleton Counties. Prior to the Civil War, Barnwell himself owned three plantations—Woodward, Cotton Hope, and Bull's Point—and 158 slaves.[7]

Robert Woodward Barnwell (1801–82).
Painting by George Gibbes Barnwell, 1859.

He was educated in private schools in Beaufort and Charleston and then went to Harvard from 1817 until 1821. He graduated at the head of his class. Returning to Charleston, he studied law under James Louis Petigru and opened an office in Beaufort in partnership with his cousin, Robert Barnwell Rhett. In 1826 he was elected to the South Carolina House of Representatives, and his tenure (1826–29) as representative for Colleton County marked the beginning of a public career that spanned the turbulent decades from nullification to secession. He served in the U.S. House of Representatives from 1829 until 1833 and was an effective ally of John C. Calhoun and Robert Y. Hayne. Hayne, like Rhett, was a cousin. Both were ardent secessionists.

A contemporary, South Carolina Gov. Benjamin F. Perry, described Barnwell thus: "No man ever enjoyed in higher degree, the respect and confidence of his constituency, and few, indeed, have deserved it as well. His eminent qualifications . . . were apparent to all. . . . [His] popularity was based upon his well-known adherence to principle, and an unalterable love of truth and justice. He illustrates in a striking degree the fact that a public man can enthrone himself in the affections of the people, without stooping to the arts of the demagogue."[8] After several years in Washington, Barnwell declined to stand for reelection and returned home, hoping, he said, to become merely "a fireside politician."

Recounting how Barnwell became president of the South Carolina College, Daniel Hollis notes that he "did not solicit the position; indeed, it sought him."[9] As a prominent planter and proponent of states' rights, Barnwell was politically acceptable, and when the new governor, George McDuffie, his former colleague in the U.S. House, offered the position, Barnwell responded: "With the exception of a sincere desire to serve the State and promote learning, I possess but little fitness for the position."[10]

Hollis continues:

> The trustees never had occasion to regret their choice. Six months after they had elected him president, they were so pleased with his performance that they chose him to fill a vacancy on the board of trustees, an honor which Cooper had failed to receive. The third president [Barnwell] was an entirely new type. He was not a Baptist academician like Maxcy nor an intellectual controversationalist [*sic*] as was Cooper. He was, instead, an indigenous South Carolina politician, and he became an excellent president. In looking about for a man to recapture public confidence in the college — the trustees had made a superb choice. His Harvard background gave him the necessary appreciation of scholarship, yet he was not such an academician that he lost touch with the public. He handled his students, the trustees, and the legislature with a deft perfection that was rewarded by an ever-increasing flow of students and by (for those days at least) a torrent of funds from the general assembly. So universally popular was he in the State that under his administration public confidence in the institution was restored and criticism almost extinguished.[11]

The governor and trustees turned to Barnwell to save the college. Barnwell's leadership and the trustees' determination to succeed resulted in an energetic building program, and the library was the culmination of that campaign.

During Cooper's tenure the campus had fallen into disrepair, but as soon as he was gone, "the legislature appropriated $20,000 for restoring the college physical plant and in 1835 all the buildings were renovated."[12] A substantial brick wall was also erected around much of the campus to remedy "the air of dilapidation and decay which the ragged wooden fences . . . always presented." In the first year of Barnwell's presidency, the legislature appropriated forty-five thousand dollars for two new dormitories, miscellaneous repairs, an on-campus faculty residence, and a portion of the money needed to build a library.[13]

On December 8, 1836, the trustees' building committee had reported that "the present building used as a library is unfit for that purpose. Besides the imminent danger which must be daily incurred in having the chemical Laboratory, the Library and mechanical and Philosophical apparatus in the same house, the present building is entirely out of repair, the sleepers and partitions in the lower part of the house being entirely decayed and ready to fall, the roof leaks and the floors are rotten. The committee recommend that a new building, entirely separate from the other buildings be erected for the use of the library"[14]

Fifteen thousand dollars of the 1836 appropriation was meant to defray the cost of building a new library. The legislature assumed the balance would be provided by a pledge of $10,000 offered by the South Carolina Society for the Advancement of Learning. Unfortunately the society's promise was not fulfilled, and Barnwell and the trustees felt they could not spend the state money unless they found the additional money needed to do a good job. By adding $11,400 from unencumbered college funds to the state appropriation and using 374,000 bricks previously purchased for other projects, they gathered resources to go ahead.

On January 30, 1837, they advertised in the Washington, D.C., *Daily Intelligencer:*

> To Contractors, Master-Masons & Carpenters. Proposals will be received by the building committee of the South Carolina College, until the 1st of March next, for building two college wings of brick 84 by 30 feet each, three stories; to be finished by the 1st of October next.
>
> Masons will state the lowest terms for which the masonry will be done; materials being furnished by the committee. Carpenters will make bids for work and materials. Lumber can be purchased at prices varying from $1.50 to $1.75 per hundred feet, delivered on the spot.
>
> A new library building will be erected during the present year, which, in materials and cost of workmanship, will equal if not exceed the two wings.
>
> Further particulars may be obtained of the South Carolina delegation in Congress, or the chairman of the committee, to whom communications on the subject may be addressed.
>
> R. W. Barnwell,
> Chairman of the committee, Columbia, S. C.
>
> To be published in the Baltimore Patriot, Richmond Whig, Petersburg Intelligencer, United States Gazette, Pennsylvania Sentinel, Boston Daily Advertiser, Boston Courier, Courier and Enquirer, and Commercial Advertiser, New York, three times a week for one month, and accounts to be forwarded to the chairman of the committee at Columbia, South Carolina.[15]

THE PROPOSAL

Mills's sketches for the library predate the advertisement, and the building committee did not solicit designs, so they must already have contacted him about the library. The earliest indications of his participation in the creation of the library are sketches in a pocket-sized notebook in which he jotted down things to remember. The notebook also contains lists of bills and payments due, notes on what he read, diverse snippets like pieces of a puzzle. It brings to life the pattern of his days.[16]

Ideas for the library cover seven sequential pages, so they were probably written all at one time. The final library drawing is dated January 27, 1837. Beside another library sketch, Mills notes, "wrote Mr Ridgeway of Columbia Sept. 19th for extension of time for Designs."[17] These scribbled notations suggest Mills had known about the project for some time, and as the new year dawned, he felt pressed to meet a deadline for finished drawings.

To understand what he envisioned, historians can use the sketches and imagine a complete, solid, three-dimensional building. Put another way, these rough drawings help to visualize what Mills saw in his mind's eye.

VERSO: Robert Mills, sketches for the South Carolina College Library, a ground plan with flanking wings, 1837. Diary of Robert Mills. Library of Congress.

RECTO: Robert Mills, sketches for the South Carolina College Library, a ground plan and west facade, 1837. Diary of Robert Mills. Library of Congress.

Robert Mills, sketches for the South Carolina College Library, east and west facades, 1837. Diary of Robert Mills. Library of Congress.

The sketches convey a great deal of information. There are two plans of the ground floor, three plans of the second, or principal, floor, three elevations of the western facade, and three elevations of the eastern facade. Details vary, but all the drawings clearly relate to the same project, and that project is obviously the library, for notations in Mills's hand include "Library Hall of the South Carolina College" as a caption. "Library" is inscribed in the frieze of one of the elevations, and "West Façade of Library Hall" appears beneath another sketch.

The first drawing related to the library is a faint outline of an elevation flanked by some numbers. On the bottom half of this page, Mills drew another small elevation and a ground plan. These latter two sketches are important, for they contain the essence of his idea; each subsequent drawing refines and elaborates on what is suggested there. These initial plans for the college library are preceded by the ground plan of a domed building flanked by "arms" reminiscent of Jefferson's library at the University of Virginia.

The small elevation that begins the South Carolina College library sequence depicts a two-story, domed building; its ground floor consists of a raised basement with five arches supporting a portico with six columns. These columns support a pediment. Above the pediment faint lines suggest that the arches, columns, and pediment form a slightly projecting central block that is capped by a dome and flanked by three vertically aligned windows on either side.

The ground plan below this initial elevation shows the shape and approximate size of the building as well as the rooms within its second, or principal, floor. Mills initially envisioned the structure as a rectangle, 105 feet long by 65 feet deep. Dots on the long sides of this rectangle represent the bases of the columns on the porticoes, and that indicates that this is a plan of the principal floor. Directly behind the porticoes is a round room 50 feet in diameter. Given the relation of this drawing to the elevation above it, the round room is directly beneath the dome. At either end of the rectangle, flanking the round central room, Mills placed two almost square rooms and a staircase. The number twenty-five appears in three of these smaller rooms, and in each he has drawn an X, corner to corner. These Xs indicate he is thinking of groin-vaulted masonry to provide fireproof construction. The "two-rooms-and-staircase" ensemble fits within the 65-foot depth of the building, so allowing for the staircases, he must have intended the rooms to be approximately 25 by 20 feet.

Larger sketches fill the facing pages that follow; to draw them he turned the notebook to make room for the length of the building. Turning the images ninety degrees counterclockwise, as he did when he drew them, makes the ground horizontal and puts the drawing labeled "West Façade of Library/Hall" on top. Mills meant for this to be the public face, or front side, of the building. It faces west, so clearly he intended for the library to front Sumter Street. This would have "closed" the Horseshoe. The elevation shown below the Sumter Street facade was meant to be the east, or campus, side of the library, the side facing into the Horseshoe.

On the drawing of the west facade, the raised basement story was to be eighteen feet high. The principal story was to be approximately thirty feet high, and the raised basement walls were to be grooved. Mills would have known that in Columbia the library would be built of brick. He must have wanted the brick exterior to be treated with ochre or grey stucco, grooved to resemble stone. The elevation of the east facade shows a wide, arched passageway in the center of the raised basement. At ground level within this archway, there are two short, vertical lines. Subsequent detailed plans of the

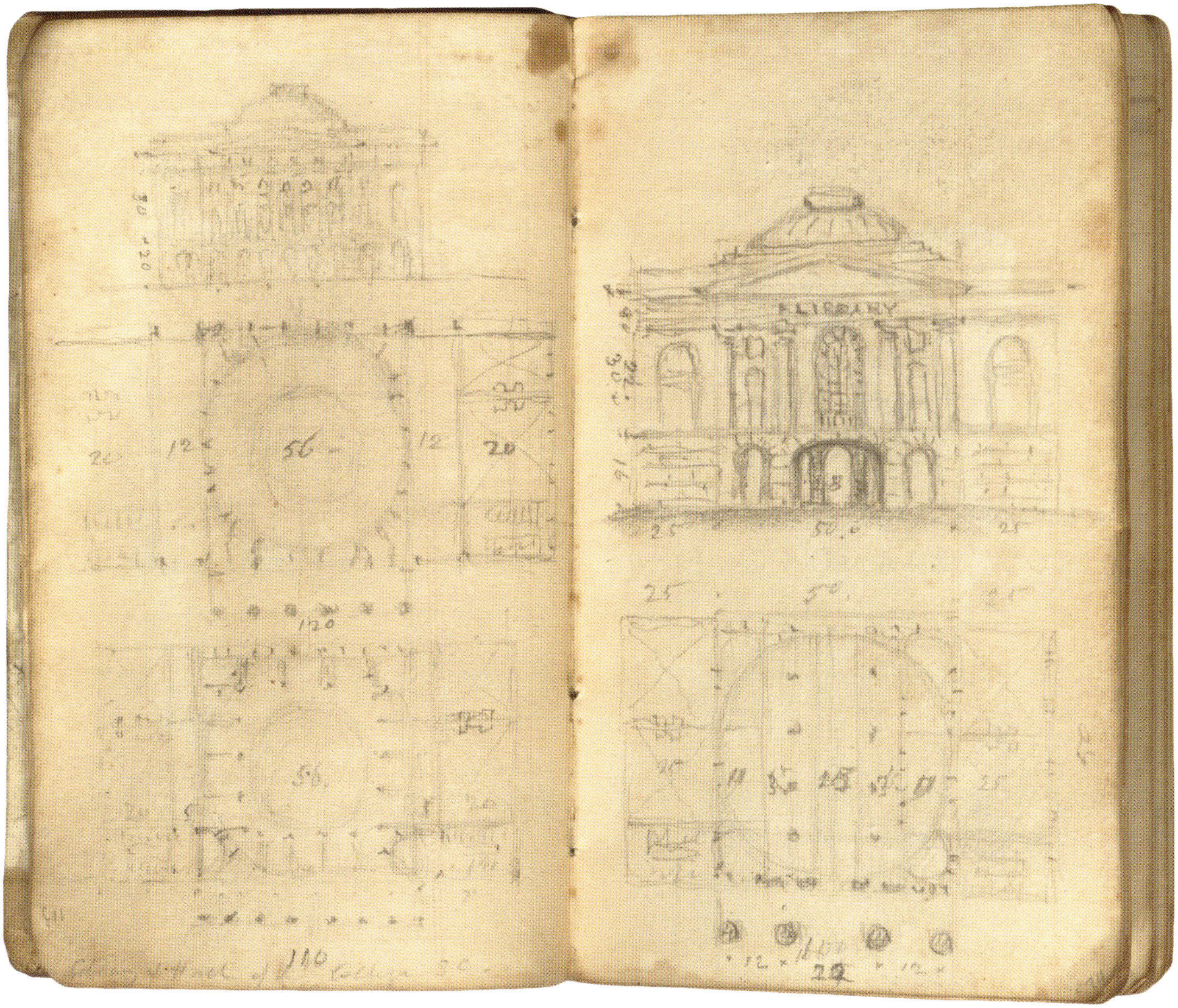

Robert Mills, sketches for the South Carolina College Library, west facade with two plans of the second or principal floor below; east facade with plan of the ground floor below, 1837. Diary of Robert Mills. Library of Congress.

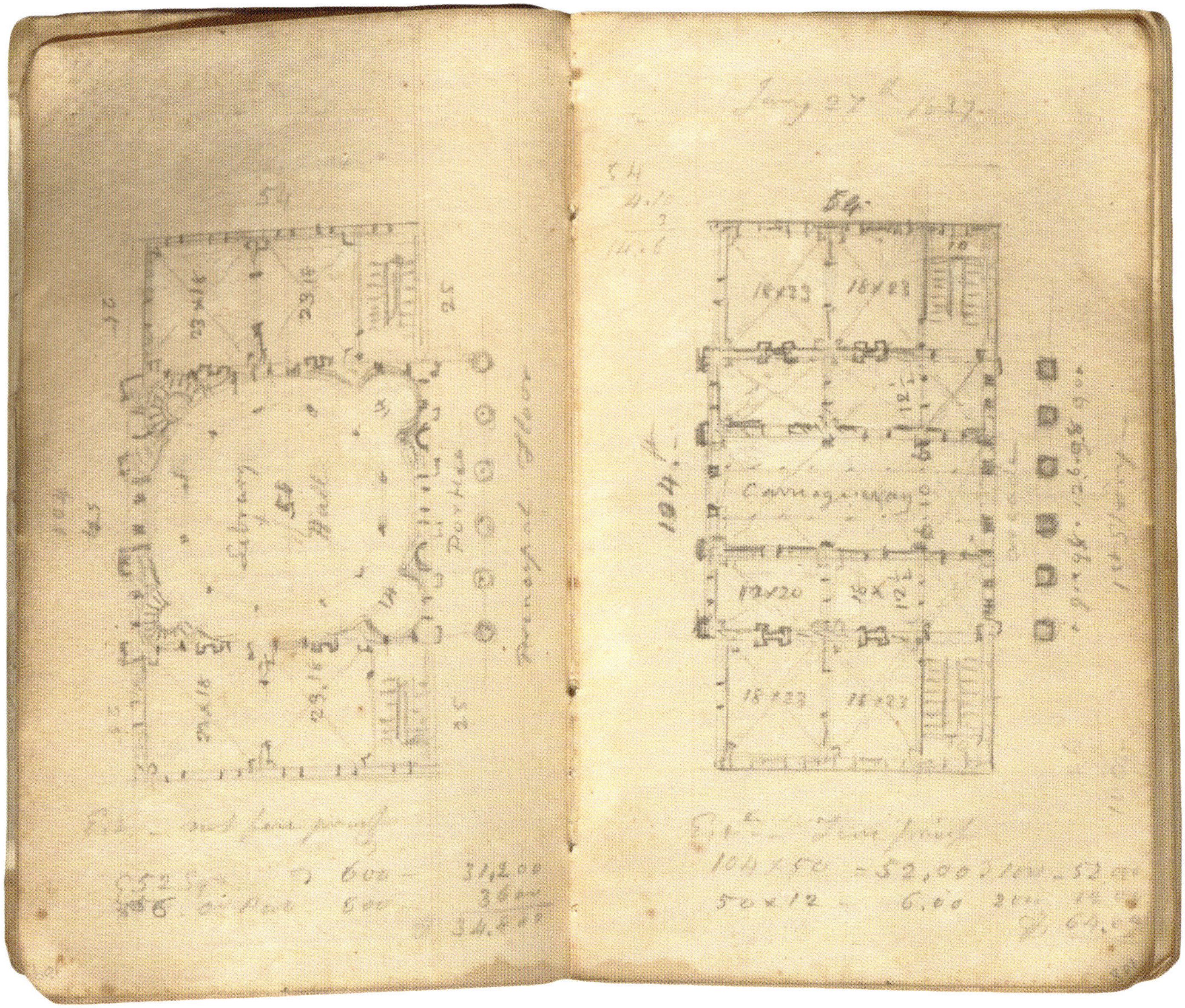

Robert Mills, sketches for the South Carolina College Library, plan of the principal floor and a plan of the ground floor, 1837. Diary of Robert Mills. Library of Congress.

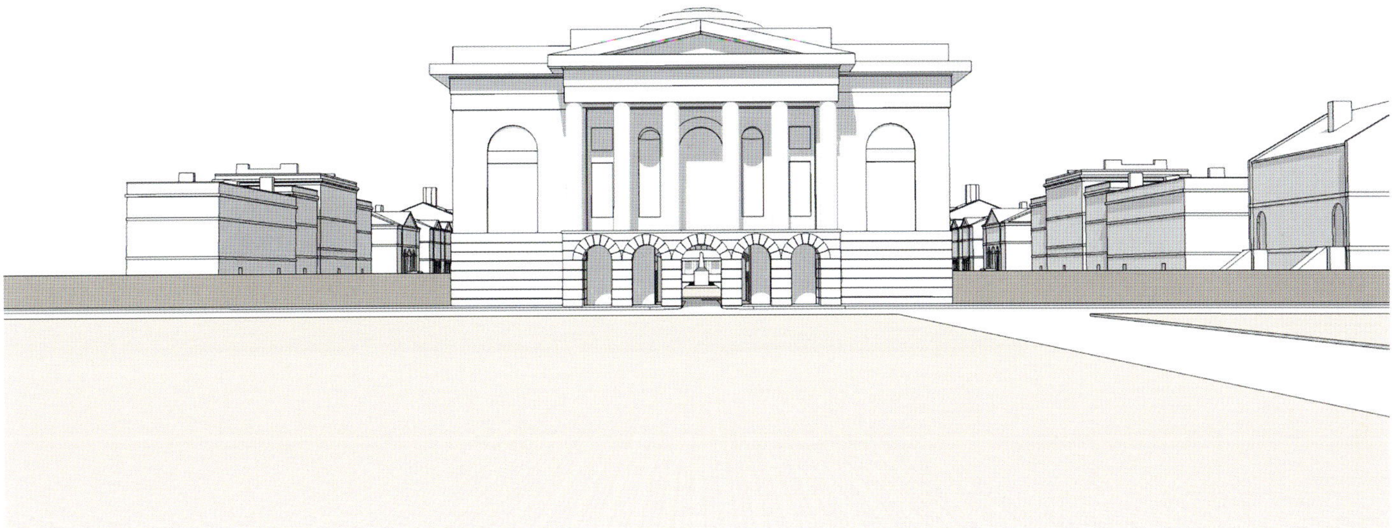

Robert Mills's proposed library viewed from the west. Drawing by Derek Gruner, University of South Carolina architect, 2016.

first floor, or ground level, show that this archway was labeled as a "carriageway" serving as an entrance to the Horseshoe. The vista through this archway would have centered on the Maxcy Monument and the president's house, which then stood in front of the present McKissick Museum. The short vertical lines inside the arch represent bollards—stout posts to keep horses and carriages from hitting the walls.

The next pair of facing pages shows two elevations and three plans. Here Mills varies some of the dimensions, but the major features, exterior and interior, remain essentially unchanged.

The final pair of facing pages contains plans of the first floor and the principal floor. Each plan fills a page and contains more measurements than the preceding drawings, for Mills's concept was becoming more specific. For example, the round Library Hall is now 56 feet in diameter, and a circle of dots within this rotunda represents the bases of columns supporting a gallery or balcony. Two curving stairs provide access to the gallery. In these two plans, the rectangular body of the building is shown as being 54 by 104 feet, and to build such a building "not fire proof," Mills estimated, would cost $34,800. He anticipated that fireproof construction, which meant vaulted masonry throughout, would cost $64,000.

There are two meticulous scale drawings of these final floor plans among miscellaneous early college records, both signed "Robt Mills arch." Unfortunately these scale drawings have survived in isolation, without any explanatory correspondence, and there is no reference to them in board

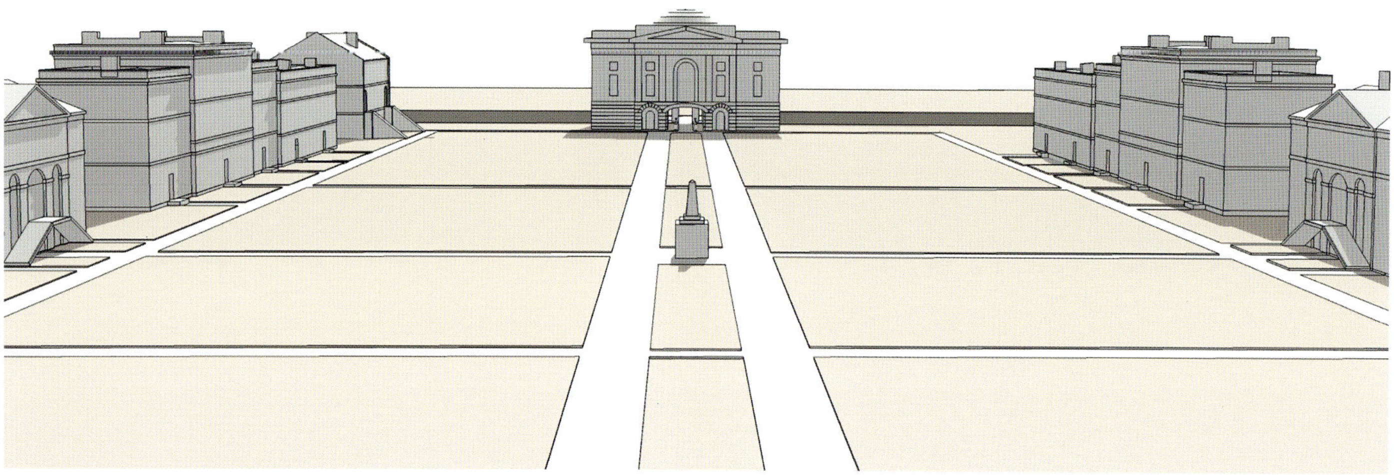

Robert Mills's proposed library viewed from the east. Drawing by Derek Gruner, University of South Carolina architect, 2016.

minutes or other memoranda. Excepting these two drawings, the records contain nothing concerning Mills's participation in the creation of the library. Nonetheless the two drawings prove Mills refined the sketches and transmitted the proposal to the college.

His initial concept was unlike any building in South Carolina. In suggesting a domed rotunda, he was thinking of Jefferson's library at the University of Virginia, and it is worth noting that twenty years earlier he had drawn plans for a similar library for a company in Baltimore. Mills's proposal was similar to plans by Benjamin Latrobe, and Latrobe's were accepted, but the library was never built. Mills's description of his proposal matches his initial concept of the Caroliniana.[18] The Baltimore library was never built, but it foreshadowed the college plan. Portions of his description of the Baltimore proposal fit both projects: "the basement or office story . . . rooms are all proposed to be vaulted and made fire proof—so as to render the upper part of the building perfectly secure from fire. . . . The Principal or Library floor . . . occupies the rotunda in the center which rises above the main walls of the building and is crowned with a dome. . . . One or more tiers of hanging galleries . . . will give access to the higher surfaces of the wall. The communication with these galleries is made easy by small stair cases in the angles."[19] The Baltimore Library Company was unable to raise enough money to construct their building, and inadequate funding no doubt explains why the South Carolina College proposal was radically altered.[20]

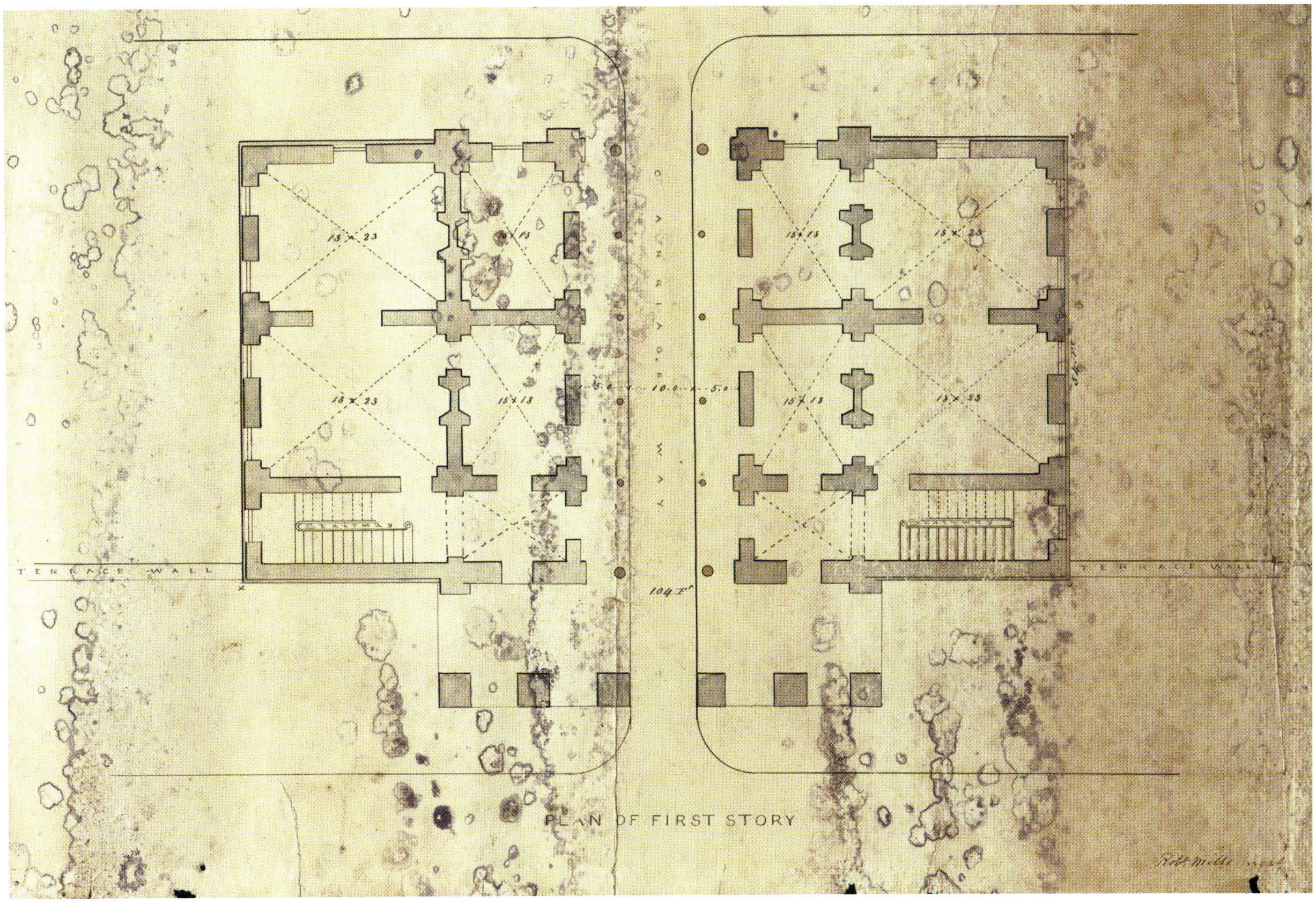

Robert Mills, ground plan of proposed library
for the South Carolina College, 1840.

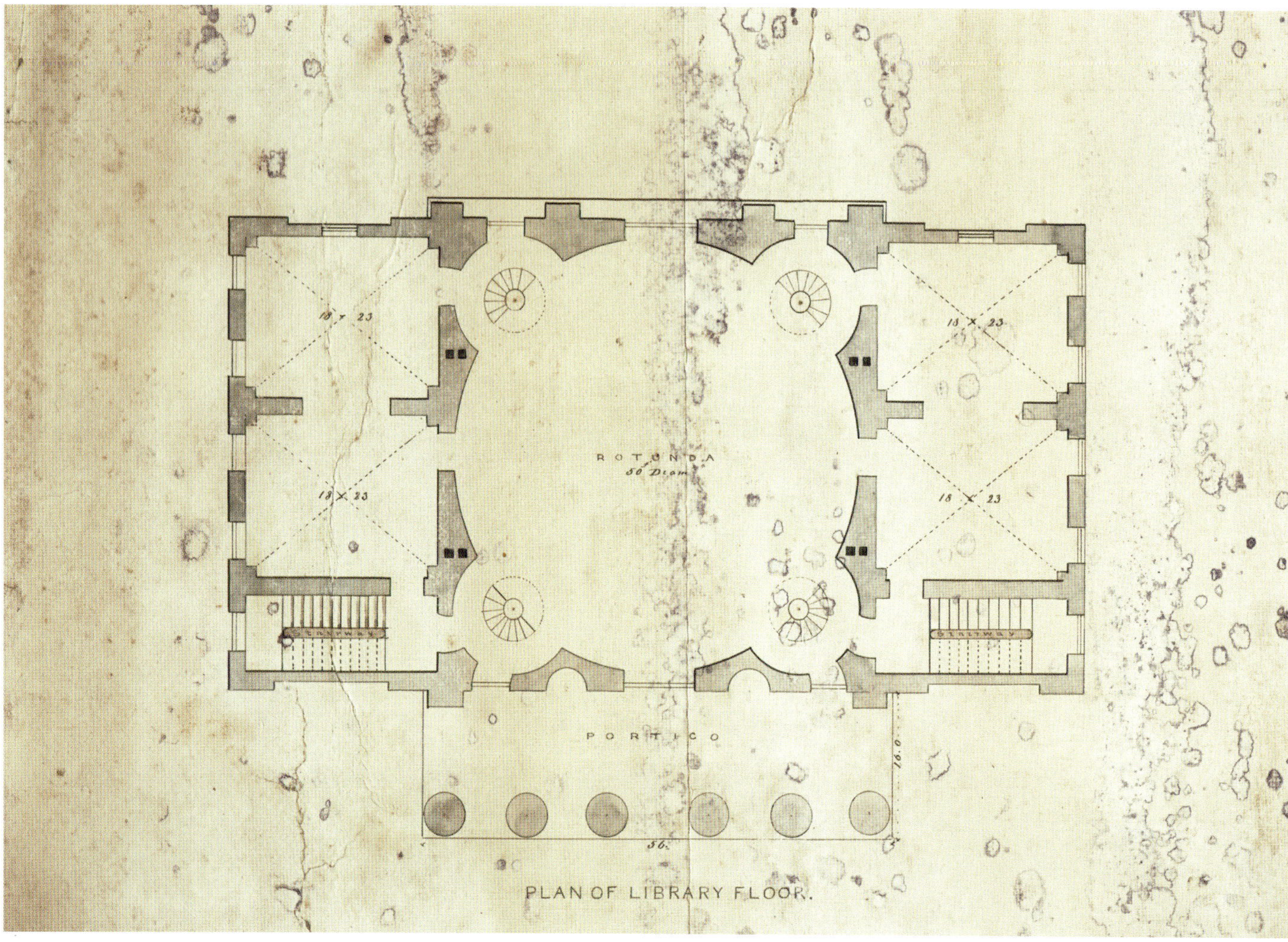

Robert Mills, plan of the principal floor of proposed library for the South Carolina College, 1840.

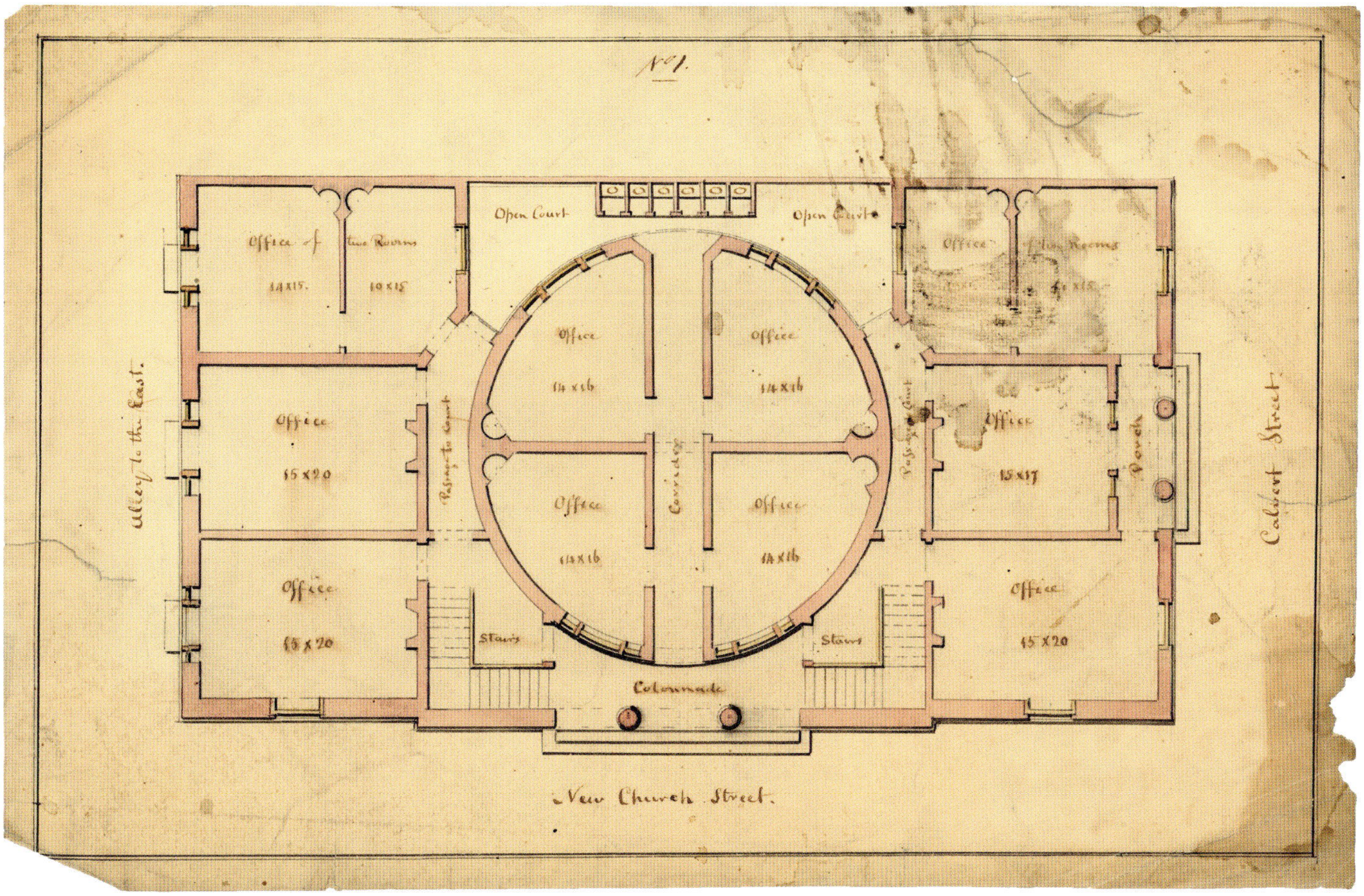

Robert Mills, ground plan of proposed library for the Baltimore Library Company, 1817.

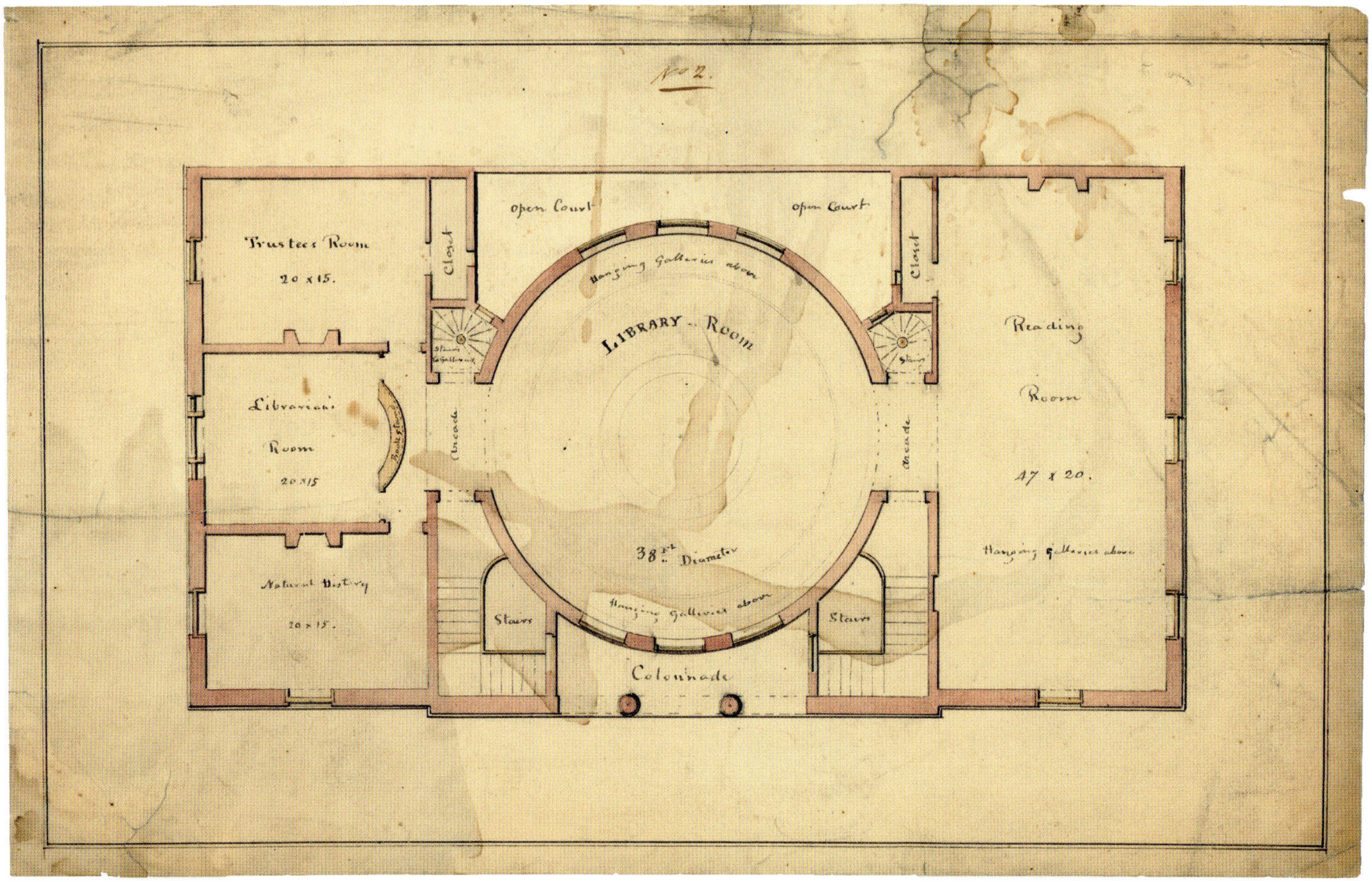

Robert Mills, plan of the principal floor of proposed library for the Baltimore Library Company, 1817. Maryland Historical Society.

THE FINAL PLAN

Setting aside Mills's initial proposal, the primary issue remains: Was he involved with the library they built, and if so, in what way?

We know he did not come to South Carolina during the planning and construction of the college library (c. 1837–1840), for on July 6, 1836, President Jackson had appointed him architect of the public buildings. While the college library was being designed and built, Mills was focusing on the creation of the U.S. Treasury building, the U.S. Patent Office, and the Federal Post Office. During these years (1837–40) he was also responsible for numerous smaller federal projects, including the design and construction of a marine hospital in New Orleans, a courthouse in Alexandria, Virginia, a jail in Washington, D.C., a library and science building for the military academy at West Point, prototypical designs for federal marine hospitals, and an improved heating system in the White House. Concurrently, at the Capitol he also undertook alterations in the House of Representatives and directed repairs to the copper sheathing on the Capitol dome. He directed the building of three new cupolas over the Library of Congress skylights and was responsible for "erecting shelves and bookcases in the committee rooms under the direction of the Committee on the Library."[21] In short, the new college library coincides with the apex of Mills's career.

During the spring of 1837, President Barnwell, perhaps joined by college committees and interested faculty and trustees, began considering a final design. Members of the library committee included A. B. Longstreet, W. F. DeSaussure, J. P. Carroll, and J. H. Thornwell. The building committee consisted of DeSaussure, G. Gregg, and Abram Blanding. Although Blanding, as an engineer, had worked with Mills, no member of either committee is known to have participated in architectural projects, so it is unlikely they designed the library.

Robert Mills, silhouette by August Edouart, 1841.
The author's collection.

Realizing that Mills's proposal was much too expensive, someone associated with the college must have contacted him. That person would have been familiar with his work, for he had designed more than thirty buildings in South Carolina during the 1820s. Barnwell had witnessed his work in the House of Representatives. Blanding, a member of the college building committee, had shared responsibility with Mills for many of the state public improvement projects, and the contractor for the new library, Charles Beck, had worked with Mills too.

In addition to the board and members of the building committee, Francis Lieber, who had joined the South Carolina College faculty in 1835, had retained his position as a member of the board of visitors of the U.S. Military Academy at West Point. In 1838 he served as chairman of the West Point Building Committee, and reporting on the state of the academy's facilities, Lieber noted "in the month of February last [1838], the building which contained the library, chemical laboratory, philosophical apparatus, and models for engineering was destroyed by fire. . . . The superintendent of the academy has submitted to the Secretary of War a plan for the erection of suitable buildings."[22]

Acting on Lieber's report, the secretary of war, Joel R. Poinsett, had Mills submit a design for a library and science building for the academy. Lieber was energetic, and given his experience at West Point, it is easy to imagine him participating in discussions concerning the South Carolina College library. The building itself provides the best reasons to believe Mills participated in the alteration of his initial plan.

Deleting nonessentials, those involved must have decided not to build the raised basement. The dome was another luxury they decided the college could not afford. Without the raised basement and its arched carriageway, the library could not serve as a ceremonial entrance to the campus, and without the dome, it was virtually impossible to create a round reading room.

In addition to providing an arched entrance to the Horseshoe, Mills meant for the eighteen-foot-high raised basement to elevate the library upon a pedestal-like base. Elevation was part of the classical tradition, and the majority of Mills's designs for public buildings are made prominent this way, raised above their neighbors.

Relative height is potentially eloquent as an aspect of design, for people often instinctively associate height with power or prestige. The psychological significance of height is confirmed when one speaks of high honors or a high court or simply says "your highness." Deleting the raised basement significantly altered the impact Mills wanted the library to make. Furthermore in Western culture the dome typically signifies a socially significant building. Mills crowned his "auditorium" churches in Philadelphia, Richmond, and Baltimore with domes, and near the end of his career he proposed a new enlarged dome for the U.S. Capitol. He wanted the library's site, height, and form to express its preeminence in the life of the college.[23]

Although it was built without the raised basement, the ground floor of the library resembles the floor plan found in Mills's proposal. Coming into the low entry hall, which would have been the carriageway, visitors face a curved staircase contained in a tower projecting from the rear facade. This configuration made it possible to develop the symmetrical, rectangular reading room on the principal floor. Mills had used stairs like this at the South Carolina Asylum (1822) and the Marine Hospital in Charleston (1831–33). Of course anyone familiar with his work could have adapted the curved staircase and other characteristic details.

The reading room provides the most compelling evidence that Mills participated directly in the final design process. The construction contract for the library mentions seven drawings, none of which have survived: "No 4 represents the alcoves and galleries, which are to be finished precisely in the same manner as the congressional library at

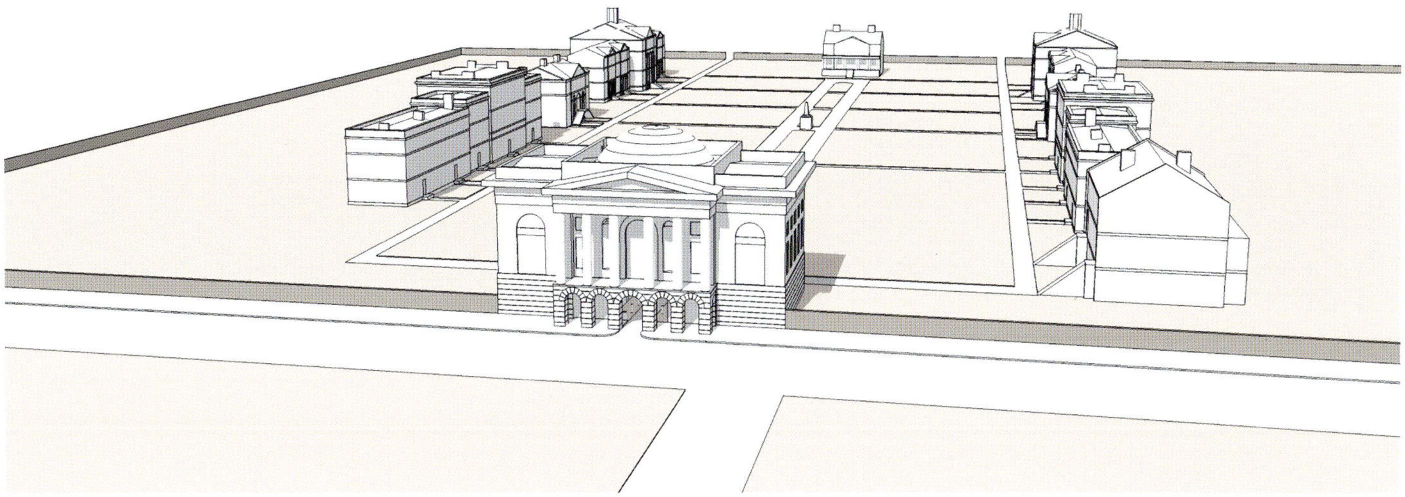

Aerial view from the southwest of Mills's proposal for the South Caroliniana Library. Drawing by Derek Gruner, University of South Carolina architect, 2016.

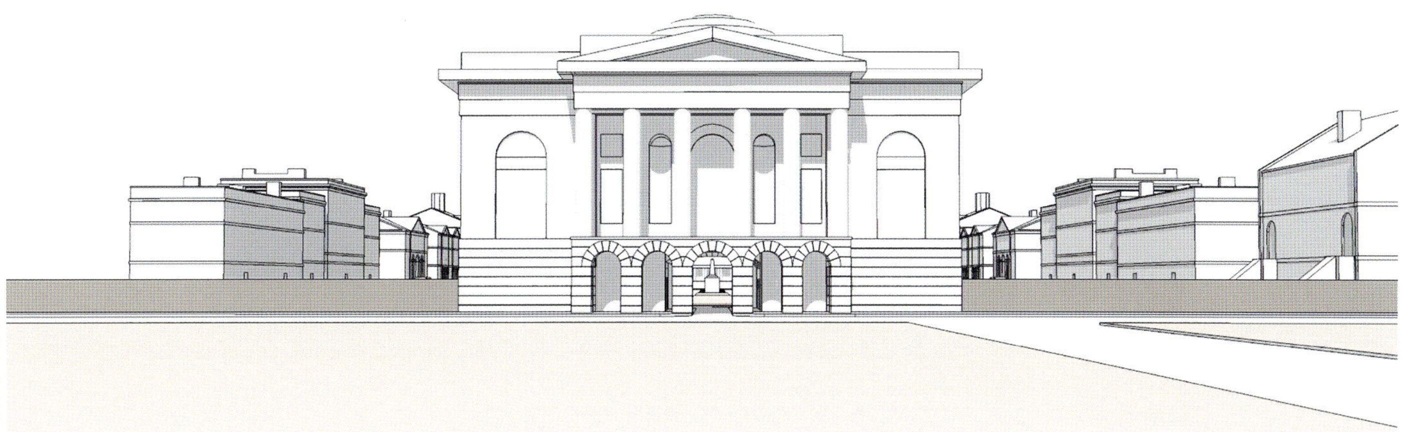

West facade of Mills's proposal for the South Caroliniana Library. Drawing by Derek Gruner, University of South Carolina architect, 2016.

South Caroliniana Library reading room, 1940. Historic American Buildings Survey.

Washington of which [illegible] is a drawing." And drawing "No. 6 represents the ceiling overhead, which is to be done in plaster in the very best stile, equal to that of the congressional library, with the exception that instead of its being coved, it is to be straight."[24]

Having accepted the need to delete the carriageway, dome, and rotunda, Mills must have reworked the principal floor to accommodate a replica of the Library of Congress. That he read there is known, for in the diary containing the South Carolina College library sketches, he notes: "For the Bridges of Scotland see the English Reports of Roads & Bridges 6 to 9—Cong Library alcove 6"[25] And again: "Sound. Ventilating &c Inman on Ventilating & Warming &c speaks of my Report on alterations in Hall of Congress in Book in Cong Library—Chap 15 no. 162—alcove 5."[26] More important, as architect of the public buildings, Mills worked on the congressional library that was then located in the Capitol. An early historian of the U.S. Capitol, Glen Brown, says that "from 1836 to 1851 all matters relating to changes in and the maintenance of the Capitol came under the supervision of Mills."[27] And Mills's 1836–40 diary contains references to work related to the library: "Pay Roll Libry and Document Room $421.25"; under the heading "Business before Com of P Bldg," "New Library Room & Repy $2,000"; and under the heading "Capitol Jany 27 1837," "opening floor in Doc R. do [same] in Library R. . . . oil for Library."[28] In addition, as previously mentioned, he built cupolas for the three skylights in the ceiling of the Library of Congress like the three skylights in the Caroliniana reading room.

Writing about the Capitol, Mills described the library:

> a door opens into the library; a splendid room, ninety two feet long, thirty six feet wide, and thirty six feet high. At the entrance are two stone columns in advance, with capitals corresponding with those in the octagon tower at Athens; and immediately opposite, fronting the outlet into the Western colonnade, are two similar columns in advance. On each side of this central entrance, and extending the whole length of the room, are a series of alcoves, ornamented in front with fluted pilasters, which, with their entablature, support two galleries, divided as below into twelve shelved recesses; above these springs

Alexander Jackson Davis, *Library of Congress Reading Room*, circa 1832. New York Public Library.

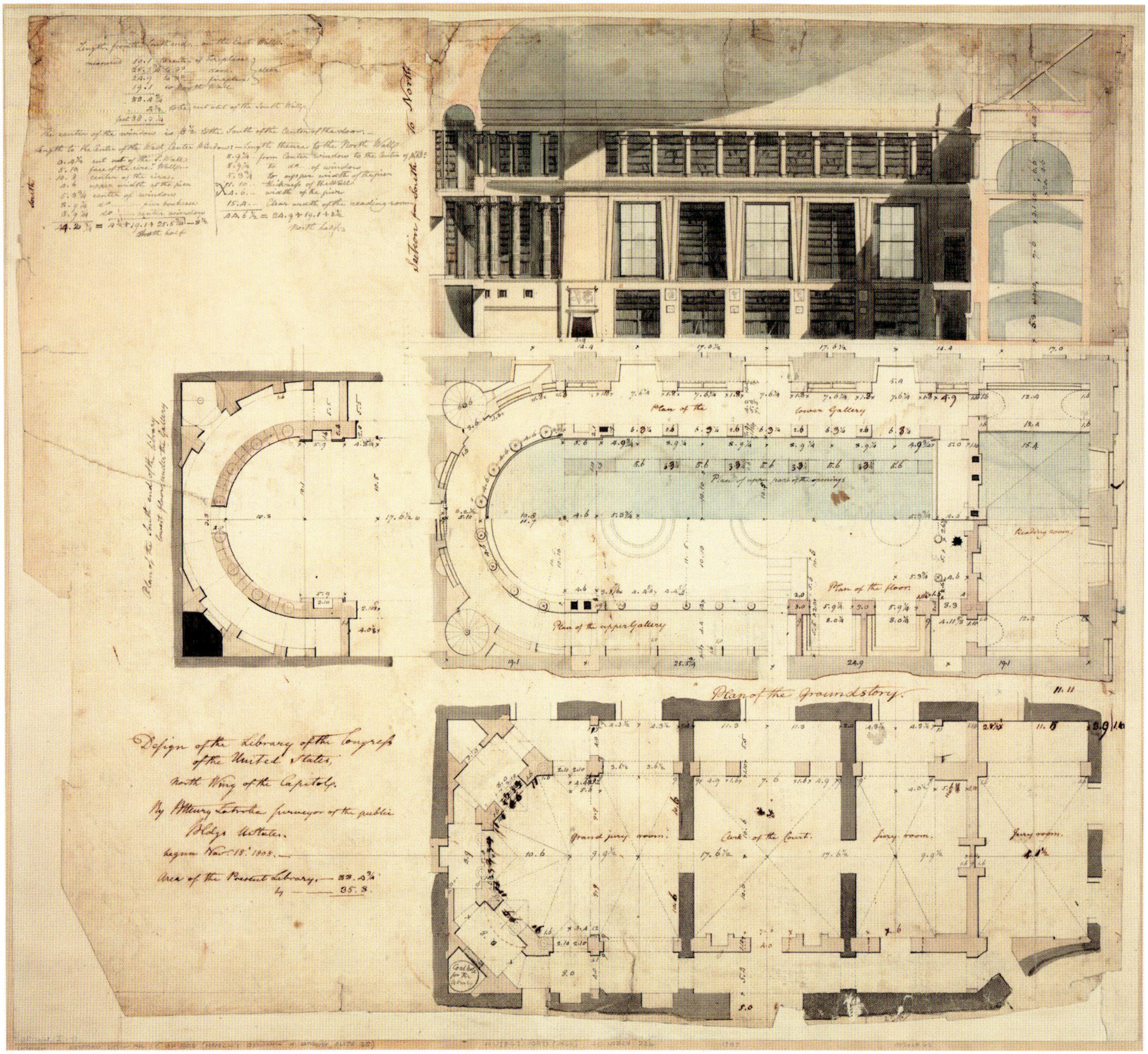

Benjamin Henry Latrobe, "Design of the Library of Congress of the United States North Wing of the Capitol," 1808. Library of Congress.

> the great arch forming the ceiling, handsomely decorated with enriched panels, borders, and wreaths of flowers, and pierced with three circular apertures, handsomely ornamented, which admit the light and ventilate the room.
>
> Each alcove has a table and chair; the cases are all wire glazed, with labels above, designating the subjects of the works they contain. The middle of the room is furnished with suitable tables containing drawers to receive large sheets of engravings, and with sofa seats; the whole placed on a Brussels carpet. The room is heated by furnaces from below. . . .
>
> The first thing that attracts the attention when entering, is the admirable order of arrangement of the different subjects embraced in this room. The several works are classed according to Mr. Jefferson's arrangement, corresponding "to the faculties of the mind employed on them." 1st, Memory, (result, history;) 2d, Reason, (philosophy;) 3rd, Imagination, (fine arts.) Labels, in large characters, point out the position of the several classes of books in the order named above; for instance, alcove No. 1 to contain works connected with history, ancient, modern and ecclesiastical; natural philosophy, agriculture, chemistry, surgery, medicine, anatomy, zoology, botany, mineralogy, technical arts; No. 4 to 8, works connected with philosophy, namely: moral philosophy, law of nature and nations. . . . The catalogue of the library now numbers about 42,000 volumes, and gives, besides a list of the books, an index to the names of authors and annotators, &c.[29]

South Caroliniana reading room balcony and ceiling detail with skylight, 1934. Historic American Building Survey.

The Caroliniana's reading room differs from the Library of Congress in that the college reading room is slightly shorter—ninety-one feet, eight inches long rather than ninety-two feet—and the congressional library had a coved (curved) ceiling, whereas the college reading room ceiling is flat.

Mills was the only person ideally situated to send detailed drawings of the congressional library to the college. Unfortunately early nineteenth-century architectural drawings were typically destroyed through use on site; consequently it is not surprising that those mentioned in the contract have not survived.

The Library of Congress described by Mills burned in 1851. His descriptions and sketches by others suggest what it was like, but the South Carolina college reading room offers a full-scale replica, and thus it expresses the aspirations of the antebellum South Carolina College.

The alcoves are often said to reflect Thomas Jefferson's library, in that it places books in specific sections, each devoted to a different type of knowledge. In fact the library at Monticello had no alcoves; nonetheless Jefferson apparently organized his bookshelves to reflect divisions of knowledge as defined by Francis Bacon (1561–1626). Christopher Wren is generally credited with conceiving the alcove library as an architectural embodiment of Bacon's categories. In the Trinity College Library at Cambridge, built in 1675, he used alcoves with a table for consultation of material in the center of each. "The alcove . . . provided natural division by subject . . . reduced distraction . . . facilitated record keeping and shelving, and it had aesthetic appeal. Small wonder that it is attractive to modern man."[30]

After the British burned the Capitol during the War of 1812, Congress acquired Jefferson's books to form the core of its new library. Charles Bulfinch (1763–1844), an architect from Boston, rebuilt the Capitol and designed the new Library of Congress with alcoves—the congressional library Mills knew. Bulfinch was following an alcove arrangement that originated in England.[31]

Architectural forms that become traditional must function well on several levels. In addition to utility and stability, recognizable building types—like the alcove libraries—evoke an emotional or psychological response consonant with their use. Christian churches, for example, usually create sight lines and pathways to the altar; courtrooms focus on the judicial bench. The alcove library presents a visually balanced and clearly defined space. Here the visitor is cloistered from the bustle of the world and free to move in any direction. As a creator of meaningful spaces, Mills must have appreciated the effect, as well as the fame, of Bulfinch's "splendid room"—the Library of Congress.

The alterations to Mills's original design made the massive Doric columns the principal feature of the facade, and emphatic columns have become an architectural cliché emblematic of the antebellum southern planter class. This is not what Mills meant to convey. The complexity of his proposal brings to mind his remark that he "always deprecated the servile copying of the buildings of antiquity. . . . I say to our artists: Study your country's tastes and requirements, and make classic ground here for your art."[32] He wanted the building—like the collections it would house—to broaden our vision.

THE BUILDER

Charles M. Beck built the college library. He was born in Massachusetts on July 11, 1792, and died in Columbia on August 12, 1861 or 1862. Precisely when he moved south is not known, but notice of the internal improvements appropriation in 1819 may have prompted him to come, for in 1820 the *Camden Gazette* praised his work on the "Sumterville" Courthouse.[33]

Beck was clearly optimistic about the state's building program. In 1821 he advertised in Boston for "six or eight" carpenters willing to move to South Carolina.[34] For the next twenty years, whenever his name appears in public records, it is almost always in connection with one of Mills's projects.

Edward Brickel White, proposed *New Chapel and Exhibition Hall, and Halls for the Euphradian and Clariosophic Societies, So Ca College*, circa 1850.

In 1822, for example, they both worked on the Saluda and the Columbia canals and the Newberry courthouse and jail. The following year Beck contracted to build the Ainsley Hall House, another Mills design. The federal census of 1830 shows Beck living in Columbia with a household of three free white males, two free white females, and two male and two female slaves. Like Mills, Beck ventured beyond construction: in 1834 he and William Jenks, who also lived in Columbia, obtained a patent for an improved method of hulling and breaking cottonseed.[35] Shortly thereafter, in 1839, Beck built the Edgefield County courthouse and was praised publicly by the Edgefield commissioners of public buildings just as the library project got underway.[36]

The college library may have been Beck's final construction job in South Carolina. The 1840 census lists him as living in Columbia and owning eight slaves. He also appears in the 1860 census, but after that the record is silent.

Finally, although Mills's initial idea was not built, it was not forgotten, for a Charleston-based architect, Edward Brickell White (1806–82), mimicked it in an unsuccessful proposal for a "New Chapel and Exhibition Hall, and Halls for the Euphradian and Clariosophic Societies, So Ca College." The date of White's proposal is uncertain, but more than a decade after the new South Carolina College library opened, he designed a ceremonial arched entrance, the Porter's Lodge (1850–52), for the College of Charleston.[37]

Edward Brickel White, Porter's Lodge, College of Charleston, 1852. Photograph by the author, 2015.

Mills's initial "archway" concept for the South Carolina College library may be reflected in the Porter's Lodge, but his reading room replica of the Library of Congress was clearly copied by George Edward Walker (1810–63) when he designed the reading room in the College of Charleston library (c. 1854). In 1854–55 Walker worked briefly as architect of the new state house in Columbia, but conflicts and controversies led to his dismissal, and he returned to Charleston, where he had been working with Edward Brickel White on the U.S. Customs House. Walker clearly visited the new library in Columbia, for as soon as he returned to Charleston, he designed a new library for the College of Charleston (1855–56). Its interior is a dollhouse, diminutive version of the South Carolina College reading room. The College of Charleston version is about seventy feet by twenty feet. As in Columbia, the entrance is in the

Towell Library Reading Room, circa 1950.
Addlestone Library, College of Charleston.

Beaufort College, 1852. Works Projects Administration, photograph circa 1938.

center of one long side, and the long walls are lined with alcoves, seven on each long side as in Columbia; both have galleries above their alcoves, and at either end of their reading rooms both libraries have fireplaces faced with veined, black Italian marble.[38]

The library was in service less than a year when ill health forced Barnwell to resign as president. He returned home to Beaufort, and while White's ceremonial arched Porter's Lodge was being built for the College of Charleston in 1852, Barnwell was serving as president of the Beaufort College; there he was responsible for the creation of a new multipurpose, temple form, Greek Revival–style building. Classrooms and offices occupied the rectangular body of the building, and the college library was located in a rotunda attached to the rear. The Beaufort College library was a round, open reading room with galleries. Like the Charleston Porter's Lodge, it was a dim architectural echo of Mills's initial proposal for the South Carolina College.[39]

CHAPTER THREE

The COLLEGE LIBRARY, 1840–1932

The aims, methods, and ideals of the library were modified as life itself underwent profound social changes. The library, in common with all social agencies, moved through alternate periods of fluidity and convention but always responded, in greater or less degree, to its environment.

J. H. Shera, *Foundations of the Public Library*

The library collection grew steadily during the 1840s and 1850s, and before the Civil War, it was recognized as one of the best in the country.

At mid-century "in New England only Harvard, Yale and Brown contained 20,000 or more volumes; Bowdoin had 13,000. . . . Amherst, Colby, Dartmouth, Middlebury, Trinity, the University of Vermont, Wesleyan and Williams each had less than 7500 volumes in their respective libraries. . . . In the South, the library of the University of Virginia was the largest, having 18,378 volumes. Six sister institutions in Virginia averaged 2270 volumes. South Carolina College had at that time one of the best selected and most generously supported libraries in the country, and numbered 17,000 volumes. Eighteen college libraries in the states of North Carolina, Georgia, Alabama, Mississippi, Louisiana and Tennessee averaged 3140 volumes."[1]

Arthur T. Hamlin, in his *University Library in the United States: Its Origins and Development,* says that "the University of South Carolina . . . led the way with the first building . . . planned for and solely devoted to library purposes (1840). It was in every way a fine building which avoided mistakes made by Harvard (1841), Yale (1846), Amherst (1853), and others. . . . The University of South Carolina was approaching the twenty-thousand-volume mark when war cut it off; more importantly, its scholarly collection was carefully selected with much history, literature, travel, and science as well as the customary theology, classics, and antiquities."[2]

After the Civil War, everything changed. State funding for the college collapsed, and during the late nineteenth and early twentieth centuries, several national trends merged and influenced the creation of a new, specialized division within the South Carolina College library.

The acquisition of John James Audubon's *Birds of North America* is often cited as a highlight of the antebellum collection. The Audubon folio also exemplifies the multiple layers of meaning found in many items in the collection.

On January 16, 1834, Audubon predicted that "our work will be the standard of American ornithology."[3] He was correct, of course. The 435 images of 497 species — 25 of them identified for the first time — and Audubon's ambition, energy, and artistry made every aspect of the project exemplary, but beyond these qualities, the folio is fascinating simply as an antebellum acquisition, for it leads to stories about South Carolinians who contributed to its creation and its purchase by the state.

The first hint that the college might acquire the folio is found in a letter Audubon wrote to his wife. He was traveling from Philadelphia to Charleston, and on October 13, 1831, he wrote Lucy, "We [Audubon's sons, John and Victor, were with him] have had for compagnon de Voyage a Colonel Preston, the nephew of the Large Colonel Preston which we knew at Louisville — an amiable Gentleman who resides at Columbia S.C. and whom we will see there for he hired a Gig last evening and pushed for home having no baggage except a carpet bag — I shall stay at Columbia 2 days as Col Preston thinks the College at least will subscribe."[4]

The "Large Colonel Preston" whom the Audubons knew in Louisville was William Preston (1770–1821), and the nephew who traveled with the Audubon party was William Campbell Preston (1794–1860), then a member of the South Carolina House of Representatives. He was later president of the South Carolina College (1845–51). If Audubon followed W. C. Preston to Columbia, he probably met Thomas Cooper and R. W. Gibbes, Cooper's teaching assistant; shortly after the probable visit to Columbia, Audubon enlisted Gibbes to carry the initial plates of the folio from Charleston to Columbia to show them to the legislature.[5]

A motion to purchase "Mr. Audubon's work on American Ornithology for the use of the College Library" was approved in the House of Representatives, "Yeas 51 Nays 50," on December 17, 1831. The resolution stipulated that "the terms are as follows, to wit, two hundred and twenty dollars on the delivery of the first volume, and a yearly subscription of sixty dollars, until its completion. The work to be completed and comprehend all the birds of America drawn to the size of life and accurately coloured in four volumes. It is expected that the whole work when completed will not exceed eight hundred dollars."[6]

The provision for an annual "subscription of sixty dollars" reflects the fact that the folio was published and distributed as a serial; this allowed Audubon to pay Robert Havell Jr., the English printer, as prints were produced. It also made the initial cost less daunting for patrons. Subscribers, like the college, were to pay in installments as they received each set of unbound prints. Audubon originally planned for each completed folio to consist of eight hundred prints, and he hoped to distribute five new images to each subscriber every two months. Production was time-consuming and complex. Audubon inspected Havell's first print — of the wild turkey — in June 1827. The final image was not printed until June 1838, so it is not surprising that nine years elapsed before he received the final payment for the college's folio.[7]

Whether or not Audubon paused in Columbia in October 1831, Charleston was his destination. There he met and was befriended by the Reverend John Bachman, a noted amateur ornithologist, and Bachman welcomed the Audubon party into his home. He provided lodging, a studio for the artist, and workspace where Audubon's son John preserved skins and mounted specimens to serve as models.[8]

Describing their time in Charleston, Audubon wrote, "It is impossible to do justice to the generous feelings of the Charlestonians, or to their extreme kindness towards me."[9] His gratitude is understandable, for in addition to providing accommodations, Bachman sought subscribers for Audubon's folio, and Audubon's sons married Bachman's daughters—John Woodhouse Audubon married Maria Rebecca, and Victor Gifford married Mary Eliza. In addition Bachman's sister-in-law, Maria Martin, painted many of the botanical specimens that provide settings for the birds and form essential elements of every composition.

On the printer's proof depicting the black-caped titmouse (plate 160), Audubon renamed the bird the Carolina titmouse and wrote, "I have, named it so partly because it occurs in Carolina, and partly because I was desirous of manifesting my gratitude towards the citizens of that State, who by their hospitality and polite attention have so much contributed to my comfort and happiness, whenever it has been my good fortune to be among them."[10]

Like many items in the college library, Audubon's folio becomes more interesting when an awareness of people and circumstances surrounding its creation and acquisition prompts researchers to explore other aspects of his work. For example, *The Birds of North America* leads to his lesser-known *Ornithological Biographies,* descriptions of bird behavior and habitat written to supplement the *Birds of North*

John James Audubon, *Birds of North America*, plate 26, Carolina parrot. Irvin Department of Rare Books and Special Collections.

America plates. His commentary on the Carolina parrot, *Conuropsis carolinensis* (plate 26), is typical:

> The Parrots in my picture are shown feeding on the seeds of the cocklebur. The bird alights on the plant, plucks the bur from the stem with its bill, and takes it from the latter

> with one foot, in which it turns it over until the joint is so placed as to meet the attacks of its bill. Then it breaks open the bur, takes out the fruit, and lets the shell drop. Once a flock has discovered a field well filled with these plants, they will eat or pluck off all the seeds, and return to the place day after day until hardly any are left. . . . The Parrot does not satisfy himself with cockleburs, but eats or destroys almost every kind of fruit, a fact which makes him an unwelcome visitor to the planter, farmer, and gardener.[11]

The Audubon birds are rarely criticized today, but when they were first shown publicly in 1826–27, several naturalists faulted them for being overly dramatic. Before *The Birds of North America* was published, most illustrations of birds—and animals and plants too—were composed as silhouettes.[12] Audubon rejected the static, "pressed-flower" tradition by using foreshortened, three-dimensional poses, often presenting multiple points of view within a single image. Critics reacted by claiming he was sacrificing accuracy in order to gain visual impact. The Carolina parrot exemplifies Audubon's attempt to bring birds to life by showing them in motion.

The animated quality of Audubon's compositions conveys—and may stem from—his emotional response to wildlife. Passages in his journals make his empathy explicit: for example, "when I close my eyes I hear the birds warbling, nay, every sound; the shriek of the Falcon, the coy Doves cooing; the whistling note of the Grackle seems to fill my ear, again I am in the cornfield amidst millions of these birds, and then, transported afar, I must tread lightly and with care, to avoid the venomous Rattler."[13]

Charles Waterton, Audubon's most acerbic English critic, pecked away at Audubon's reputation for several years.[14] He

John James Audubon, *Birds of North America*, plate 21, mockingbird. Irvin Department of Rare Books and Special Collections.

ridiculed the mockingbirds with the rattlesnake in their nest (plate 21) by insisting that snakes never pursue their prey and that rattlesnakes' fangs are never extended the way Audubon presented them. In 1835 Waterton wrote:

> I have been the midst of snakes for many years: I have observed them on the ground, on trees, in bushes, on bedsteads, and upon old mouldering walls, but never in my life have I seen a snake pursue a retreating prey. I am fully satisfied in my own mind that it is not in a snake's nature to do so. A snake would follow its retreating prey in a tree with just about as much success as a greyhound would follow a hare through the mazes of a thick wood. . . . I beg leave to draw attention to plate 21. . . . The mouth of the rattlesnake is wide open and the fangs are the first things to attract the inspector's notice. . . . The artist, in his note . . . says that he confined a rattlesnake for three years in a cage. Did he never once get a sight of the fangs all that time?. . . . If he can produce one single solitary fang of any snake, great or small, with the point turned upwards, I will submit to be sent to the treadmill for three years.[15]

Audubon needed credibility as a naturalist in order to sell *Birds.* Authors signing their letters "R. B." and "Audubon Jr." defended him in English journals, and to rebut Waterton either John Bachman or Audubon himself obtained a testimonial letter about a climbing rattlesnake from Thomas Cooper:

> October 21, 1833
> Mr. Audubon
> Dear Sir or Madam: About three weeks ago, my son and two of my black servants, observed a very large rattle snake climbing up the fence that separates my garden from the road, at my country house. The snake put himself in the attitude of striking, whereupon one of the men ran for a gun, and shot the snake on the last rail but one of the fence. The snake was 4.3 long, as thick as my wrist, and had seven rattles.
>
> I am Dear Sir
> Your Obedient servant
> Thomas Cooper[16]

Like many manuscripts, this testimonial offers multiple layers of meaning. It indicates that Cooper had a son, a country house, and two black servants and that he knew or knew of Audubon and the "climbing rattlesnake" controversy. Cooper's "rattlesnake note" is also a final, fragmentary bit of information tangentially related to the antebellum library's acquisition of the Audubon folio.

When the folio was purchased, pressure for secession was building like a thunderhead. The war would affect the college, and it is worth remembering that as early as 1827, Cooper proclaimed the time had come to "calculate the value of the Union"; that as a member of the U.S. House of Representatives, Robert W. Barnwell had advocated nullification; and that later as president of the college, he said a better library would help South Carolina be educationally "independent of other states."

Although there was no specifically secessionist or racist curriculum, the library's collection was used by Cooper and others to support the proslavery, secessionist point of view. Robert Henry, professor of moral philosophy, for example, urged students to study the arts as the hallmarks of high culture. He cited the inspirational literature and monuments of Egypt, Greece, and Rome as evidence of racial superiority.[17] Politics tinted pedagogy, and the effect of these lessons spread beyond South Carolina, for alumni settled throughout the South. "Between 1830 and 1860, South Carolina led all states in the Union in percentage of out migrant population. Almost half of the alumni left the state, and nearly all went to the lower South." They became legislators, preachers, and teachers. "[South Carolina] College alumni served as antebellum governors of Georgia, Florida, Alabama and Mississippi. More than a dozen alumni were sent to Congress from Georgia, Alabama, Mississippi, Louisiana, and Texas." Alumni participated in every secession convention. One alumnus wrote that the proslavery, secessionist influence of the college was so great "as to give it historical significance."[18]

As the new college library opened, South Carolina established two military schools in 1842 — the Citadel in Charleston and the Arsenal Magazine Guard in Columbia.[19] Other southern states did likewise; it was a sign of the times. The Virginia Military Institute was created in 1839, and the Seminary of Learning and Military Academy was established in Louisiana in 1859 (it would become Louisiana State University). William Tecumseh Sherman was the Louisiana school's initial superintendent.[20]

On the South Carolina College campus, the corps of cadets personified the growing militancy throughout the South. They marched on what became known as Davis Field (the site of the fountain in front of the current Cooper Library). Their weapons, provided by the state, were kept under lock and key on the lower floor of the library, perhaps in the closet beneath the spiral staircase leading to the new reading room or in one of the rooms that flanked the entrance hall.

Despite growing political tension off campus, the college and library flourished during the 1840s and early 1850s. The mid-nineteenth-century library catalog (1849) is 151 pages long. It has no trace of the old Baconian categories of knowledge. This catalog lists books alphabetically by author or by title if the author was unknown. One surviving copy was bound with blank pages on which the librarian recorded acquisitions. The librarian's copy shows that 1,850 volumes were added to the collection between 1848 and 1858. Consequently, as Patrick Scott has observed, "Taking account of multivolume sets, holdings before the War significantly exceeded 20,000 volumes."[21] The library grew just before the war to accommodate a growing student body. The enrollments of 1848 (221), 1849 (237), and 1858 (201) represent plateaus that were not exceeded for another quarter century.

Bound mid-nineteenth-century shelf lists survive for several of the alcoves, and they tell something about the organization of the collection in the new library prior to Reconstruction. For example, an author list for the "South Gallery" (the balcony) shows that it was the "Medical Alcove," but this is the only collection that can be assigned to a specific location, for which alcove the shelf list numbers refer to is unknown. Alcove five held "translations"; alcove nine was devoted to poetry, literary criticism, and literature; civil law, political economy, and statistics were grouped into alcove ten; alcove eight was devoted to Latin and philosophy; alcove eleven to theology. And alcove twelve contained books on rhetoric, logic, and modern languages.[22]

The antebellum librarians used ledgers — one for students and another for faculty — to record books borrowed. These ledgers show who was reading what just before the war. For example, the most distinguished member of the faculty, Francis Lieber (1800–1872), borrowed around 250 books during the period 1846–56. Specific connections between his reading and writings are not readily apparent; nonetheless the record is evocative.[23]

Lieber had joined the South Carolina College faculty in 1835 as a professor of political economics and history.

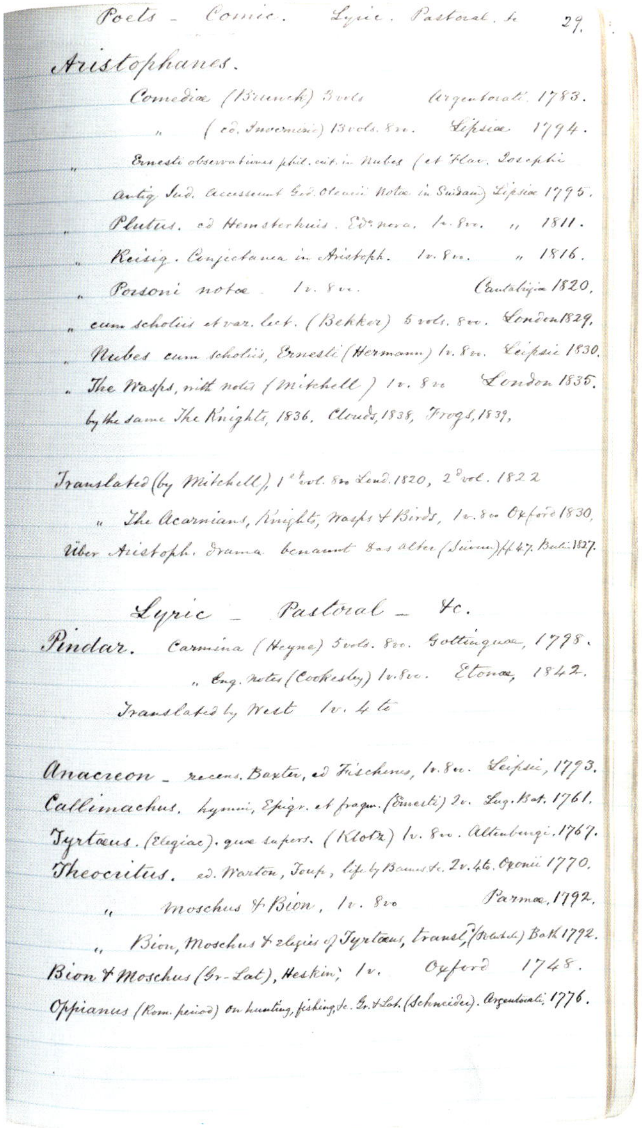
Poets – Comic. Lyric. Pastoral. &c. 29.

Aristophanes.
Comediæ (Brunck) 3 vols Argentorati 1783.
" (ed. Invernizi) 13 vols. 8vo. Lipsiæ 1794.
" Ernesti observationes phil. crit. in Nubes (et Flav. Josephi Antiq. Jud. Accessunt Ed. Olearii Notæ in Suidam) Lipsiæ 1795.
" Plutus. ed Hemsterhuis. Ed. nova. 1v. 8vo. " 1811.
" Reisig. Conjectanea in Aristoph. 1v. 8vo. " 1816.
" Porsoni notæ 1v. 8vo. Cantabrigiæ 1820.
" cum scholiis et var. lect. (Bekker) 5 vols. 8vo. London 1829.
" Nubes cum scholiis, Ernesti (Hermann) 1v. 8vo. Lipsiæ 1830.
" The Wasps, with notes (Mitchell) 1v. 8vo London 1835.
by the same The Knights, 1836. Clouds, 1838, Frogs, 1839,

Translated (by Mitchell) 1st vol. 8vo Lond. 1820, 2d vol. 1822
" The Acarnians, Knights, Wasps & Birds, 1v. 8vo Oxford 1830.
Über Aristoph. drama benannt das alter (Süvern) Berlin 1827.

Lyric – Pastoral – &c.
Pindar. Carmina (Heyne) 3 vols. 8vo. Gottingæ, 1798.
" Eng. notes (Cookesley) 1v. 8vo. Etonæ, 1842.
Translated by West 1v. 4to

Anacreon – recens. Baxter, ed Fischerus, 1v. 8vo. Lipsiæ, 1793.
Callimachus. hymni, Epigr. et fragm. (Ernesti) 2v. Lug. Bat. 1761.
Tyrtæus. (Elegiae). quæ supers. (Klotz) 1v. 8vo. Altenburgi. 1767.
Theocritus. ed. Warton, Toup, life by Bowness &c. 2v. 4to. Oxonii 1770.
" Moschus & Bion, 1v. 8vo Parmæ, 1792.
" Bion, Moschus & elegies of Tyrtæus, transl. (Polwhele) Bath 1792.
Bion & Moschus (Gr-Lat), Heskin; 1v. Oxford 1748.
Oppianus (Rom. period) on hunting, fishing, &c. Gr. & Lat. (Schneider). Argentorati 1776.

South Carolina College Library records.

Francis Lieber, carte-de-visit by A. A. Turner at D. Appleton & Co., New York, circa 1865.

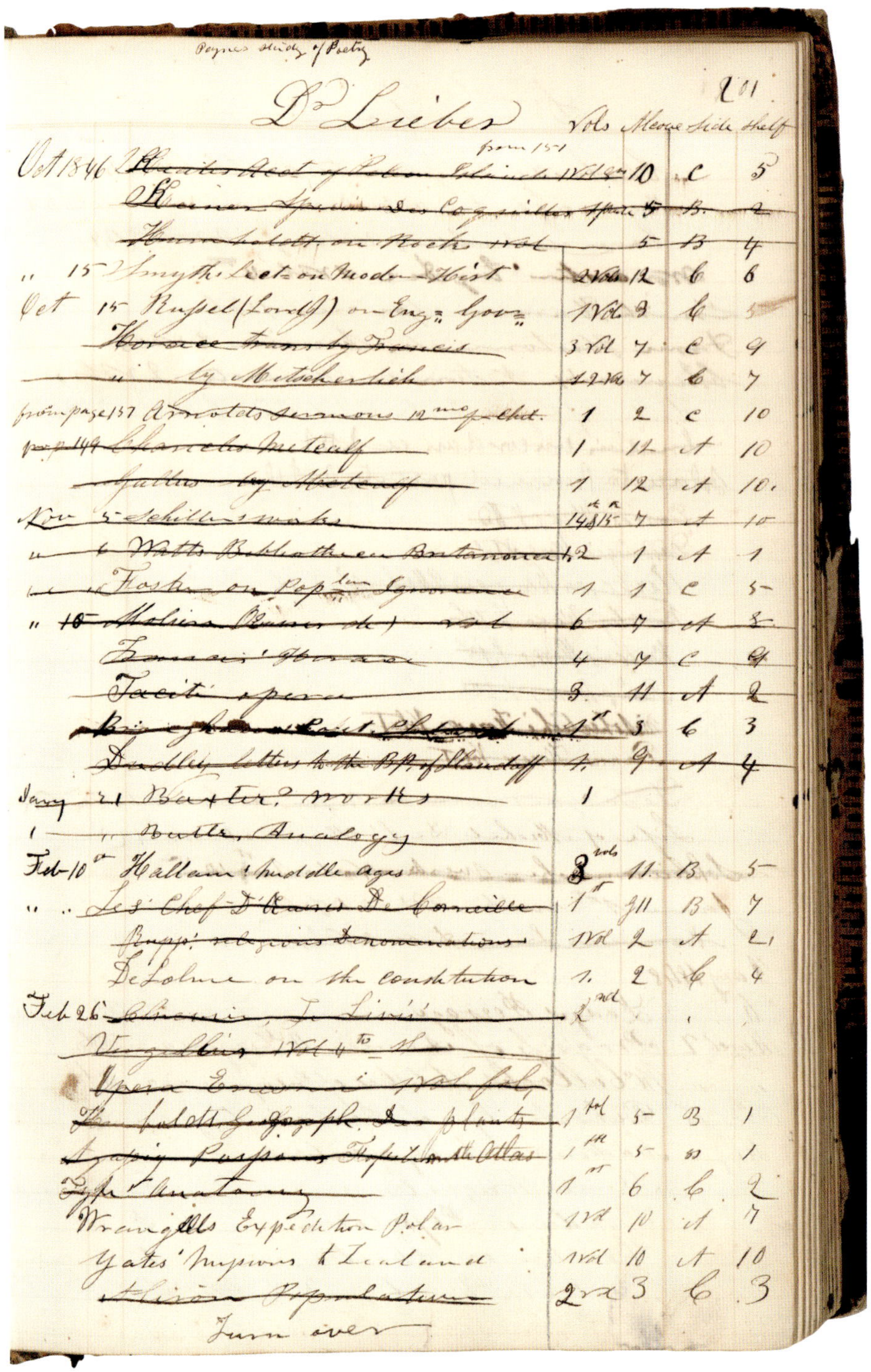

South Carolina College library checkout record for Francis Lieber.

Oscar Lieber, ninth plate daguerreotype, circa 1857.

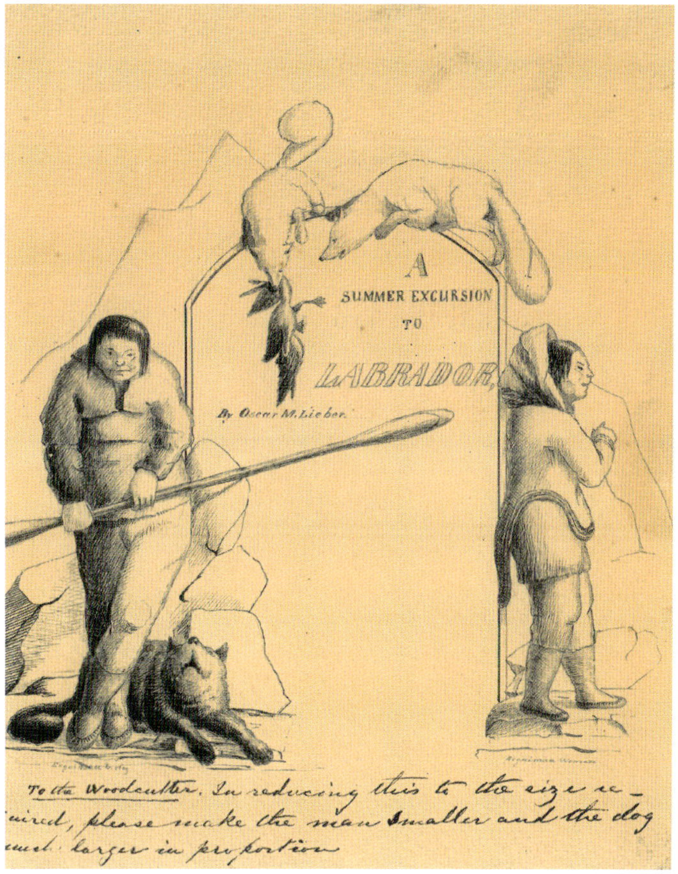

Oscar Lieber, *A Summer Excursion to Labrador*, 1860.

Unfortunately as a unionist he found life in the South increasingly difficult, so he moved to New York in 1856. During the two decades he lived in Columbia, he published internationally and corresponded with prominent Americans and Europeans. His papers in the Caroliniana demonstrate how meaningful manuscript collections can be. This one collection of 1,242 items of personal and professional correspondence contains contemporary comments on slavery, travel, family life, philosophy, art, linguistics, politics, and education. Letters invite scholars to consider biases, to watch themes develop and evolve across a sequence of documents, to relate manuscripts to printed material, and to link the writers' first-person observations to events in the larger world. The Lieber collection exemplifies the type of source material needed for "scientific history."[24]

Time mutes the significance of details, but many of the Lieber papers retain the power to bring the past alive. Those dealing with abolition, secession, and the war are especially evocative, and this is not surprising, for two of Lieber's sons, Hamilton and Norman, fought for the North. (Hamilton lost an arm.) Their eldest son, Oscar — a promising geologist who studied in Germany; published; worked on geological surveys in Mississippi, Alabama, and South Carolina; and traveled to Labrador with a scientific expedition before the war — fought for the South and was mortally wounded at the Battle of Eltham's Landing.[25]

Today Francis Lieber is remembered primarily as the author of the Lieber Code. These rules of military conduct (written at the request of President Lincoln) are "said to have contributed significantly to the first Geneva Convention in 1864 and even the 1949 Geneva Conventions."[26]

Concerning libraries, "this then, was the picture until the Civil War. . . . A major principle was separation of books from readers. Shelving was in alcoves, with galleries for expansion. Light and ventilation were provided by windows and skylights; gas lighting, which became normal in the latter half of the century, was provided only very slowly. There was little heat. Emphasis was on the protection, not the use, of books. A notable exception to nearly all the above and a shining example of enlightened librarianship was the University of South Carolina, but it was far from the mainstream and its example apparently had no influence on the important institutions of the North."[27]

Secessionist demonstrations, bonfires, speeches, and parades occurred frequently in Columbia throughout the late 1850s. Students were drawn to the turbulence like moths to a flame, and it appears that virtually all of them participated in the campus riots of 1856 and 1857. Robert W. Gibbes, Thomas Cooper's former assistant and publisher of the *Daily South Carolinian* newspaper, thought the students' excitability and lawlessness might be attributed in part to the times: "disobedience, resistance to law, and to authority, has been so often inculcated by great men and editors, that it is not wonderful that boys should have regarded it as chivalric to be disobedient."[28] Nobody died in these two upheavals, but the students bore arms, and this led the trustees to disband the corps of cadets temporarily on June 11, 1857. They also concluded the college needed stronger leadership, so they forced the college president, Charles F. McKay, and for good measure the entire faculty, to resign.

Some of the old staff was reinstated; several new professors were hired, and Augustus B. Longstreet was elected by the trustees to succeed McKay as president. During this period of administrative transition, nothing notable happened in or to the library.

When the war began, John Hillary Gary (1840–63) was student-captain of the recently revived South Carolina corps of cadets, and just as Audubon's folio represents a high point of the antebellum library, Gary's family papers in the Caroliniana provide a vivid glimpse of life on campus at the outset of the war. The Gary papers also show how diverse types of ephemera — letters, pictures, notes, and clippings — can be assembled like pieces of a puzzle to present a coherent picture.[29]

In addition to the picture of John H. Gary wearing his cadet uniform, the collection includes snippets from the minutes and rolls of the Clariosophic Literary Society. Literary societies were then an important part of student life (intercollegiate sports and fraternities came later). Speaking before his peers, Gary debated "whether the progress of civilization

Captain John H. Gary, in uniform of South Carolina College cadets, copied circa 1868 from a daguerreotype by Wearn & Hix in Columbia.

diminishes the love of martial glory." Eight months later he addressed the question "Should the South Secede from the Union upon the election of a black republican to the presidency?" He must have been high-spirited, for the society's "Critic's Book" cites him "for laughing aloud, for disturbing the 3rd critic and for leaning against the curtain"; for "leaving the hall door open and for laughing while answering to a report"; for "putting his hat on in the hall"; for "answering the roll out of order"; and "several times for leaving the hall door open."[30]

He was elected captain when the trustees and faculty reluctantly approved the revival of the corps of cadets in 1860, and upon hearing that Fort Sumter had been bombarded, Gary asked the governor and the college administration to allow the cadets to join the fray. The college administration refused. They kept the guns locked in the library.[31]

Nonetheless Gary and virtually the entire student body took the train to Charleston. They ostensibly went as individuals, for the corps did not have permission to leave campus. Gov. Francis Wilkinson Pickens had them serve briefly as his bodyguards, then he sent them to Sullivan's Island, where they patrolled the beach (April 12–13, 1861) within sight of Fort Sumter. Mary Boykin Chesnut visited their camp and wrote, "South Carolina College had volunteered to a boy. Professor Venable (The Mathematical) intends to raise a company from among them for the war, a permanent company. This is a grand frolic, no more—for the students at least!"[32]

When the spring term ended, Gary enlisted on June 6, 1861, as a second lieutenant of artillery. His unit helped capture a Federal gunboat on the Stono River, and he quickly rose to the rank of captain. He was wounded during the defense of Fort Wagner on James Island and died on August 17, 1863.

The faculty and president of the college were successful in preventing the cadets from serving as a unit, but in the spring and summer of 1862 most of the students enlisted, and classes ended for the duration of the war. On June 16, 1862, the governor and executive council informed the trustees that college buildings, excepting faculty residences and the library, would be used by the Confederacy as a hospital.

The trustees continued to meet in the library twice a year (typically May and November or December). They may have taken some comfort in routine, for their minutes scrupulously record mundane reports. During the war the librarian's reports usually began by noting, "No appropriation was made by the Legislature for the purchase of books; consequently, no addition has been made to the library."[33] An exception was 1862 when the book budget was $8.00. (The money was not spent.) C. Bruce Walker, the librarian, did begin a new catalog. He also recommended pasting "a paper containing the number of its alcove [illegible] and shelf" inside the cover of each book. He tended to leaks in the roof, a skylight, and the portico; he had the reading room whitewashed and its plaster repaired. He also tried to retrieve books checked out by Columbia residents.

Union troops entered Atlanta on September 2, 1864, and Mary Boykin Chesnut was incredulous that Columbians appeared paralyzed, unwilling or unable to take action. In her diary she wrote: "The men who would not join Noah in his ark-building must have left no descendants. They do not count Sherman among the devastating forces of nature. I do believe they forget his existence." Later she wrote that "deep waters are closing over us; and we . . . are like the outsiders at the time of the Flood. We eat, drink, laugh, dance, in lightness of heart!"[34]

Nobody in Columbia knew where the Federal troops would go or when they might appear. Sherman divided his forces in Savannah, and he ordered Gen. Oliver Otis Howard to capture the capital of South Carolina. He commanded Howard to spare private property, asylums, and libraries: "[Order No. 26] General Howard will cross the Saluda and Broad Rivers as near their mouths as possible, occupy Columbia, destroy the public buildings, railroad property, manufacturing and machine shops; but will spare libraries, asylums, and private dwellings."[35]

Federal troops entered the city on February 17, 1865, and Howard posted a guard detail at the entrance to the Horseshoe. As darkness fell, the city burst into flame, and burning embers fell on campus. The roofs of Flinn Hall (then located where the War Memorial Building is today), the president's house, Rutledge, and DeSaussure all caught fire. Patients—almost two hundred sick and wounded—stumbled or were carried from the two big buildings, and one of the nurses, Mary Amarintha Snowden, led her young son, Yates, onto the Horseshoe. Spectral figures scrambled onto rooftops to fight the flames. Firelight flickered across facades on the Horseshoe, but disaster was averted. The library building escaped unscathed, but the librarian later informed the trustees that ninety-seven books, borrowed by Columbia residents, had burned in homes throughout the city.[36]

After the war, while the State House was being made habitable, the racially integrated Reconstruction South Carolina Senate convened (1867–69) in the library reading room.[37] Here, and in Longstreet Theater where the House met, they drafted the new state constitution, which provided for "the maintenance of the State University" and stipulated that "all the public schools, colleges and universities of the

State, supported in whole or in part by the public funds, shall be free and open to all the children and youths of the State, without regard to race and color." For good measure the Reconstruction legislature passed an act in 1869 stating that there should be no "distinction in the admission of students or the management of the University on account of race, color or creed."[38]

The postwar Board of Trustees was appointed in 1868. They also wanted the college to become a "university," and this meant replacing the antebellum emphasis on Greek, Latin, and rhetoric with a curriculum more immediately relevant to contemporary society. The faculty and student body were integrated in 1873. Racial integration, and to a lesser extent the new curriculum, prompted many faculty members to resign. The librarian resigned too.

The trustees hired Erastus W. Everson (1837–97) to replace Walker as librarian. They also hired Richard Theodore Greener (1844–1922) as professor of mental and moral philosophy, sacred literature, and evidences of Christianity.[39]

Everson was a Union veteran, and Greener, a Harvard graduate who soon would replace Everson as librarian, was the university's first African American faculty member. Neither remained in the library for long. Everson served as librarian and secretary of the faculty from October 1873 until the summer of 1875. Greener took over for the remainder of the year. Their experiences, both at the university and beyond its walls, reflect the turmoil of the time.

Everson was born in Massachusetts. He enlisted in 1861 and was wounded at Bull Run and Fredericksburg. When the war ended, he was in South Carolina, and for eighteen months (1866–67) he worked for General Howard inspecting Federal troops. He then transferred to the Freedman's Bureau

Erastus Everson, circa 1861.

Richard Theodore Greener, circa 1880, by Larry Lebby, courtesy University of South Carolina Law School.

and traveled across the upstate for three years arresting "bush whackers" and collecting taxes. In Laurens in 1871 he ran afoul of the Ku Klux Klan and was lucky to escape with his life. Testifying to a federal committee about the Klan, Everson noted he "carried seven bullets" in his body.

Everson was not trained as a librarian; nonetheless he started the first card catalog of the library's holdings, though he did not finish it, for he slipped away without giving notice in May 1875. He went back to Massachusetts and is thought to have worked there as a newspaperman until his death.[40]

Richard Theodore Greener was born in Philadelphia. His father went west, ostensibly looking for gold, and disappeared. His mother moved the family to Boston when he was young and enabled him to attend Oberlin, then Andover and Harvard. Having studied history, political ethics, and metaphysics, in 1870 he became the first African American to graduate from Harvard, and he did it with honors. He was the principal of the Institute for Colored Youth in Philadelphia and the Sumner School in Washington, D.C. In Washington he also worked for Frederick Douglass at the *New National Era*. James A. Bowley, a new trustee of South Carolina College, recommended Greener, and when he was hired, Gov. Franklin J. Moses praised the college, saying, "For the first time in the history of South Carolina one of the literary chairs in her highest institution of learning is worthily and acceptably filled by a colored Professor."[41] After Everson had been gone about a month, the trustees' minutes note, "the Faculty on June 14, 1875, voted 'to request Prof. Greener to attend to the correspondence of the University during the absence of a Librarian and take charge of the keys of the Library subject to the order of the Library Committee.'"[42]

Greener informed the board that "Major Everson, shortly before his departure, had begun a new catalogue of the Library, but had only progressed far enough to throw everything into disorder." He continued:

> I determined to apply myself during the vacation to a complete re-organization of the books in the Library — no

> slight task—and make it possible for my successor to go at once about the preparation of a new card catalogue according to the latest methods now in vogue in the best Libraries.
>
> In accordance with this design and by the aid of three college students whom I hired to assist me, we have rearranged all the books in the library, corrected many misclassifications of Major Everson owing to his ignorance of Greek, Latin or French, added new shelving and brackets, put all the busts into place and hung ten portraits belonging to the Euphradian Society upon the walls. While this work was in progress, I wrote an account, forty pages of M. S. for the Bureau of Education at Washington on the origin, gifts to, valuable and curious books in and a detailed statement of the Legislative appropriations to the Library from 1803 to the present time.
>
> In order to be received at Washington, this work was to be ready by the 1st of September, otherwise our Library could have had no suitable notice in a book shortly to be issued by the Bureau on the Libraries of the United States.[43]

A synopsis of Greener's report on the library was published by the Federal Bureau of Education as "part of the exhibit made by this Office at the Centennial Exhibition."[44] Greener's photograph album preserves the best visual record of the library during his time in South Carolina.

In addition to teaching and serving as librarian and secretary of the faculty, Greener was active in civic affairs. He spoke to a teachers' meeting in Chester, read a paper on John Milton in Charleston, was a member of the Richland County Board of Health, and served on a legislative commission on public education. Campaigning for the Republicans in 1876, he spoke in Newberry, Anderson, Walhalla, Greenville, Pickens, Laurens, Columbia, and Lexington. Amid all this activity, he found time to read law and received a law degree from the university in 1876.

Greener was an energetic advocate for civil rights, and the election of the Hampton Democrats in South Carolina in 1876 must have dashed his hopes for positive change in South Carolina. The new Democratic legislature lost no time in stripping away African Americans' rights. They also installed an all-white Board of Trustees at the university, and these trustees forced the entire faculty to resign. The university closed in 1877 and reopened in 1880 as an all-white institution.

Greener left South Carolina. His departure was one of many signs that the Jim Crow era had begun.[45]

The centennial prompted Melvil Dewey to invite librarians to gather at the exposition in Philadelphia. One hundred and three delegates responded. They founded the American Library Association and published Dewey's decimal classification system in their new *Library Journal.* Librarians mark 1876 as a milestone in the development of their profession.

The centennial also stimulated a broad interest in local history, and this would ultimately influence the creation of the South Caroliniana library; a more direct influence was an emphasis on document-based "scientific history" promoted by Johns Hopkins University (founded in 1876). Social and political turbulence in South Carolina would also affect the university and its library. These factors intermingled, fugue-like, as the twentieth century began and the University of South Carolina prepared for its own centennial.

The Exterior of the Library, Prof. Richard Theodore Greener's photograph album, circa 1874. Courtesy Widener Library, Harvard University.

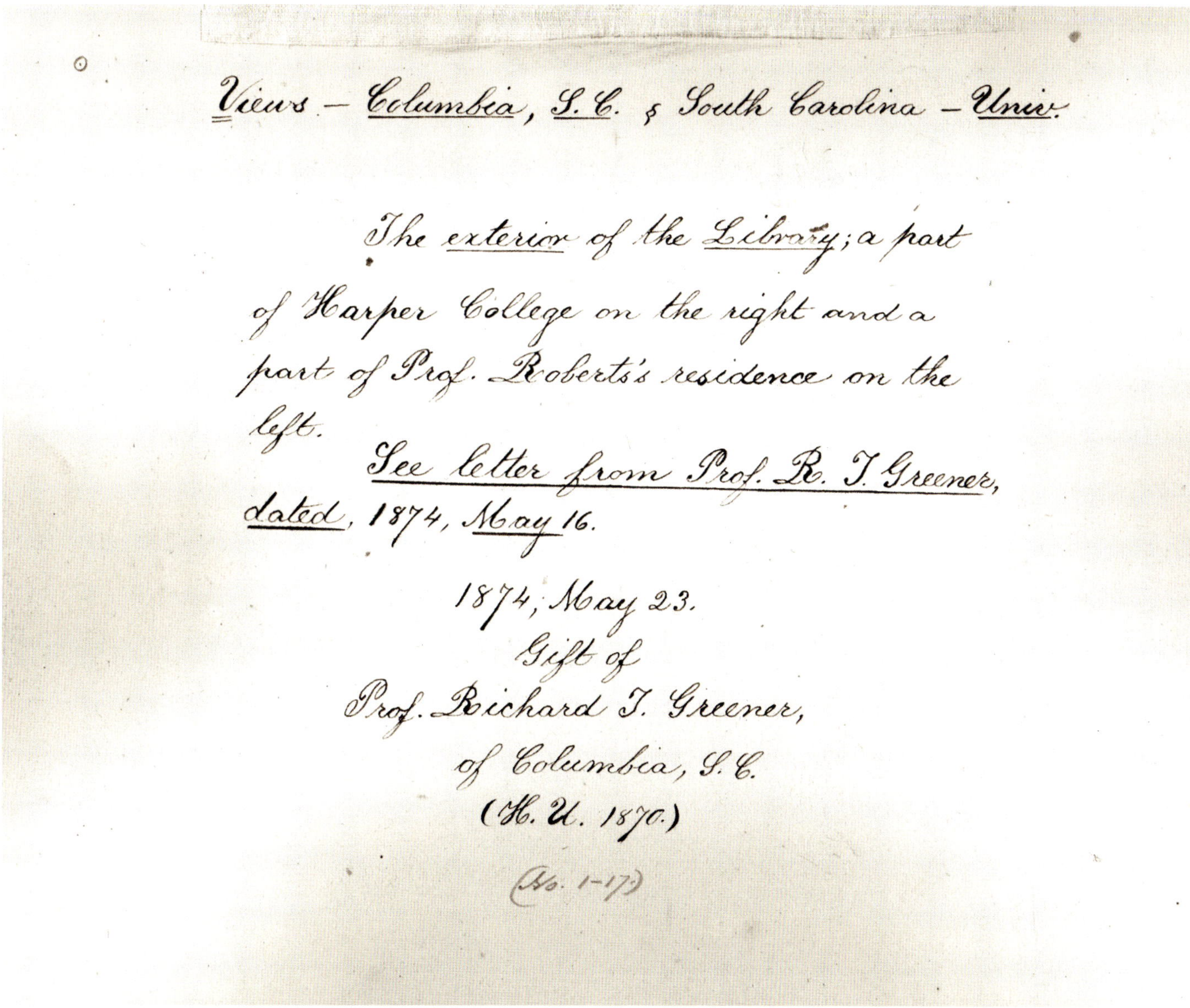

Views — Columbia, S.C. & South Carolina — Univ.

The exterior of the Library; a part of Harper College on the right and a part of Prof. Roberts's residence on the left.

See letter from Prof. R. T. Greener, dated, 1874, May 16.

1874, May 23.
Gift of
Prof. Richard T. Greener,
of Columbia, S.C.
(H. U. 1870.)

(Ho. 1-17)

Professor Greener's caption, *The Exterior of the Library*, circa 1874. Courtesy Widener Library, Harvard University.

The Reading Room, Professor Greener's photograph album, circa 1874. Courtesy Widener Library, Harvard University.

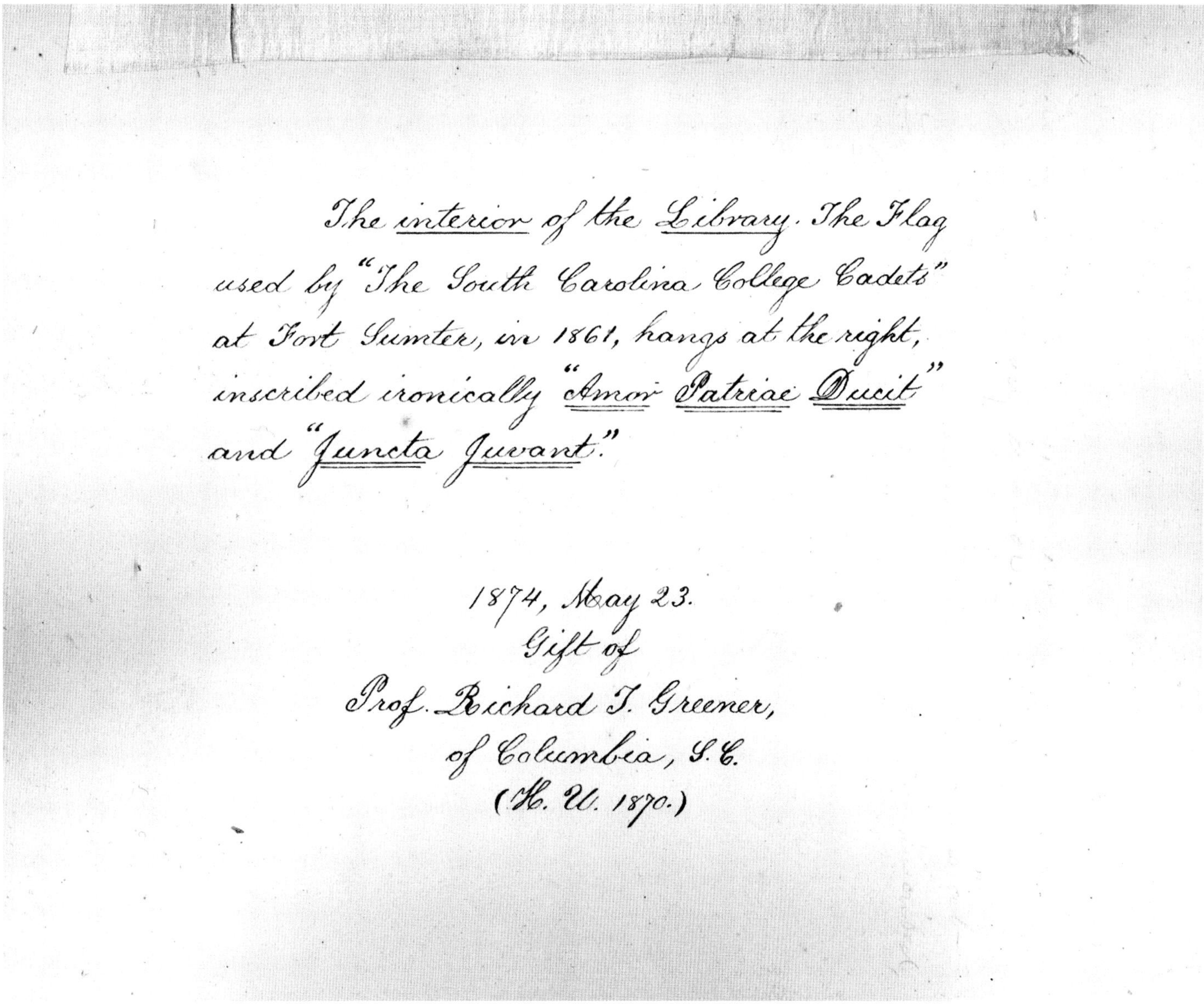

The interior of the Library. The Flag used by "The South Carolina College Cadets" at Fort Sumter, in 1861, hangs at the right, inscribed ironically "Amor Patriae Ducit" and "Juncta Juvant."

1874, May 23.
Gift of
Prof. Richard T. Greener,
of Columbia, S.C.
(H. U. 1870.)

Professor Greener's caption, *The Interior of the Library*, circa 1874
Ill: 3.11 facade. Courtesy Widener Library, Harvard University.

The National Centennial Exposition in Philadelphia included a full-size replica of the turret of the *Monitor,* Native American crafts, a Colonial New England kitchen, George Washington's carriage and "relics" (clothes, crockery, and furniture), and a pioneer frontier camp complete with hunters in costume and a tethered bear and deer. Most of the northern states had individual buildings: for example, Massachusetts's "structure occupies one of the most prominent positions. . . . it is built after the style of houses common in colonial times, and of course presents a rather quaint-looking appearance that could not fail to attract general attention."[46] With the exception of Greener's report, South Carolina did not participate in the National Centennial Exposition.[47]

Anniversaries promote reflection, and immediately after 1876 historical societies popped up around the country like summer mushrooms after rain. Nationwide there were only sixty-five of them in 1865, but there were two thousand in 1900. "The real flowering of local history," say Carol Kammen and Norma Prendergast, "occurred after the Centennial Celebration."[48] For the next half-century, Americans often lived in Colonial or Georgian Revival–style homes furnished with period style and reproduction furniture. Genealogy became a popular pastime. Roadside historic markers were placed to preserve and promote communal memory. Visiting historic sites became a recognized form of tourism. Whole villages and streetscapes were preserved, restored, or re-created, and the market for all sorts of antiques flourished.

At the same time the centennial stimulated interest in American history, the practice or writing of history was being transformed by new teaching methods. Johns Hopkins University was established in 1876, and before it opened, Daniel Coit Gilman, its first president, visited London, Zurich, Dresden, Vienna, Berlin, Freiburg, and Edinburgh to observe Germanic seminars. Johns Hopkins's curriculum featured small classes in which advanced students used primary materials to conduct original research. In an intimate setting, the students presented papers to their professor and peers. Historical writing in which each fact was substantiated by reference to a primary source was soon called "scientific history." By the turn of the century, Johns Hopkins's seminar model was emulated in colleges and universities across the country. Historians and aspiring historians came to believe that original, historic manuscripts — primary sources — were vital to their craft.[49]

Collecting old manuscripts was not a wholly new phenomenon. Americans have systematically saved evidence of their heritage since the late eighteenth century. The Massachusetts Historical Society, established in 1791, was perhaps the first organization to acquire and preserve manuscripts programmatically. Jeremy Belknap, an early member, said, "We intend to be an active, not a passive, literary body; not lie waiting, like a bed of oysters, for the tide (of communication) to flow in upon us, but to seek and find, to preserve and communicate literary intelligence, especially in the historical way." Explaining a trip to Connecticut looking for documents, he wrote, "There is nothing like having a good repository, and keeping a good lookout, not waiting at home for things to fall into the lap, but prowling about like a wolf for the prey."[50]

After the national centennial, collectors sought "prey" in South Carolina. People with money and an interest in manuscripts, antique furniture, or architectural woodwork found opportunities in the post-Reconstruction South; so many came hunting bits of history that Carolinians called the phenomenon "the second Yankee invasion." This invasion entailed the loss of heritage as outsiders purchased various aspects of the cultural landscape.

Between around 1885 and 1935, wealthy northerners converted some 112 former plantations totaling around 345,000 acres into winter homes and hunting preserves.[51] The Vanderbilts, Huntingtons, Winthrops, and their ilk hunted deer and quail, ducks and geese, and they typically posted the land. Northerners also bought and dismantled houses. They reinstalled historic Charleston paneling and ironwork in residences and museums in Minnesota, Michigan, New York, and Delaware.

Manuscripts were taken away too. Duke acquired historic documents from the South Carolina families of William Watts Ball, Francis W. Dawson, Thomas Rhett Smith Elliott, the Hemphills, John P. Grace, John Jackson McSwain, and James Henry Rice Jr. The Southern Manuscript Collection at the University of North Carolina at Chapel Hill also collected actively and obtained South Carolina papers from the Elliott-Gonzales family, the Boykin family, John Ewing Colhoun, Alexander Cheves Haskell, Mitchell King, Alexander Robert Lawton, the Manigault family, William Porcher Miles, the Singleton family, John Rutledge, the Grimball family, and John and Keating Simons Ball.[52] These losses alarmed historically minded South Carolinians. J. Rion McKissick, professor of journalism at the University of South Carolina, bemoaned pillage by "literary bootleggers from outlandish parts."[53]

During the late nineteenth and early twentieth centuries, the state was struggling financially, and as the century ended, agrarian populists, led by Benjamin Tillman, took control politically. They stifled the old South Carolina College's ambitions to become a full-fledged university by establishing rival institutions — Clemson, Winthrop, and South Carolina State — that competed for state and federal funding. The agrarians also directed the trustees of the old college to drop recently established programs in agriculture and engineering and to focus on the liberal arts.

The library suffered through these years of financial constraint and administrative turmoil: "no acquisitions were made in the 1880s aside from a few gifts."[54] Things barely improved during the 1890s; the book acquisition budget in 1893 was only ninety dollars; two years later it was seventy-one dollars. In 1898, as an economy measure, Frank C. Woodward, president of the university, took on the role of librarian and treasurer. He then appointed his clerk, Margaret H. Rion, librarian, and she did yeoman's work until 1912.

The university celebrated two centennials. In 1901 speeches and banquets commemorated the legislation that had established the college; then in 1905 a three-day extravaganza of sermons, orations, responses, and processions honored the opening of classes in 1805. Like the national centennial, these celebrations prompted thoughts about the future. Speakers did not dwell on troublesome contemporary politics or financial problems; instead they described opportunities for growth and change to help the state in years ahead.[55]

Immediately following the second celebration, two issues of the university *Bulletin* contained essays by faculty members suggesting ways to improve instruction and serve people across the state. The professors proposed a multifaceted university museum; their ideas foreshadowed the creation of the Caroliniana Library.

In the first essay, Andrew C. Moore, chairman of biology, presented the costs and benefits of a museum, and noted that the initial cost would be minimal, for the college already owned Thomas Cooper's geological collection and shells gathered by Joseph LeConte. These two collections, together with nineteenth-century portraits and marble busts, would provide the nucleus of a university museum. Moore was actively involved in public education, and he emphasized that a museum would serve the children throughout the state, for "the tangible and visible are valuable aids in attracting and fixing the attention" of students.[56] The museum would distribute educational kits, which, in addition to creating goodwill, might prompt donations. David S. Martin, a geologist, wrote the second essay. It described Cooper's collection and placed it in a national context.

The third essay focused on Native American artifacts, some three thousand to four thousand items, donated to the college by Dr. J. W. Babcock, whose father formed the collection after seeing exhibits at the Centennial Exposition and the Smithsonian. August Kohn, a college trustee, was the principal author of this essay, and he noted that the Babcock ethnographic collection was one of the three best in the country. An addendum by Edwin L. Green, historian of the college, noted that other institutions actively sought Native American artifacts and exhorted that "we owe it to the history of South Carolina that all that remains of her ancient population should be preserved—preserved within her borders."[57]

The conceptual cornerstone of the Caroliniana Library, the fourth essay, was by Yates Snowden (1858–1933), head of the history department. After acknowledging the potential of the existing collections of minerals and artifacts, Snowden observed that "it is singular, that in all its hundred years of splendid service, no effort has apparently been made to gather documents and MSS, relating to the history of the State. The College library, for example, contains now but a single MSS book, a small volume prepared by the Hon. John Drayton, in 1807, entitled *The Carolina Florist.*" He continued:

> It is the intention of the Department of Political Science and History . . . to establish a depository for MSS of all sorts, relating to history, biography, bibliography, natural and exact science, and any and all letter books, business account books, educational data, unpublished catalogues of libraries, public and private; old wills and inventories of estates, bills of sale, accounts current, and more particularly of the now rare "plantation books," and letters dealing with the economic life of the people during the slavery regime and during the War Between the States.

He went on to note that although public records were being "collected and classified by Mr. A. S. Salley, Jr., the Secretary of the Historical Commission of South Carolina," and despite the fact that the South Carolina Historical Society, established in Charleston in 1855, had important manuscript collections, much remained to be done. Many documents remained in private hands, vulnerable to "loss by fire or theft."[58]

The October 1906 *Bulletin* consisted of two essays by Edwin L. Green; both are devoted to the library. In the earlier *Bulletin,* Snowden announced his determination to collect written material related to life in South Carolina; Green linked this idea to a facility dedicated to Caroliniana.

Green's essay, "A New Library Building," begins by noting that the

> present library building . . . is too small for the needs of the University. . . . The ordinary needs of the University demand an enlarged building. But there is now being collected what is to be of the greatest benefit to the

> future fame of South Carolina, all books, pamphlets, manuscripts, everything that will in any way preserve the history of this State. For it there should be a special hall — Carolina Hall — or a special room in the library, wherein should be kept, not only things written, but also the portraits of distinguished South Carolinians, and why not also keep here specimens of old furniture, old plate, costumes, all things that would illustrate in the most complete way the life of the people of South Carolina from the mountains to the sea? This building should be made of brick and metal work, having no wood at all about it, in order to insure the greatest safety possible from fire.[59]

Green, like professors Moore and Martin, was thinking of a multifaceted state museum. Snowden, on the other hand, was primarily interested in manuscripts and published material relevant to South Carolina.

The trustees responded by deciding "that one-half of the appropriation for books shall now and each year hereafter be first reserved and applied, if as much be necessary, for the purchase of old or rare books, newspapers or other publications, connected with or relating to South Carolina; and that Mr. Kohn on the part of the Board, and Profs. Snowden and Green, from the faculty, be appointed a standing committee to carry out this resolution."[60]

Prompted perhaps by Snowden, Green, and Kohn, the librarian, Margaret H. Rion, began gathering state-related materials into one alcove, which by 1923 was called the "Carolina Alcove."[61] This collection was considered special, for "early in the new century one of the library's reading-room alcoves had been set off with a grilled gate to house the most valuable books of special South Carolina interest."[62] If that alcove could be identified today, it would be marked as the birthplace of the Caroliniana Library.

Yates Snowden's 1906 proposal justifies his reputation as one of the founders of the Caroliniana Library, but he is also remembered for his distinguished private collection of state-related material and a long career as a beloved professor. The son of a Confederate surgeon, he was born in Charleston. His mother brought him to Columbia during the war, and she was working as a nurse in Rutledge and DeSaussure the night the city burned. After the war Snowden attended the College of Charleston and subsequently worked as a reporter for the *Charleston News and Courier.* He briefly operated a used bookstore in Charleston with Alexander Samuel Salley Jr., a fellow newspaperman, before joining the college faculty as a historian in 1905.[63]

Snowden's bookstore partner, Salley, played a dark role in the early years of the Caroliniana. The two men's approaches to the practice of history were very different. Snowden represented the old school. He was a polished storyteller who "determined his facts, particularly those pertaining to the Civil War and reconstruction, from osmosis."[64] He never earned a college degree, and although he took courses at Columbia University in 1904 and was awarded an honorary doctorate by the College of Charleston in 1910, he remained disdainful of the new insistence on graduate degrees and meticulous documentary research.

Salley, on the other hand, was a devotee of scientific history. He participated in the post-centennial formation of historical societies in the South, the United Sons of Confederate Veterans in 1895 and the Southern Historical Association in 1896, and in 1899 he was hired as secretary, treasurer, and librarian of the South Carolina Historical Society in Charleston. Within a year he was editing the society's *South*

Alexander Samuel Salley Jr., circa 1900.

Carolina Historical and Genealogical Magazine. The magazine exemplified, and Salley personified, Johns Hopkins's reverence for original documents.

In 1905 an arm of the South Carolina secretary of state's office, the South Carolina Historical Commission, "a moribund . . . organization with no staff," advertised for a secretary to organize historic and current state records. Salley applied, claiming, "I am the only person in South Carolina who has adopted scientific historical research as a profession and who makes a livelihood exclusively thereby."[65] He got the job, and for forty-four years, until forced to retire, he ruled the state archives as a fiefdom. The commission consisted of five members appointed by the governor. They were empowered to collect, preserve, index, and publish material related to the history of the state and to make their collections at all times open to inspection and examination, for the purposes of historical research, and although the legislation stressed official state records, they were authorized to accept deposits by private parties of any historical material of any kind.

Salley was autocratic and pedantic and had no interest in working with others. Alone in the dank, dark basement of the State House, he worked among boxes and piles of papers, slowly and methodically, for fourteen years. He antagonized people who wanted to use the public records. Despite the broad authority defined by the legislation that created the commission, he did nothing to encourage the preservation of private records, and his restrictive policies made it obvious that the university needed to establish its own collection to support teaching and research.[66]

CHAPTER FOUR

COLLECTING CAROLINIANA

With the rarest exceptions, the death of each human individual is followed in a short time by complete oblivion. . . . Even family recollection or tradition quickly becomes dim, and soon fades utterly away. . . . men accounted famous at their deaths slip from living memories and become mere shadows or word pictures . . . which too often distort or misrepresent the original.

Charles W. Eliot, "John Gilley, Maine Farmer and Fisherman"

On June 17, 1905, Margaret H. Rion, who was simultaneously serving as librarian and university treasurer, informed Yates Snowden of his selection "to the professorship of History and Political Science." From that day forward, his career can be traced through correspondence in the Caroliniana's Snowden Collection.[1]

A gregarious, enthusiastic personality shines through his papers. The Snowden Collection consists of some seventeen thousand items, including letters from book dealers, newspapers, other academicians, students, colleagues, and people interested in the history of South Carolina. Incoming correspondence from 1905 until 1932 illuminates Snowden's interests and reputation. A 1929 letter from a former student provides a sense of closure: "It never occurred to me that you were a proper candidate for retirement . . . that you could be retired from anything."[2]

The stream of queries addressed to Snowden demonstrates a widespread interest in Caroliniana; a sample includes a letter from John R. Commons in New York thanking Snowden for help "in searching for early labor papers"; Laura A. White wrote from the University of Wyoming about her planned research trip to South Carolina; another letter came from William O. Scruggs at Louisiana State University concerning Snowden's interest in Charles Frederick Henningsen. Charles W. Ramsdell at the University of Texas wrote thanking Snowden for copies of two diaries;

Prof. Yates Snowden, undated.

correspondence also arrived from Princeton, the University of North Carolina, the University of Virginia, the Carnegie Institution, Harvard, and the University of Chicago.[3]

Other people in Columbia were interested in Caroliniana too; Samuel Chiles Mitchell, president of the university beginning in 1909, was one of them. Mitchell received a letter from William E. Dodd, a distinguished historian at the University of Chicago. Dodd wrote thanking him for the loan of "the Cooper material." Dodd also noted that he planned "to get in touch with all such collections of papers as those mentioned in your letter bearing both upon the religious and secular life of the south, and then to have my students work them when I find them ready." He hoped to come to Columbia and to visit collections in Kentucky and Tennessee.[4]

Dodd's work reflected his German Ph.D. (Leipzig, 1900). He grew up in rural North Carolina and became one of the earliest of the scientific historians to focus on the American South. President Mitchell and Professor Dodd certainly knew one another by reputation; perhaps they were acquainted, for Mitchell's Ph.D. in history was from Chicago. Robert Lee Meriwether (1890–1958), the principal creator of the Caroliniana Library, studied with Dodd, and Meriwether's subsequent work, and the library he envisioned, both manifest the best aspects of the new approach to historical writing and research.

Snowden and a circle of friends were creating private collections of state-related material for more than a decade before Meriwether joined the faculty in 1919. The early collectors included August Kohn, a university trustee and prominent businessman. Kohn, Snowden, and Salley had worked together as young newspaper reporters in Charleston. Salley and Kohn had grown up together in Orangeburg. Kohn's daughter recalled that "Papa was perhaps closer to Yates Snowden than to any one person outside of his family . . . [and] Papa was largely responsible for having Mr. Snowden give up his newspaper work to become history professor at the University."[5] Snowden and Kohn were appointed by the trustees in 1905 to the committee to purchase Caroliniana. The Gonzales brothers, Ambrose and William, were collectors too, and Helen Kohn Hennig's biography of her father conveys the joy these friends found in locating and saving old newspapers, pamphlets, rare books, and manuscripts — the

August Kohn's bookplate, circa 1935.

Catalog cards, undated.

stuff of history.[6] Dr. James Babcock, a bibliophile who first recommended collecting Caroliniana to Kohn, and Harry Watson, editor of the *Greenwood Index,* also collected, and they were later joined by J. Rion McKissick. All of these men became benefactors of the Caroliniana Library.

Without fanfare, shortly after the university's centennial, Margaret H. Rion began gathering Caroliniana into one alcove.[7] The alcove she set aside has not been identified, but the card catalog can be celebrated as her monument within the library. Building upon what Everson and Greener had begun, she completed the shift from shelf lists to a card system. According to an article in the university's campus newspaper, the *Gamecock,* she cataloged thirty thousand books over a period of two years without assistance.[8] Her work demonstrated an awareness of national trends and a dauntless commitment to the library.

In 1910 she wrote President Mitchell that

> the library is one of the most important departments of a college—"the treasure house" "the central feature," etc, but . . . it has not been so recognized in this institution. Ever since I have been here . . . economy has been the cry. Dr. Woodward, who first recognized the importance of the library, said to a friend of mine—I propose to economize on the library by getting a woman to fill the office of librarian and treasurer. He offered me the place in connection with the clerkship in his office, which I held for $35. I would not take less than $50. Other departments are supplied with assistants "at a living salary" without hesitation. . . . The only way to get the library catalogued is to spend some money . . . it should have a sufficient staff of workers and room to place the books so as to be readily available.[9]

Margaret Hunter Rion, copy of an 1885 photograph.

The "unsatisfactory conditions at the library, as to equipment, facilities, etc.," persisted, so Rion resigned.[10]

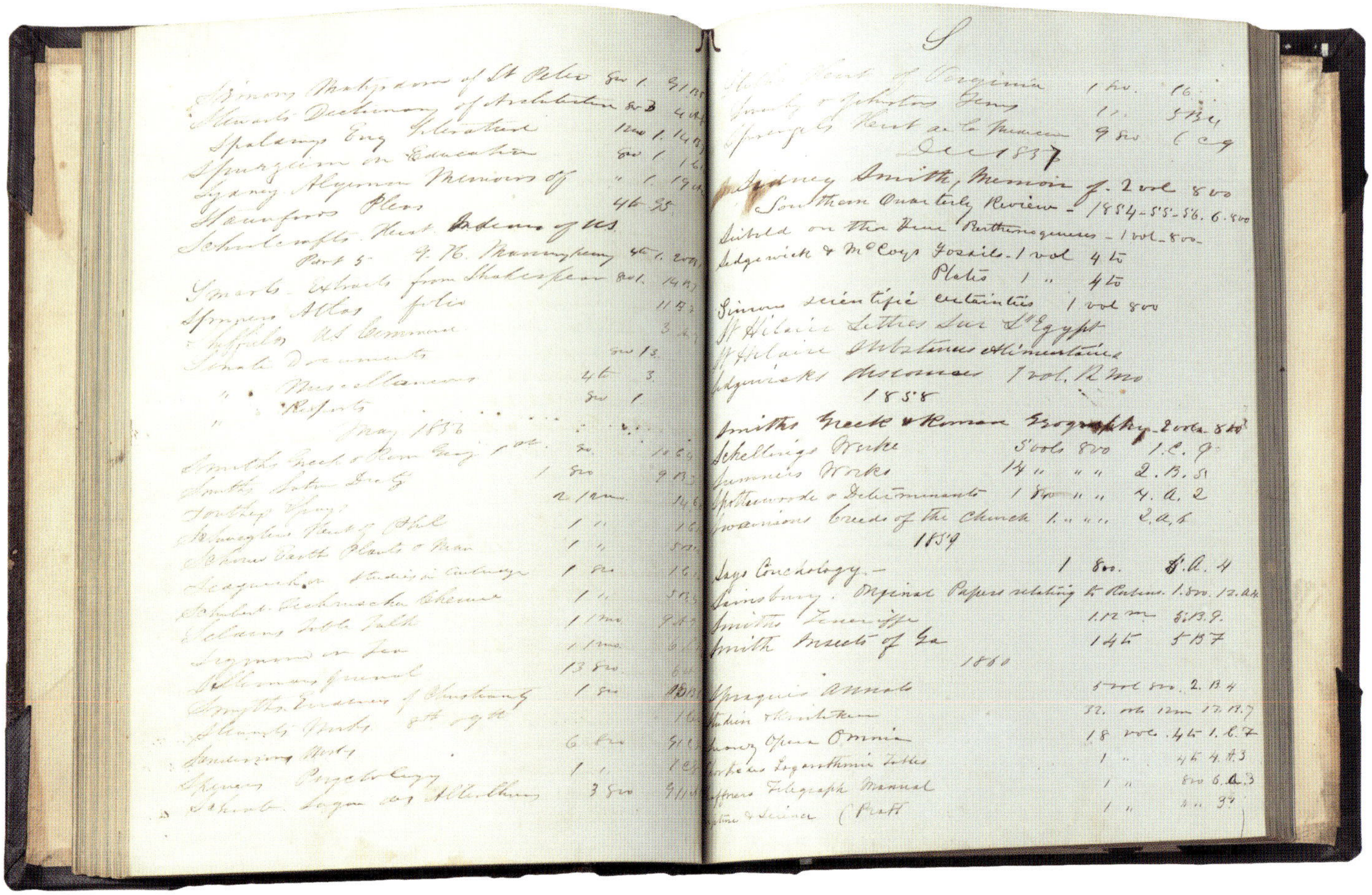

South Carolina College Library shelf list, circa 1860.

As late as 1898, the library was using handwritten, separate shelf lists for each alcove.[11] President Mitchell informed a correspondent in 1909: “We have no printed catalogue of the library.”[12] Work on the card catalog may already have been underway in 1909, for a draft of the 1911–12 librarian’s report notes that “the work of cataloging, to which our main effort is directed shows great progress, and threatens to overflow the recently acquired addition to the catalogue cabinet [illegible] cards have been added 1571, of these 800 were done previously, but had to be corrected and revised before ready for the catalogue.”[13]

Prior to the late nineteenth century, finding aids in most libraries consisted of lists arranged alphabetically by authors’ last names. Librarians often prepared several lists, each being devoted to a specific type of subject matter or location, but due to the difficulty of adding new items to the lists, in a growing collection shelf lists were quickly out of date.

The national Centennial Exposition was important to American libraries in several ways. The advantage of cards over lists was publicized, and the federal Bureau of Education's 1876 *Report* contained the first public explanation of Melvil Dewey's classification systems as well as Charles A. Cutter's essay "Rules for a Printed Dictionary Catalogue." Dewey organized a national meeting for librarians at the exposition; 103 attended. They founded the American Library Association, and the next year the new ALA began publishing the *American Library Journal* to "discuss problems and costs of cataloging, difficulties of cooperative indexing, formulation of rules and codes, purchase of supplies and equipment. . . . The conference at the Centennial in Philadelphia was the foremost event leading to a new level of maturity of the library profession."[14]

After Margaret Rion resigned, her successor, Robert W. Kennedy, and his assistant, Elizabeth D. English, who had been Rion's assistant, continued to gather state-related items together. In 1923 they issued *Author List of Caroliniana in the University of South Carolina Library,* an inventory of approximately twenty-three thousand books and pamphlets "in the Carolina alcove."[15] They appended a list of relevant photographs, busts, and paintings and three manuscripts.[16] This list may be the earliest university publication to use the term *Caroliniana.*

To define *Caroliniana,* Kennedy and English consulted Snowden, Kohn, Salley, and Dr. George A. Wauchope.[17] They decided to include anything written by a native South Carolinian, items written in or about the state, old or rare South Carolina imprints, issues of the university *Bulletin,* and M.A. theses. The 1923 Kennedy-English list provides a gauge of the state-related portion of the university library prior to the formation of the Caroliniana Library. Only a few manuscripts and pictures are mentioned, and the authors knew their list was already out of date when it was published, for they noted plans to append a separate list of "the Abney Library presented to the University last spring."[18]

In 1921 President William S. Currell had informed the board that the library needed a "fire-proof annex": "it would be nothing short of criminal for a great state like South Carolina to allow her most treasured legacies of the past to perish in the flames." He suggested a committee be created to examine "the congested condition" of the library, but nothing was done.[19] Currell resigned in 1922, and the trustees elected William Davis Melton (1868–1926) as his successor. The new president reported to the Board of Trustees in December 1924 that the library "is a veritable fire trap. . . . The building has no proper reading rooms, no storage room, no work room, no room for books reserved for the use of the departments, no department room, no seminar rooms, no administrative office, no modern equipment and convenience whatsoever, and the library force is wholly inadequate for present demands."[20] The library was on the new president's agenda.

Born in Chester County, Melton graduated first in his class from the university law school in 1892. He practiced briefly in Chester, then moved to Columbia and quickly established himself as a lawyer, businessman, and politician. He wrote

Reading room of the South Carolina College Library, circa 1890–1910.

city ordinances establishing the municipal water and sewerage systems, the fire department, and the police commission. He was president of the City Development Company and a principal in the Columbia Real Estate and Trust Company and the North Columbia Land Company. Melton also served on the boards of several local banks and insurance companies. He had a sterling reputation as a manager, and like the trustees he believed the growing university needed thoughtful and systematic planning.

Melton told the trustees:

> Upon assuming the presidency of the University, I made my first examination of its buildings, its equipment, its faculty, its courses of instruction, and its methods, I can think of no better word to describe the impression made upon me than the word — chaos — a confused mass with no organization, no system, no intelligent direction — a veritable case of "every man for himself and the devil take the hindmost" — the equipment old, worn and inadequate, the grounds badly kept and the buildings and plant rapidly deteriorating. It seemed to me an institution that, like Topsy, "never was born — never had no father, nor mother, nor nothin" — was raised by a speculator with lots of others — and had just grow'd.[21]

In his first formal report to the trustees, President Melton observed that rapid, unprecedented growth in enrollments was putting pressure on every aspect of the university. (The student body of 621 in 1921 more than doubled in four years to 1,419 students enrolled in 1925.) New dormitories, classroom buildings, and academic programs needed to be funded; consequently maintenance was deferred. The president said he had "requested an appropriation of $30,000 for an extension to the library building," but he "candidly admitted that the needs of a classroom buildings and additional dormitories are greater at this time."[22]

❖❖❖

President Melton's experience as a real estate developer brought him into contact with the architect who would design many buildings for the university, including the wings of the Caroliniana library.

John Carroll Johnson (1882–1967) was born in Sweden, grew up in Chicago, studied at the Art Institute of Chicago, and received academic architectural training at the Armour Institute. As a child he saw the 1893 Columbian Exposition, the Chicago World's Fair, and he kept a scrapbook devoted to it for the rest of his life. When Johnson was eighteen years old and still a student, he worked in the Chicago architectural firm of William Le Baron Jenney. Jenney was a prominent pioneer in the development of tall buildings — skyscrapers — based on the use of internal steel frames instead of traditional masonry load-bearing walls.[23]

Upon graduating from the Armour Institute in 1906, Johnson left Chicago and broadened his experience by touring major cities in America, working in an architectural firm in Washington, D.C., and obtaining a B.S. degree from the University of Pennsylvania. Like many young American artists and architects, he toured Europe to visit and sketch architectural sites, then he came to South Carolina in 1910 to work for Charles Coker Wilson (1864–1933) and his partners, Edwin D. Sompayrac and James B. Urquhart. Johnson was their chief designer for two years.

The Wilson firm had an extensive private practice; they worked for the state, too, and had recently completed the

J. Carroll Johnson, circa 1925.

South Carolina State House. C. C. Wilson had been appointed university architect in 1907, and he held the position until it was abolished in 1915. Before Johnson joined the firm, Wilson had prepared a development plan for the university, had restored several of the older buildings, and had designed Davis and LeConte Colleges (LeConte is now called Barnwell). While Johnson was a member of the Wilson firm, they were creating the Thornwell dormitory. Wilson's commissions and contacts brought Johnson onto the campus.[24]

In 1912 Johnson and Urquhart formed their own office and worked together for five years. After they dissolved their partnership, Johnson practiced alone until his death in 1967. The quality of his residential work in and around Columbia impressed William D. Melton, and upon becoming president of the university, he turned to Johnson as the de facto university architect.

Over a period of forty-two years, from 1912 until 1954, Johnson worked on twenty university projects. Before Melton became president, Johnson had designed Thornwell College (1912) and Woodrow College (1913) and was responsible for extensive renovations on the Horseshoe (1918–26). At first Melton directed him to concentrate on repairs and renovations, then he had Johnson develop an athletic facility — a football field, track, and bleachers — on Davis field where the Corps of Cadets had marched. Melton died in 1926; the athletic facility was renamed Melton Field, and for its entrance Johnson designed a gate featuring handsome, urn-capped pillars that inspired the gates that have become a feature of the campus landscape.

Shortly before he died, President Melton secured appropriations for additions to the Steward's Hall, a field house for indoor athletic events, an expansion of the library, and a new classroom building. He assumed Johnson would design these

Melton Memorial Gate, designed by J. Carroll Johnson, 1928.

projects. One of C. C. Wilson's first cousins was a member of the Board of Trustees, however, and another, Professor Edward C. Coker, was chairman of the faculty committee on buildings and grounds. The latter apparently prevailed upon the acting president, Leonard T. Baker, to assign the wholly new buildings to Wilson and to authorize Wilson to act as an adviser to Johnson on the expansion of the library. Johnson protested, and the trustees reversed Baker's decision. They awarded the commissions to Johnson, but it was a close and bitter thing.[25]

Those involved with the expansion of the library had to consider the budget and the allocation of space for books, readers, additional offices, storage, and processing. Everyone was committed to fireproof construction and the preservation of the architectural character of the old building. Johnson's approved design suggests they also wanted the new exterior to be compatible with the historic Horseshoe and the familiar interior to remain undisturbed. President Melton had sent Johnson, Edward C. Coker, and Robert W. Kennedy, the librarian, to visit libraries at Duke, North Carolina State, and the University of North Carolina. This tour may have influenced Johnson's plans; however, his earlier work had already demonstrated his vision of the campus as an architecturally harmonious whole, and his early experience with the Jenney firm foreshadowed the prefabricated iron stacks in the east wing.

President Currell had spoken of a fireproof annex for the library, suggesting a separate building or perhaps a single wing. Johnson's plan, however, entailed two wings, one attached to the east end of the Mills building and the other to the west end. As he designed them, the Horseshoe facades of the wings match the public face of the old library. The west elevation of the west wing, clearly visible from Sumter Street, matches the exterior of the historic library, but the

Harry Dodge Jenkins, *University of South Carolina Library*, watercolor, 1927.

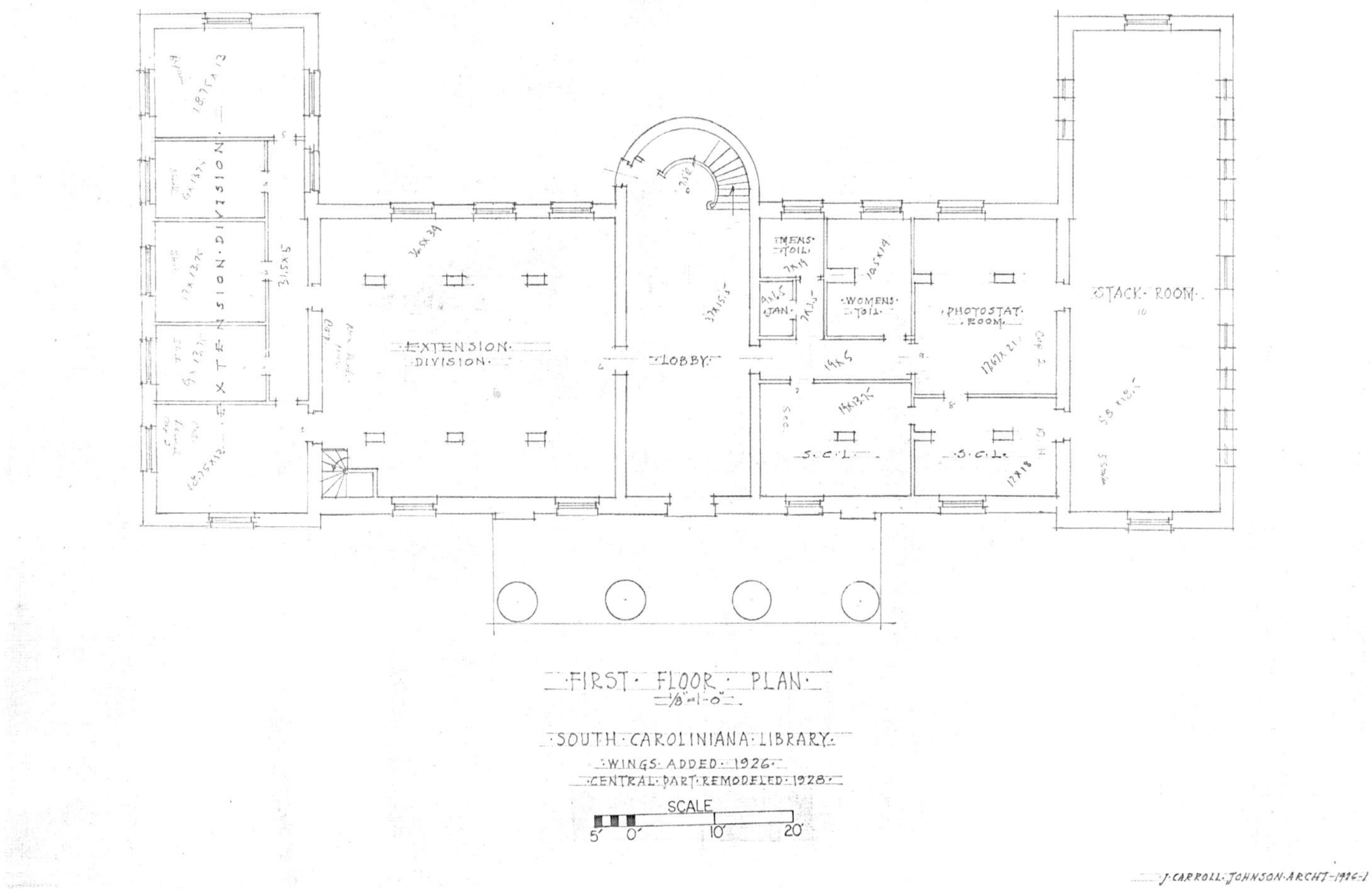

"First Floor Plan South Caroliniana Library Wings added 1926 Central part remodeled 1928. J. Carroll Johnson Archt 1926–1928."

east elevation of the eastern wing is partially hidden by Elliott College; consequently the windows here are functional. Entering the library from the Horseshoe, the only visual hint of the additions is a shadow line created by the thirteen-inch projection of the wings beyond Mills's facade.

The ground floor of the west wing contains offices. The second floor of this wing, adjacent the west end of the "Library of Congress" reading room, consists of a single large room intended as a museum, exhibition, or meeting space. For visual balance and symmetry, Mills had placed a pair of

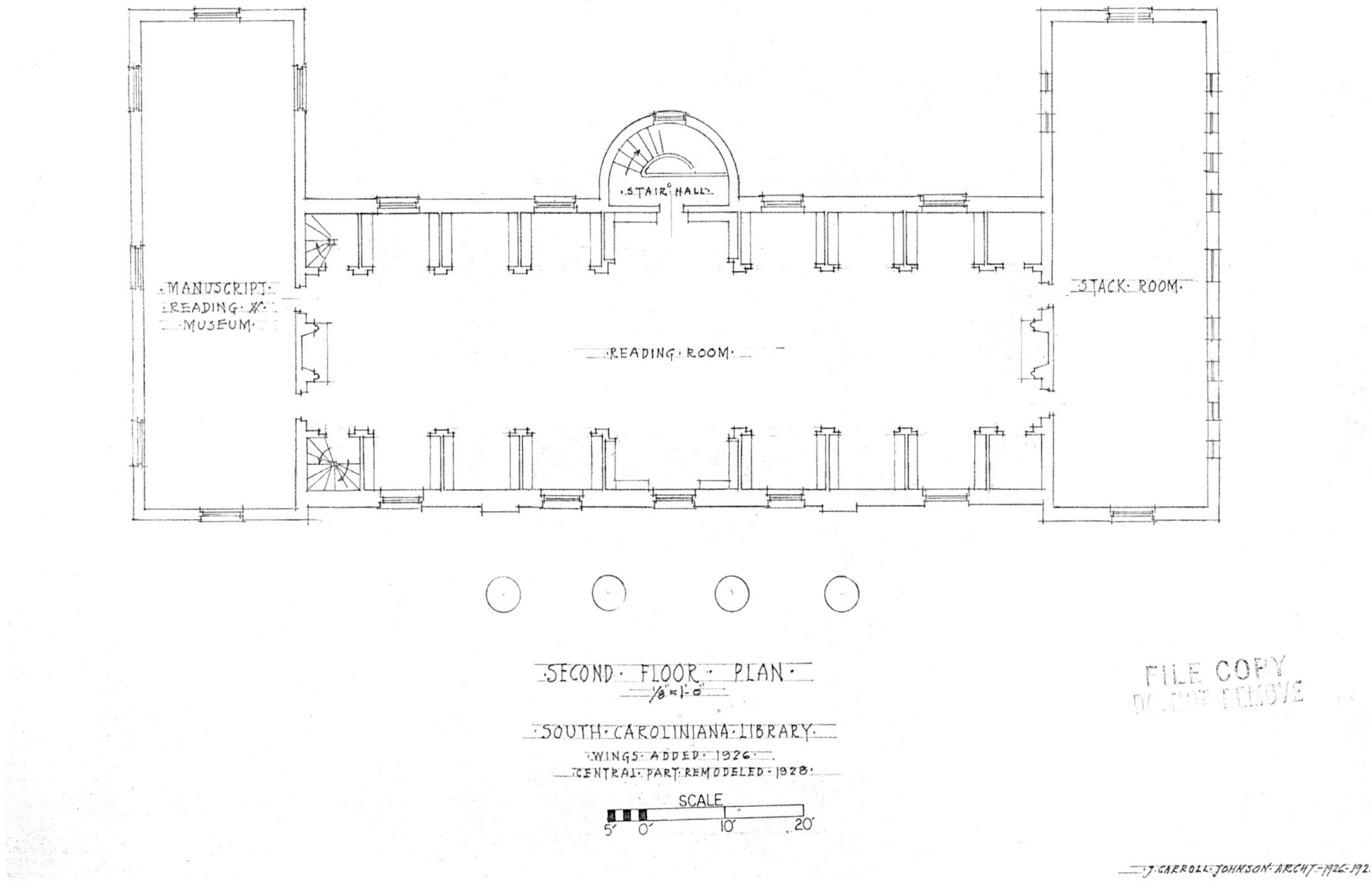

"Second Floor Plan South Caroliniana Library Wings added 1926 Central Part Remodeled 1928. J. Carroll Johnson Archt 1926–1928."

false doors at either end of the reading room; Johnson converted the false doors into real openings providing access to the wings. Above the large room in the west wing, level with the reading room balconies, a suite of small offices became the second home of the Caroliniana material. When the wings were completed, an article in the *Gamecock* announced "Treasure House of South Carolina Writings Is Placed in Fire-Proof Room" and "Misses English and Rion Realize Need of Collection of S. C. Material." Collections "which were previously crowded into an alcove in the main

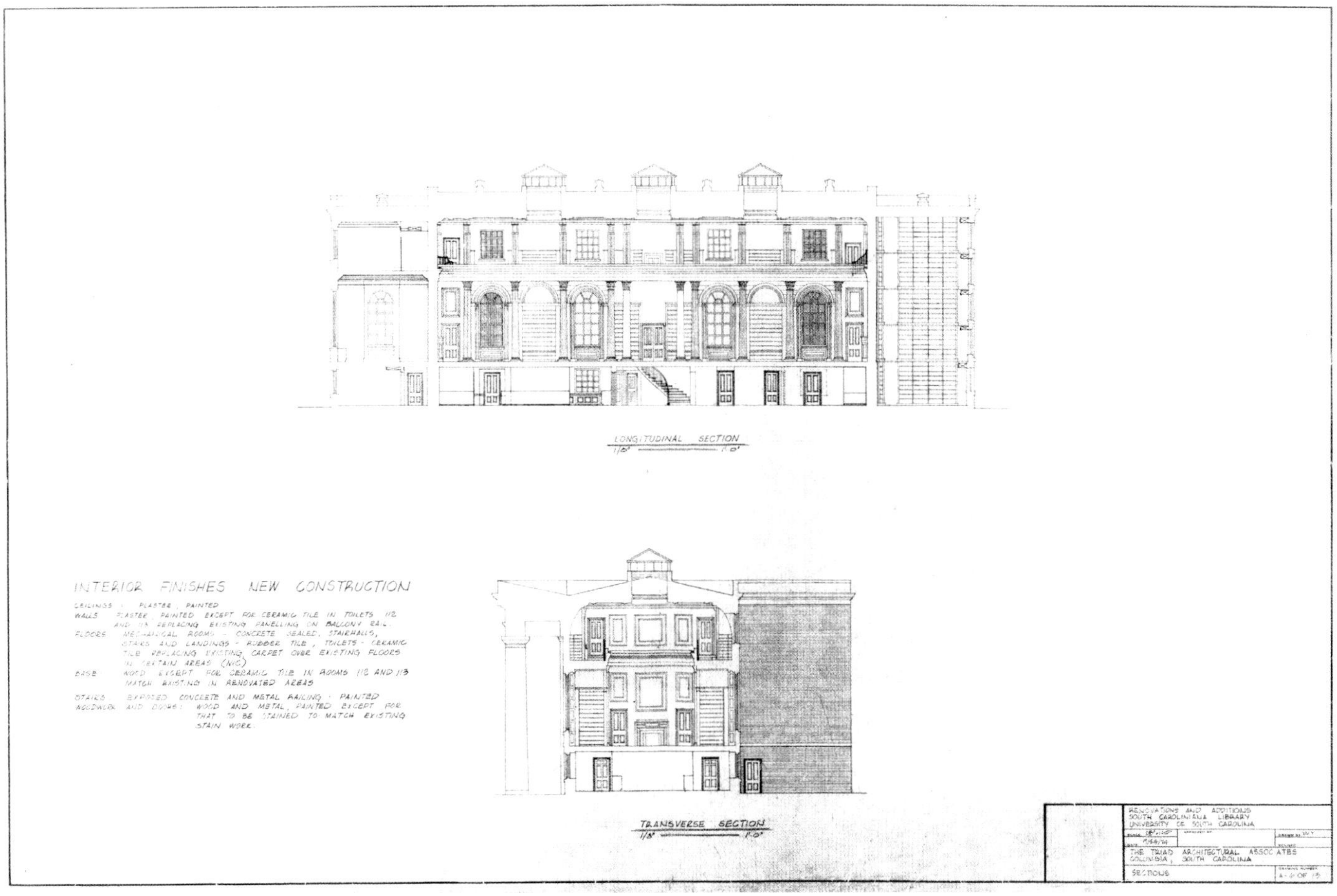

Renovations and additions to the South Caroliniana Library, University of South Carolina, Triad Architectural Associates, drawing by Wayne Young, 1974.

part of the library, have . . . been moved into new quarters, a room about 25 feet wide and 65 feet long, located on the third floor of the building over the museum room."[26]

The east wing has always been devoted to book stacks. It is essentially a vertical, rectangular box; the exterior brick walls match the historic old library, but the interior is filled with a prefabricated cast-iron frame. The cast-iron, adjustable metal bookshelves and marble paneled floors or aisles are integral parts of the frame. There are five levels, and each has a floor-to-ceiling clearance of only seven feet, so ladders

Book stacks, east wing. Photograph by Hunter Clarkson, 2016.

are not needed to reach any of the books. The shelves can be adjusted vertically; they are each three feet long, and there are 135 of them on each of the five levels. The system provides 2,025 lineal feet of shelving room for approximately 16,200 books.

This metal frame and shelving has roots that reach far beyond campus. Snead and Company of Jersey City, New Jersey, made the stacks. Angus Snead Macdonald (1883–1961), president of the company from 1915 until 1952, produced the most widely used prefabricated metal book stacks in America. His system was used at the Library of Congress (c. 1897), Widener Library at Harvard (1915), and the New York Public Library (c. 1910).[27] The use of cast iron and steel prefabricated book stacks originated in France and England; early examples include S. Genevieve in Paris (1843–50) and the British Museum in London (1854–56). Several systems of this type were patented in America in the late nineteenth century, and they became popular quickly, for in addition to being considered fireproof, they were well suited to the concentrated weight of larger and larger collections; they also required less space than load-bearing masonry and were therefore economical.

The metal bookshelves consist of slits and bars, which was thought to enhance the circulation of light and air. The vertical posts of the metal frame support the shelves and the aisles between the book stacks. There are no wall-to-wall

Book stacks, east wing. Photograph by Hunter Clarkson, 2016.

floors, so openings in the floor of each level also allowed light to penetrate and air to circulate. Unfortunately the absence of solid horizontal floors creates a fire hazard, for if books catch fire the stack area becomes a chimney; consequently the system fell into disfavor in the mid-twentieth century.[28]

Snead stack systems were installed in 164 academic libraries in the United States during the period 1916–30, and the University of South Carolina is listed in an inventory of their installations. (So is Clemson.) Snead book stacks were also placed in more than 200 American public libraries as well as libraries in nine foreign countries.[29]

President Melton and the trustees told Johnson to "complete the plans and specifications for the addition of fire-proof wings to the library" on August 16, 1926. Work began that fall, and the wings were completed by June 1927.[30]

⁂

The new wings did not solve the library's problems, and construction dust must have still been in the air when the trustees' minutes noted that "it was intended, after the additions were made and the books transferred to them, to remodel the first floor of the old Library and use it as a reading room. It is absolutely necessary to make this improvement. The floor, which has probably been there over seventy-five years, is rotted out and ants are destroying the books." Several months later President Davison McDowell Douglas told the trustees that "the new part of the Library, I understand, is absolutely fire proof. The old part should be repaired and made as near fireproof as it is possible to do. . . . The University of South Carolina, the head of the educational system of the state, has a Library that has not in it even one lavatory or toilet. It does seem to me that these defects should be rectified and the building improved as soon as it is possible to do so, and I would recommend to the Board that an architect be employed to draw up plans and get bids that might be submitted to the Board at its next meeting in June."[31] Still later he noted that "for the past two years the library has been torn up and the use of the building greatly curtailed."[32] Edward Coker, C. C. Wilson's cousin, moved to approve Johnson's plans for the renovation, and Johnson was authorized to proceed on June 13, 1928.[33]

Within two years, despite new wings and a renovated ground floor, President Baker declared that "the University Library is totally inadequate in staff and equipment for the demands made for its service."[34] In 1935 he reported that "so great is the need for space that valuable books are piled up on the floors of rooms for lack of shelving." He concluded this lament on a lighter note, informing the trustees that Francis Lieber's granddaughter had visited and donated a bust "now mounted in the Library," and "the excellent service of Professor Meriwether as chairman of the Caroliniana Committee in collecting material is progressing satisfactorily, and many very valuable additions are being made to this division of the Library."[35]

Robert Lee Meriwether's research and writing always focused on South Carolina history. As an undergraduate he studied with David Duncan Wallace at Wofford, then took courses with W. E. Dodd and M. W. Jernegan at the University of Chicago and finished his Ph.D. coursework at Columbia University. His mentors were known for their use of primary sources, and he acknowledged that his own study of the South Carolina backcountry "began with settlement and frontier studies" at Chicago.[36] Meriwether's belief in the value of manuscripts was the catalyst that created the Caroliniana Library.

After a brief stint teaching in Alabama and a tour of duty during World War I, he came to the university as an associate professor in 1919. He was on the "Caroliniana collection" committee with Kohn and Snowden when the library's wings were completed. Snowden was then chairman of the history department (Meriwether would succeed him in 1929), and they promoted graduate research using primary material from the Caroliniana collection and from the state papers controlled by Alexander Salley for the Historical Commission.

As secretary of the Historical Commission, Salley had been indexing, organizing, and selectively publishing state documents for twenty-five years, pecking away at the mountainous backlog of state papers with little clerical help and in poor working conditions. These mitigating circumstances notwithstanding, he discouraged inquiries, offended the representatives of historically minded organizations, and offered no help to people who wanted to preserve private or county records.

In 1912 Gov. Cole Blease had tried to abolish the Historical Commission, but Salley had thwarted him by convincing the legislature to replace the governor's appointees with history department chairmen from Clemson, Winthrop, the

Robert Lee Meriwether, circa 1945.

Citadel, and the University of South Carolina and representatives chosen by the United Confederate Veterans and the South Carolina Historical Society. As chairman of the history department, Snowden was on the Historical Commission, and when Meriwether became chairman of the department in 1929, he automatically took Snowden's seat.[37]

Footnotes and bibliographies in Meriwether's dissertation and in theses by his graduate students record their research in Salley's lair.[38] As a member of the Historical Commission, Meriwether had a key, but others found access difficult, and once inside, they had little space to work. Records were crowded into the basement of the State House "at grave risk of destruction" and in "conditions [that were] nothing short of a disgrace to the state." The commissioners submitted a damning review of the situation to the legislature.[39] Meriwether, then chairman of the Historical Commission, was Salley's supervisor, and although the review praised several aspects of Salley's work, by and large it condemned his stewardship. Salley and Meriwether stopped speaking to one another. Their mutual antipathy became legendary. Nonetheless, despite criticism from many quarters, Salley kept his job and controlled the state archives for another eighteen years.[40]

At the university, as librarians moved things into the new wings, President Douglas asked a faculty committee to "survey the library situation."[41] Meriwether was a member of this committee too, and they issued a thorough report dealing with twenty-three aspects of the library. Concerning the building, they observed that despite the new wings, there was not enough space for books, readers, or study carrels. They suggested converting Johnson's new museum room into a reserved-book reading room. They also recommended attaching small, counter-like tabletops to windowsills in the fireproof book stacks for faculty and graduate students to use as desks. Their most radical proposal, "as a temporary relief for the present overcrowding," was to convert "the West Wing of Elliott College adjacent to the Library . . . into an annex . . . connected with the Main Library by a corridor leading from the second (or third) floor of Elliott. . . . The annex proposed

Alexander Samuel Salley Jr., 1949.

would provide three large halls measuring approximately 25 by 45 feet. One of the rooms should be equipped for reserve book reading. The other may be devoted to current magazines and periodicals. The third floor would serve for storage of books and material of minor value."[42]

The 1931 Special Library Committee report also emphatically advocated concentrating on the collection of Caroliniana: "The University should make its library the greatest collection of Caroliniana, owing this duty, first, to the state as its chief center of study of South Carolina past and present, second, to its students, who are more interested in South Carolina subjects than in any others, and, finally, to itself, because of the distinction that the possession of such a collection would confer on the Library and the institution." They added the university should "campaign actively for gifts and loans of material, and in view of the intense interest of Duke University and the University of North Carolina in South Caroliniana, the collecting of this material be pushed with utmost vigor."[43]

In addition to serving as chairman of the state's Historical Commission and participating in President Douglas's library committee, Meriwether initiated the organization of the South Carolina Historical Association in 1930. The seventy people attending its first meeting in Hartsville, South Carolina, "were . . . members of the faculties of the universities, colleges, high schools and preparatory schools of the State, but there were present in addition to these several persons who [were] not engaged in teaching." They created a permanent organization to promote "historical studies in the state of South Carolina, a closer relationship among persons living in this State who are interested in history, and the preservation of historical records."[44] The featured speaker at this initial meeting was William E. Dodd, Meriwether's former professor.

The new association decided to publish a journal, so a committee prepared and distributed "Instructions to

Contributors." This style sheet stipulated that "each statement of fact must have a reference to a foot-note which indicates the source of the information."[45]

The association is still active; its members meet annually, and their journal, *Proceedings,* contains carefully researched, thoroughly documented essays focusing on South Carolina history. Inasmuch as the association was founded to encourage document-based history, it was part of a national trend. Walter Muir Whitehill, director of the Boston Athenaeum, observed that "ever since the establishment of the American Historical Association in 1884 regional replicas of it were frequently . . . established. They represented, in general, the professional approach to history. . . . They had no truck with antiquarianism or genealogy, being rather concerned with the interpretation of history. The phrase 'historical association' came to connote such an organization."[46] The South Carolina Historical Association's commitment to documentary research "and the preservation of historical records" foreshadowed the creation of the Caroliniana Library.

The South Carolina Historical Association was created as an off-campus organization; concurrently, on campus, projects sponsored by the federal WPA (initially Works Progress Administration and later, beginning in 1939, Work Projects Administration) dramatically accelerated the development of the Caroliniana collections. Before there was a Caroliniana Library, the faculty committee appointed to "build up the South Carolina Collection" cooperated with various WPA programs including the Federal Historical Records Survey, the Civil Works Administration, the National Archives, the Work Projects Administration Thrift Shop, the Federal Writers' Project, and the Historical Project. WPA workers across the state pumped a veritable flood of material into the university library.

WPA personnel "copied about 120,000 pages of South Carolina courthouse, church, school and society records, private diaries and graveyard inscriptions"; made "a complete inventory of the public records of the State"; copied tombstone inscriptions; bound wills; and "sorted and mended" approximately 100,000 county newspapers.[47] The WPA workers also produced more than 1,100 photographs of places, people, and things.[48] To process this material, the WPA also "furnished typists and a trained cataloger to aid in cataloging books and pamphlets." They bound loose items and made more than 6,000 specially designed boxes for the storage of manuscripts and pamphlets. Two WPA administrators, Flora Belle Surles and Dr. Anne King Gregorie, should be remembered as having been "chiefly responsible for the invaluable contribution made by these projects to South Carolina history."[49]

Robert Kennedy, the university librarian, struggled to accommodate this influx of material, much of which was fragile, unwieldy, or both. By 1938 Caroliniana-related items outgrew the third floor of the west wing, and "one of the stack rooms of the east wing of the library was given over to South Carolina manuscripts and newspapers." Even this did not solve the problem, and the excess was placed in "fireproof storage space on the campus" in other buildings.[50] To aid in the processing and storage of this material, Prof. G. F. Lipscomb, head of the chemistry department, formulated a paste specifically for document boxes, and Prof. A. C. Carson, head of the physics department, made a humidity chamber to flatten documents.[51] Ground-floor rooms, designed as offices, became workshops for conservation, cataloging, and microfilming.

In 1937, at the height of WPA activity in the library, Meriwether and Prof. Harry Davis, a member of the Caroliniana Committee, contacted President J. Rion McKissick

Works Progress Administration, *A Good Catch*, Georgetown County, circa 1935.

"about our proposed University Caroliniana Society." Seeking McKissick's permission to announce their intention, Meriwether suggested they invite potential members to a meeting, and he appended Davis's thoughts on the organization of the society. McKissick agreed, and the initial gathering convened in Columbia on February 14, 1937. "More than fifty persons" attended, and M. L. Bonham presided. Meriwether explained that the goals of the new organization were "to support and extend the work of the Caroliniana Committee of the University," to collect and preserve Caroliniana, to cooperate with other archives within the state, and to facilitate research. They distributed an explanatory leaflet and sought members. The response was gratifying. Before Thanksgiving the new society had 137 members.[52]

Works Progress Administration, *Among the Spindles*, Greenville County. Photograph by Bill King, circa 1935.

Farm Security Administration, African American woman and children in doorway with laundry on line, Charleston County. Photograph by Marion Post, circa 1935.

Works Progress Administration, *Farmer with Cabbage*, Richland County. Photograph by Lincoln Highton, circa 1935.

Farm Security Administration, *Shrimp Boat "Mary Pickford,"* Beaufort County. Photograph by Marion Post, circa 1935.

The creation of the Caroliniana Society fortuitously coincided with the university's efforts to enlarge its library. In 1933 President Baker had begun exploring the possibility of obtaining federal funding "to erect an administration building, an auditorium, a classroom building, an annex to the library, to enlarge the infirmary, and improve the heating plant."[53] The state authorized required matching money in 1935, and President Baker and then his successor, J. Rion McKissick, began applying for federal assistance to build what they described as "an addition to the library" or an "extension of the present structure." They cited the need for more space, fireproof construction, and "our priceless collections of books, newspapers, pamphlets and documents, many of them relating to South Carolina and to South Carolinians."[54] The library as it is today was saved by the failure of repeated requests in 1933–36 for money to build additional wings.

While the university was trying to expand the library, A. S. Salley secured funding to build a facility for the state archives. Meriwether was instrumental in obtaining the university trustees' permission to place the archives on university property at the corner of Sumter and Pendleton Streets, a lot conveniently adjacent to the old library. The state archives moved into the new building (the War Memorial Building) in 1935.[55] Its proximity to the Caroliniana collection helped researchers but also diminished the space that might have been used to expand the old library.

When he first began thinking about building a new university library, McKissick wrote the South Carolina Senate that "an adequate library is the greatest physical need of the University." He noted that the old library was not fireproof, and a "mere enlargement of [it] would be only a temporary solution of our problem because of limitations of space surrounding it. We need a much larger building than could be constructed as an addition to the existing structure. . . . It is conservatively estimated that there are from 3,000 to 5,000 volumes for which there is no shelf space. Many of these are piled up on the floor. The University's excellent collection of material about South Carolina is increasing so fast that there is no shelf space or other proper place to put part of it . . . consequently much of it was inaccessible to students." McKissick continued: "If such a structure can be built, I propose to use the present library as a student activities building where students may spend much of their leisure time, instead of going off the campus and up [*sic*] street. They now have no adequate common meeting place under a roof, no place where they can take visiting parents and friends. If we had such a place where students could congregate, play harmless games, read current periodicals and magazines, and spend leisure hours, I believe it would be for the moral betterment of the student body."[56]

President McKissick appointed a special faculty committee to consider "various questions in connection with the planning and construction of the new library." Several members agreed with the president that the old library should become a student union building, for the reading room would make a grand ballroom, and the ground floor offices could easily be converted into lounges; two members felt it should be used as a gallery and studios for the art department, and four members (professors Green, Meriwether, Crow, and Norwood) "favored its use as a Caroliniana library."[57]

Funding for a new, separate library building was obtained on October 26, 1938, and the trustees chose an architect from Nashville, Henry C. Hibbs (1882–1949). They authorized a subcommittee comprising Hibbs, McKissick, and Prof.

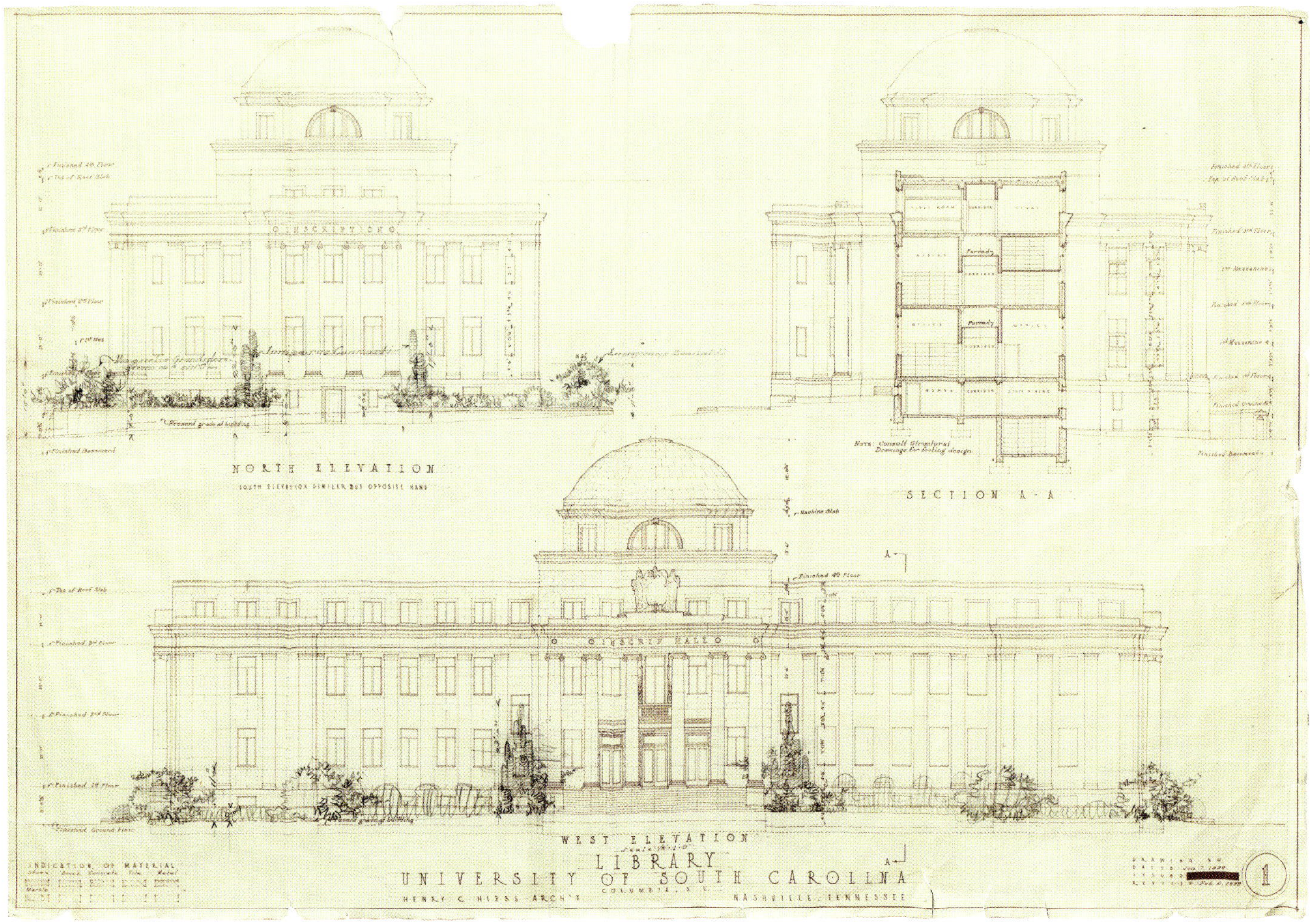

"West Elevation, Library University of South Carolina." Henry C. Hibbs, architect, 1940. Facilities Management, University of South Carolina.

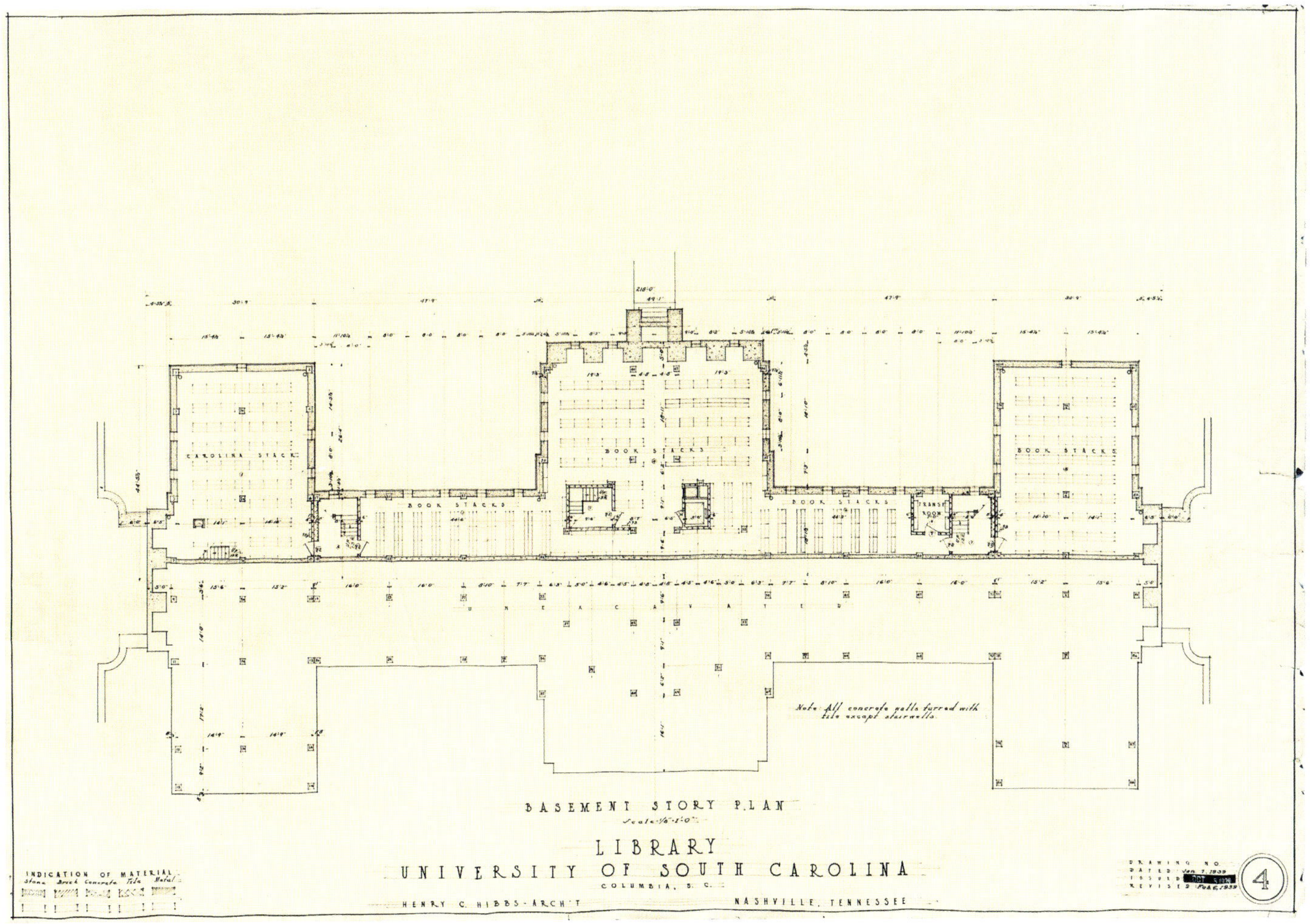

"Basement Story Plan, Library University of South Carolina," Henry C. Hibbs, architect, 1940. Facilities Management, University of South Carolina.

University Library (later McKissick Library) with partially demolished president's house in foreground, circa 1940.

Robert L. Sumwalt to select an appropriate site. President McKissick laid the cornerstone on November 6, 1939, and the building was officially opened on Alumni Day, June 2, 1941.[58]

While work on the new library was underway, trustee Harry R. Hughs moved that "the Board set aside the present library building for use of the University Caroliniana Society upon completion of the new library building, the terms and conditions to be hereafter provided by the Board."[59] Hughs's motion carried. One of the trustees, Edwin Seibels, "asked to be recorded as voting no," for he observed that Mills's building was not fireproof, and he suggested the old library should be used as a central administration building.[60] Meriwether and acting librarian R. H. Wienefeld proposed detailed "terms and conditions" to McKissick, and the trustees ratified the Caroliniana's use of the building and its relationship to the university on December 11, 1940.[61] Before the trustees' approval was announced publicly, Meriwether wrote to McKissick concerning how he thought the Caroliniana Library, housed in the Mills building, should operate.

❖❖❖

The fourth annual meeting of the University South Caroliniana Society convened in Mills's Library of Congress reading room on April 17, 1940.

Imagine the scene: a golden evening light bathes the alcoves; Meriwether and the staff have displayed "interesting and representative pieces of Caroliniana . . . spread over the balconies, over the main reading room, in the temporary Manuscripts Room of the stacks and in the present South Carolina Room."[62] There is a rippling, expectant murmur as members and guests find seats. The president of the society, Chief Justice M. L. Bonham, speaks first, then President McKissick rises and announces the university will turn over the old library to the society "as soon as practicable." Meriwether and a few others knew the "terms and conditions" had not been approved; nonetheless it must have been a happy evening.

❖❖❖

Robert Kennedy, who had been the university librarian for twenty-eight years, was apprehensive. He foresaw "heavy responsibilities" and "knotty problems . . . incident to the removal to the new library." Citing poor health, he submitted his resignation on May 14, 1940, and R. H. Wienefeld succeeded him as acting librarian.[63]

Wienefeld had done his undergraduate and graduate work at Johns Hopkins, and Meriwether hired him as an historian in 1931.[64] They collaborated and sent President McKissick a memorandum proposing the "terms and conditions" governing the relationship between the university and the Caroliniana Society, and although Wienefeld signed it as acting librarian, Meriwether must have been the principal author.[65] In presenting the memorandum to the trustees on December 5, 1940, President McKissick endorsed it as being "both practical and desirable" and in "the best interest of both libraries."[66] The trustees agreed that "when the new library building is completed and occupied space in the old library building [will] be allotted as follows: the first floor to be used for administrative offices as assigned by the Committee on Buildings and grounds of the Board of Trustees; the second and third floors to be devoted exclusively to the housing and administration of the South Carolina Collection."[67]

The relationship between the South Caroliniana Library and the university was announced and defined over a period of many months. May 19, 1941, could be considered the Caroliniana's official birthday, for that is when Meriwether signed receipts for items "received of R. H. Wienefeld, Acting Librarian." These receipts—bound catalog-like lists—provide a baseline inventory of the collection as it became the Caroliniana Library.[68] Meriwether became the director in 1941, and the staff organized things over the summer. In October they held an open house for the public.[69] Just before Christmas (December 14, 1941), President McKissick told the trustees the Caroliniana was in operation and growing rapidly.[70]

CHAPTER FIVE

The SOUTH CAROLINIANA LIBRARY

No documents, no history; no history, deep ignorance of the present.

CHARLES A. BEARD, quoted in University South Caroliniana Society Report of the Secretary and Treasurer (1938)

LIKE A SPRINTER, the Caroliniana started quickly. President McKissick told the trustees in 1942: "One of the most notable recent developments at the University is our separately-housed South Carolina library, containing 2,220,800 items, the largest collection of books, pamphlets, newspaper files and manuscripts related to our state in the world with the possible exception of that in the Library of Congress."[1]

Depression-era federal programs accelerated the identification, organization, and preservation of historic resources. Prior to the 1930s, various states, private societies, and individuals had treated historical materials differently, but federal coordination codified national standards, created schedules, and provided resources. In many respects the Caroliniana still reflects the aims and methodologies of the Historical Records Survey, the Federal Writers' Program, and the National Historical Records Publications Commission—Works Progress Administration agencies and programs designed to gather and preserve historical data.

Head of the history department and chairman of the Caroliniana Committee Robert Meriwether and James Harold Easterby, head of the College of Charleston's history department, implemented the federal Historical Records Survey in South Carolina in 1935. They set up offices in

Anne King Gregorie, circa 1940.

the university library and ensured that copies of everything would become part of the Caroliniana collection. They hired Anne King Gregorie, one of Meriwether's former students, to direct the work.

Gregorie was from Mount Pleasant, South Carolina, and knew the state well. After completing her M.A. thesis with Meriwether, she had entered a Ph.D. program at the University of Wisconsin, and as a graduate student she worked on the calendar of the Lyman Draper Papers at the Wisconsin Historical Society. She returned to South Carolina and became the first woman to earn a Ph.D. in history from the University of South Carolina; she then taught briefly at Arkansas College and returned home to work on a biography of Gen. Thomas Sumter.

When Gregorie joined the Records Survey, she was "forty-eight, healthy, white haired, eager as a hound on the scent."[2] The project's goal was to create a central collection — excluding state records managed by Alexander Salley — of all public and private historical documents in South Carolina, including wills and inventories, church, club and family records, and epitaphs. Gregorie directed typists, trained workers to inventory material in each of the forty-six courthouses throughout the state, assembled office equipment and supplies, dealt with federal forms and correspondence, and published indexes for the records of fourteen counties before World War II ended the project in 1942.

The WPA projects were primarily designed to provide employment, but the mission of the Historical Records Survey, and to some extent the Writers' Project, reflected national acceptance of the importance of document-based, scientific history. The new National Archives, opened in 1936, assured ongoing federal participation in the preservation of historical data, and the Society of American Archivists, founded in the same year, promoted (and continues to promote) rigorous standards of archival management.

Eric Gugler, the architect who designed the Oval Office for Franklin D. Roosevelt, organized a dinner at the Century

Club in New York on June 7, 1948, honoring Meriwether. Why Gugler convened the group is not known, but his guest list is tantalizing. He was interested in historic buildings, and two weeks after the dinner, he and Meriwether corresponded about fireproof iron shutters, so they must have talked about the Mills building. Talbot F. Hamlin was a guest too. Hamlin was an architect, architectural historian, and librarian at the Avery Architectural Library at Columbia University. His recently published *Greek Revival* defined the style in the United States and praised Mills as "the first American designer who realized that the new country demanded a new, an American, architecture."[3] Hamlin, however, did not mention the South Carolina College library in his book, for the diary drawings had yet to be identified, and the measured drawings were unknown. Julian Parks Boyd was also in attendance. Boyd had traveled up from Princeton, where he was librarian. He was also a founding member of the Society of American Archivists and was active in the American Historical Association. His work on the papers of Thomas Jefferson would set the scholarly standards for all subsequent historical editing projects. Boyd was born in Converse, South Carolina and, at Meriwether's request, had delivered the 1941 annual address to the Caroliniana Society. In that speech he praised the accomplishments of the federal Historical Records Survey in South Carolina.

James H. Easterby, who had organized the South Carolina survey program with Meriwether, attended the dinner too, so Gugler probably wanted to recognize the survey work in South Carolina. In any case the dinner, guests, and thank-you notes all confirm Meriwether's national reputation. Looking ahead, Boyd's *Jefferson Papers* would inspire the capstone of Meriwether's career, the editing and publication of *The Papers of John C. Calhoun*.[4]

Boyd began working on the *Jefferson Papers* shortly after he addressed the Caroliniana Society. In 1950, at a ceremony in the Library of Congress, he presented the first volume to President Truman. Truman was impressed and "expressed the hope that the papers of other American leaders would also be published." He directed Philip M. Hamer, director of the National Historical Records Publication Commission, to make available "writings of men whose contributions to our history are now inadequately represented by published works."[5]

Hamer was born in Marion, South Carolina, and when faced with developing a national program for the publication of historical papers, his "steps turned early to South Carolina, for there was one man there with whom I knew I had to confer . . . my former classmate at Wofford, my longtime friend, respected colleague, and distinguished member of the faculty of the University . . . Bob Meriwether. . . . It was under the tall trees of the University of South Carolina campus, just in front of the South Caroliniana Library. There on that summer day of 1950, the Calhoun papers project was really conceived, although it was many conferences and some two years later before it came officially into being."[6]

Hamer's plan for the National Historical Records Publications project was approved the following year, and work began on the papers of John and John Quincy Adams, Benjamin Franklin, James Madison, Henry Clay, James K. Polk, and Woodrow Wilson. Sponsoring institutions included Harvard, Yale, the American Philosophical Society, Columbia University, and Vanderbilt. Hamer wrote that "*The Calhoun Papers* project was the first of these enterprises to be established . . . [and it] has the distinction of being the first of these projects to have a volume published."[7]

Meriwether finished the first volume of the *Calhoun Papers* but died on August 24, 1958, before it was published.

Reviewers praised it, saying it "plowed new ground" and was a "monument" to both Calhoun and his editor. Like *The Papers of Thomas Jefferson,* Meriwether's *Calhoun* presents historical editing at its best. Altogether he had gathered some 3,000 documents (the first volume contains 159). As a historical editor, he had to determine the authenticity of each item, then transcribe, organize, and annotate the collection with notes to make names, places, and events meaningful to the reader.

The first volume of *The Papers of John C. Calhoun* demonstrates Meriwether's encyclopedic command of the facts, his relentless attention to detail, and his stamina. Subsequent editors have maintained Meriwether's high standards. His commitment and enthusiasm have proved to be infectious.

Harvey S. Teal met Meriwether just before the Calhoun project got underway. In October 1948, as a student seeking part-time work, Teal ventured into the library, and Meriwether hired him on the spot. Although he has never been a full-time employee, over a span of sixty-eight years, Harvey has participated in virtually every aspect of Caroliniana operations, including processing incoming material; microfilming newspapers and manuscripts; preparing packets of historic materials for teachers and students; answering queries; maintaining contacts with donors, dealers, and appraisers; adding things to the collection; and finally, producing a scholarly book—the indispensable reference on photography in South Carolina in the years 1840–1940, *Partners with the Sun,* based on his own research.[8]

Teal's starting salary was forty-five cents an hour; after several semesters, when he may have been making fifty or fifty-five cents an hour as a trusted employee, he began microfilming historic materials. "There was no such thing as a Xerox machine at the time, so if you wanted a photo copy you usually went through the micro-film process. Then you took the microfilm and made an enlargement of it on light sensitive paper, you developed that paper in chemicals, and then you had to fix it and wash it and dry it. Finally, you could hand someone a copy of a document."[9]

When Meriwether began working on the Calhoun project, he and Teal disassembled the microfilm camera stand and took it to Clemson, South Carolina, to film a large cache of Calhoun papers. Back in the library, Teal developed prints from the film in a room adjacent to Meriwether's office. Proximity encouraged spontaneous exchanges, and Meriwether often shared his enthusiasm when he found or received something interesting. Teal recalled the day "someone had brought in a copy of the *Parker's Ferry Gazette,* the real thing. Meriwether was so excited he was floating off of the ceiling." The 1780 *Gazette* was a patriot newspaper, and this was the first copy to come to light. Teal recalled another occasion "when someone brought in a book of . . . sheet music . . . from the Confederacy. . . . Meriwether was extremely excited about that because these were actual period pieces of sheet music . . . probably 50 or 75 pieces. . . . So you had all of a sudden an item that Meriwether was sharing with me that dealt with the whole Confederate Period; the printing and the music and the burning of Columbia, all of those were topics that were unfolded or that you would be led into when you examined this sheet music."[10]

Meriwether's wife, Margaret Babcock Meriwether, often worked as a volunteer in the library. She concentrated on images and objects. One of her long-term projects was preparing an index of WPA photographs, and her work made

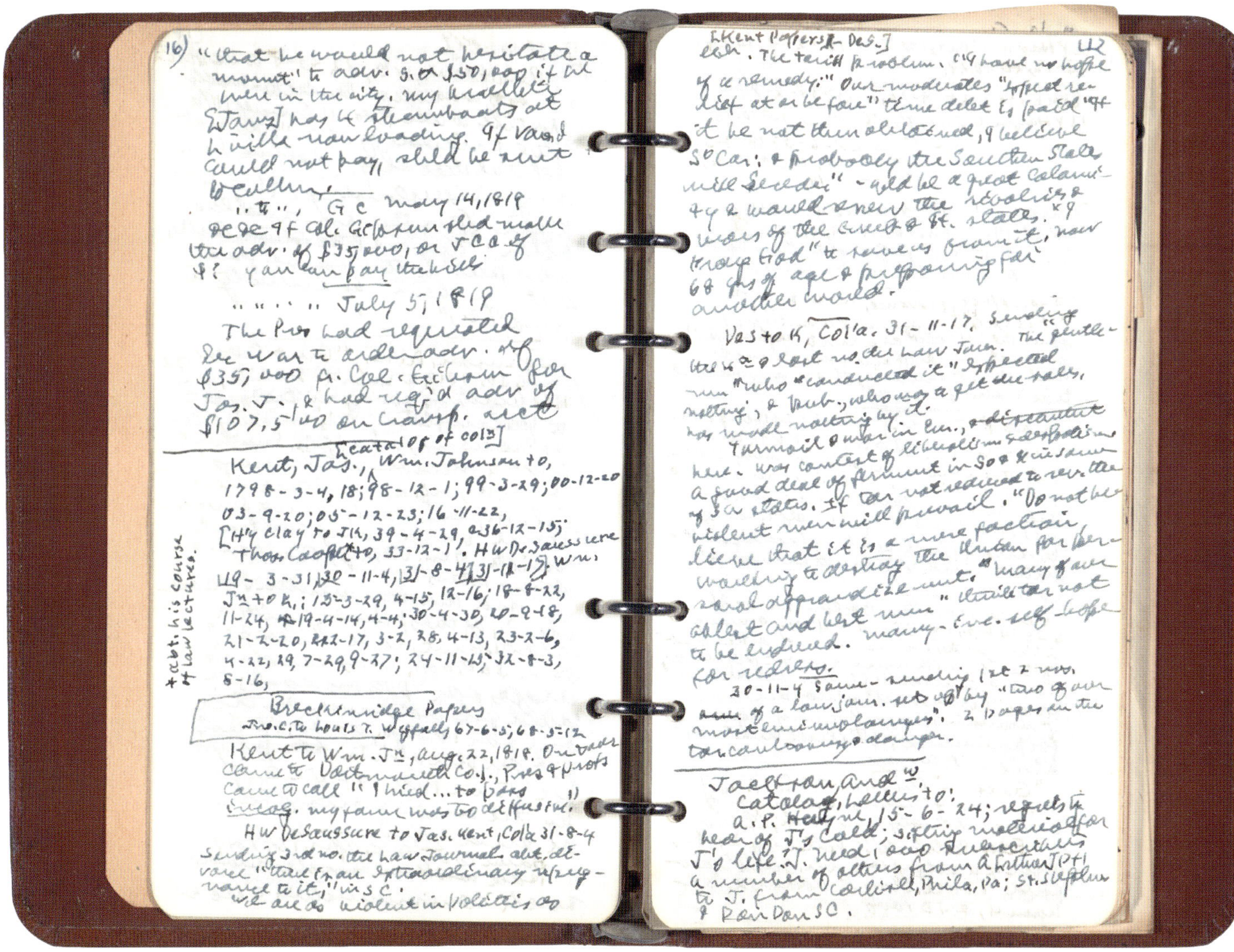

Robert Lee Meriwether's notebook, circa 1958.

Harvey Teal. Photograph by Hunter Clarkson, 2016.

Teal aware that little was known about photographers in South Carolina during the period 1840–1940. He decided to explore the topic, and after working for ten years, he produced the definitive book on the subject.[11] This research prompted him to visit other archives and museums, to join the Daguerrean Society, to meet collectors, and to establish a far-flung network of relationships that ultimately benefited the Caroliniana.

For example, one of the treasures in the collection is Mary Boykin Chesnut's famous Civil War diary. It was known that she had an album of photographs containing images of people mentioned in the diary, but the whereabouts of the album were unknown. An out-of-state collector asked Teal for information about unrelated Civil War–era images; he responded, and in the course of several telephone conversations, the collector mentioned the Chestnut album and the possibility that it was going to be taken apart and sold piecemeal. Teal helped a donor purchase it intact and bring it home.[12]

After graduating from the university, Teal taught history and civics in public schools and served as president of both the Kershaw County Historical Society and the South Caroliniana Society. He finished his career at the South Carolina Department of Education, where he was responsible for the development of television-based instruction in many states. Bringing students into contact with facsimiles of historic documents was a hallmark of his work. In many respects his life beyond the library has been a living testament to Meriwether's influence.

When Meriwether died, Erwin Lester Inabinett (1925–2004) succeeded him and served as head of the library from 1958 until 1983. Known to everyone as Les, he was in the U.S. Navy in World War II. After the war he received a B.A. in history from Pepperdine and came to the university in 1950 as a history graduate student. He worked for Meriwether in the library and as an editorial assistant on the *Calhoun Papers*. After Meriwether's death Inabinett's early years as head of the Caroliniana coincided with the civil rights movement, and the racial tension of the time was manifested in the Penn Center episode.

The Penn Center, on Saint Helena Island, South Carolina, was established in 1862 to provide education and improve the lives of local African Americans. When Inabinett became head of the Caroliniana, the center had been operating for a century. For several decades it had been nurturing the effort to improve race relations in South Carolina. In 1961 Courtney Siceloff, director of the center, approached Inabinett about donating its archives to the Caroliniana. Inabinett accepted, for although the library had antebellum plantation records, it had little to document the post–Civil War African American experience or the struggle for civil rights. He visited Penn Center several times to review the archives, and their trustees discussed having a ceremony at their spring meeting to celebrate the transfer.[13]

A month before the Penn Center spring meeting, at a gathering of Saint Helena community leaders, "the question was raised as to whether these records, if acquired by the Caroliniana Library, would be accessible to Negroes."[14] They contacted Inabinett. He checked "with a superior whose name I will not name — and I was absolutely forbidden to take the collection. I was forbidden to even pursue the matter further."[15] Consequently Elizabeth Siceloff, wife of the Penn Center director, wrote Inabinett that "Mr. Patton [of the Southern Historical Collection at the University of North Carolina] . . . made a hurried trip here, on the day of the Board meeting."[16]

The chain of correspondence concerning the Penn Center episode is incomplete, but letters from the director and his wife, Elizabeth, confirm that they did not blame Les Inabinett or the Caroliniana for the racist restrictions.

Although the library lost the Penn Center papers, it did receive several major collections during Inabinett's early years. The acquisition of the A. S. Salley collection of William Gilmore Simms material — manuscripts and publications — made the Caroliniana the major repository of work by the state's major nineteenth-century author. The following year the Henry Plimpton Kendall (1878–1959) estate donated an important collection of early cartography focusing on South Carolina and adjacent states. The Kendall Collection contains some 290 maps dating from the sixteenth through the nineteenth centuries and more than 2,300 related books. In 1965 the library received the papers of the former governor and U.S. senator Olin D. Johnston — approximately 200,000 items — marking the beginning of the effort to obtain and preserve the papers of modern South Carolina politicians. These collections and others acquired during Inabinett's tenure significantly improved and expanded the library's holdings. Nonetheless little was done during the 1960s to address the lack of material related to post–Civil War African American history.

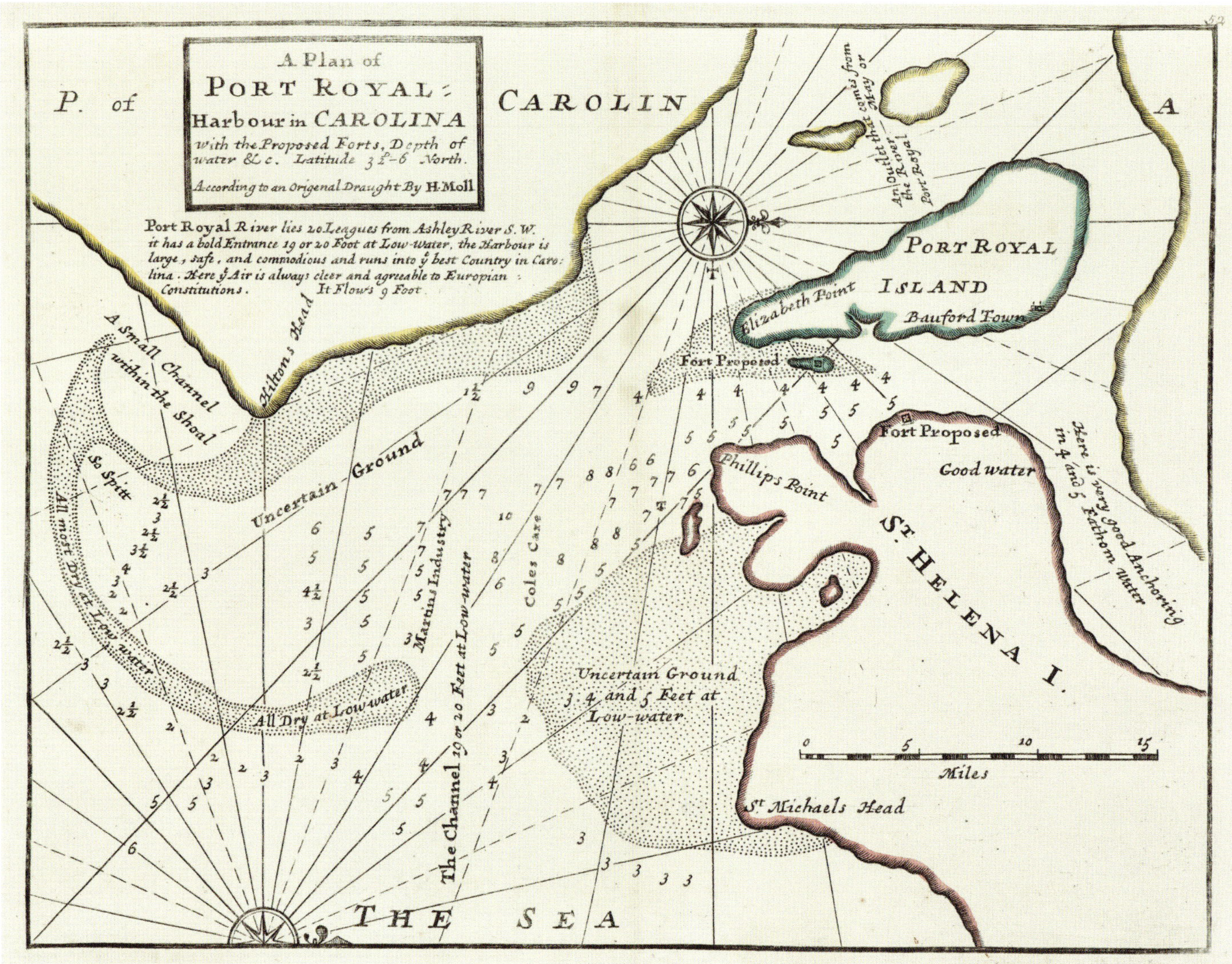

Plan of Port Royal Harbor by R. Moll
[Herman Moll], circa 1732.

The garden directly behind the Caroliniana was developed during Inabinett's tenure. The Columbia Garden Club envisioned "a Memorial garden which will link the beauties of the past with the needs of the present" to honor "dignitaries of the university as well as deceased members of the club."[17] Richard K. Webel of Innocenti and Webel, New York, designed the original garden focusing on old roses. The waist-high iron gate at the garden entrance to the Horseshoe was dedicated to Dr. J. Rion McKissick.

Inabinett and his staff were processing the newly acquired collections when Allen H. Stokes Jr. entered the library for the first time. As a Wofford undergraduate researching the use of leased convict labor, he was in the reading room on November 22, 1963, when President Kennedy was assassinated. Allen returned the following fall as a history graduate student, and in addition to his own work, he did research for Gustavus G. Williamson, a USC history professor, and for Dr. Benjamin Mays. In 1969 he began a graduate assistantship with Clara Mae Jacobs, "the library's first full-time manuscripts cataloger [who] handled, read, and cataloged every manuscript collection for more than twenty years." Allen was hired as her assistant in the manuscripts room on March 1, 1972. She retired later that year, and he became head of the manuscripts division. (When Inabinett retired in 1983, Allen became the third director of the Caroliniana after a national search.)[18]

Libraries evolve as society changes, and in the early 1970s, Thomas L. Johnson began collecting material related to the civil rights movement for the Caroliniana. Johnson had been a graduate student in the English department, and in a class taught by James Meriwether (son of Robert L. Meriwether), he became interested in the writings of James McBride Dabbs.[19]

Dabbs had been a student at the university during the brief presidency (1909–13) of Samuel Chiles Mitchell, an articulate advocate of progressive racial and economic policies. Mitchell's liberalism foreshadowed the analysis of race relations expressed in Dabbs's writings as well as his participation in church affairs and his work with the Southern Regional Council and the South Carolina Council on Human Relations. While writing a dissertation about Dabbs, Johnson became aware that records of the two councils' civil rights activity in South Carolina from around 1945 to 1970 might be acquired by one or more organizations in Wisconsin or Boston. He alerted Kenneth Toombs, head of the university library system, and Toombs authorized him to acquire the records.

Toombs was impressed by Johnson's initiative and sense of what might be historically relevant. He hired Johnson in 1973 as the Caroliniana's first full-time field archivist. Les Inabinett was head of the Caroliniana at the time, and Johnson recalls:

> Les did a first-rate job organizing and facilitating use of collections, but he never had enough time, space, or money to do what was needed. Kenneth Toombs, head of the university library, hired me, not the Caroliniana, so my position was somewhat irregular. In any case, Les Inabinett left me alone, and I defined my own mandate. The Caroliniana had slavery records, but little later material. In the 1970s black history and race relations were becoming key areas of research, so I developed vertical files of newspaper clippings about the civil rights

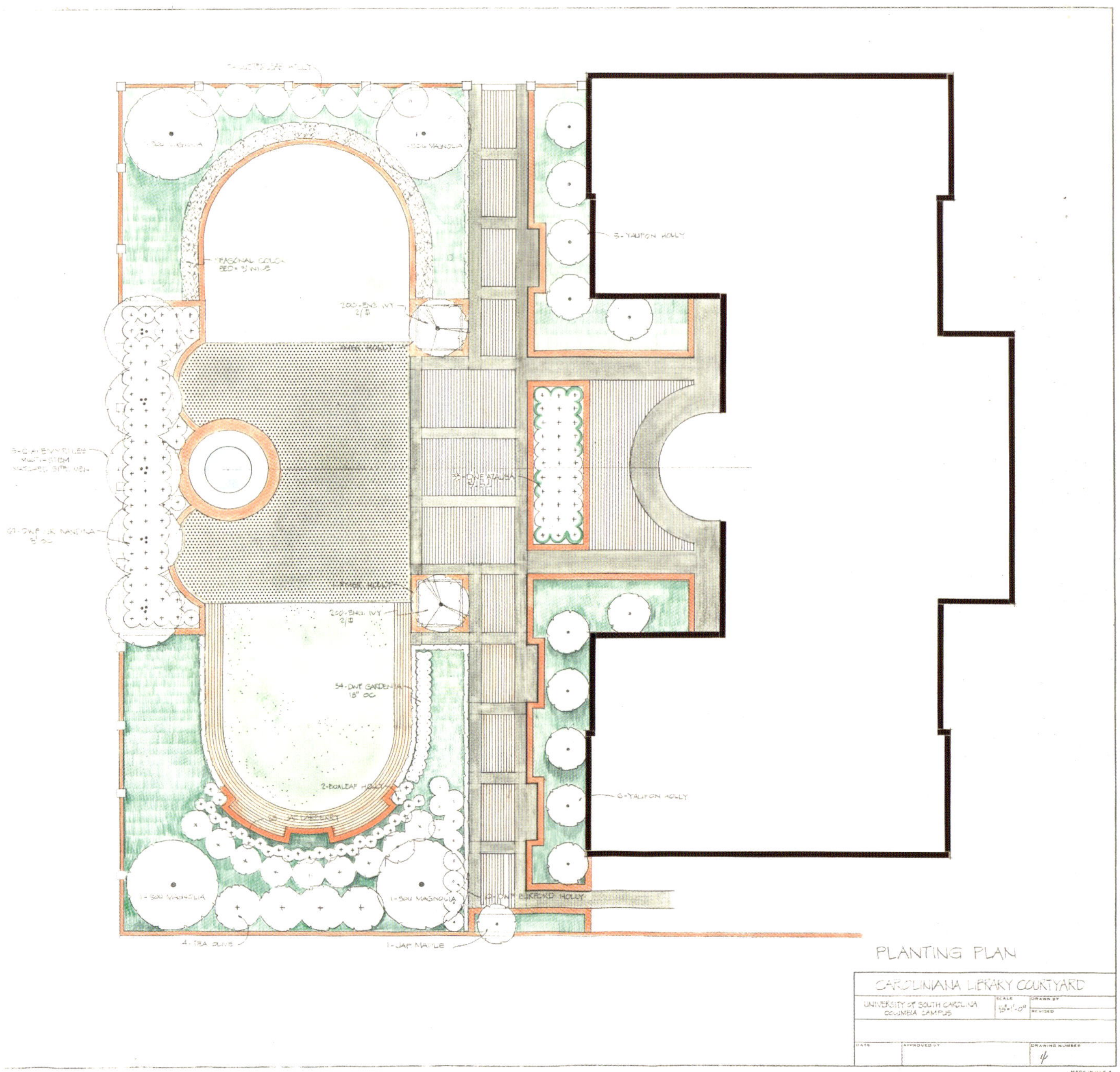

Planting plan, Caroliniana Library courtyard.
Drawing number 4, circa 1982.

Richard Samuel Roberts, circa 1930.

Wilhelmina Telitha Minne Roberts, circa 1919.

movement. I also obtained individual collections of the papers of Joseph DeLaine, James T. McCain, John Richards McCrae, Arthur J. Clement, Modjeska Simkins, Merton Simpson, and the well-known collection of glass-plate negatives by Richard Samuel Roberts, the African American photographer who worked in Columbia during the period 1920–1936. The Roberts Collection is important, and I will tell you how it happened.

One of my neighbors told me a Columbia family had their father's negatives stored under their house. She introduced me to the photographer's descendants, and over the course of more than two years, especially when Roberts's children came back to visit during the summer, we examined and cleaned negatives on tables set up in their backyard. Phillip Dunn, a professor in the art department, monitored the cleaning and agreed to make prints

Richard Samuel Roberts Family, Columbia.
Photograph by Richard Samuel Roberts.

as a trial. We were elated to find that many of the negatives were in excellent condition; equally exciting, older friends of the Robertses were able to identify many of the sitters. It was a long, complex process. The Roberts family had often talked about honoring their grandfather by publishing his photographs, but they were all working. With their support and sponsored by the Caroliniana, we were able to mount an exhibition at the Columbia Museum of Art and publish *A True Likeness.* The exhibition has traveled, and the book has gone all over the world.

Reminiscing about expanding the focus of the Caroliniana's collection, Johnson continued:

> I also obtained documents related to women's rights, the Equal Rights Amendment and the League of Women Voters, the NAACP, the Ku Klux Klan, and the papers of Bryan Dorn. Many of those things have moved from the Caroliniana to the Hollings political collections. I focused on artists, too, and arranged for the acquisition of Sigmund Abeles papers. He is an internationally known printmaker from South Carolina. The Jabbo Smith collection is notable too. He grew up in an orphanage in Charleston and became a famous jazz trumpet player. Edmund Yaghjian, Jesse Redwing "Jay" Bardin, and Catherine Heyward were all prominent painters here in the mid-twentieth century, and we added them to the collection. We also obtained material from the opera composer Carlisle Floyd, and the actress Joanne Woodward, and a number of writers. Being a field archivist was a wonderful job.[20]

By the late twentieth century, the historic Mills building could no longer accommodate the growing collection. Les Inabinett recalled, "That old building was a curse and a blessing at the same time. It was wonderful, you know, having the old building to operate in, but it never was built for an ever-expanding collection of Caroliniana. There [were] just terrible limitations to it."[21] He viewed the need for additional space as a crucial problem. Fortunately a combination of off-site storage, administrative changes, and two expansions of the Thomas Cooper Library improved working conditions at the Caroliniana.

University president Thomas F. Jones announced the first Cooper Library addition in 1972, and when the enlarged library opened in 1976, the 1940 McKissick Library became the home of the University Archives and McKissick Museum. The Caroliniana transferred treasured objects to the new museum, and in Inabinett's opinion "it was a happy day when we could divest ourselves of those things — because we really did not have the facilities or staff for making the most of that material."[22]

George D. Terry (1950–2001) was the first director of the new museum. A versatile, visionary administrator, he wrote that the mission of the museum was to "document and interpret the cultural heritage and natural environment of the South Eastern United States."[23] He knew that the creation of McKissick Museum was the realization of dreams that had been expressed by the faculty in 1906. A substantial gift from the Graniteville Corporation helped the university develop the Graniteville Room in Cooper Library as a new home for rare books transferred from the Caroliniana.[24]

Moving objects and university records to McKissick Museum improved working conditions at the Caroliniana, but the sheer volume of modern politicians' papers remained

Thomas Cooper, circa 1830.
McKissick Museum.

Presentation pitcher, inscribed "Alumni of S.C. College to Francis Lieber, December 1, 1856." Coin silver by Nathaniel Hayden and G. W. Whilden, Charleston, S.C.

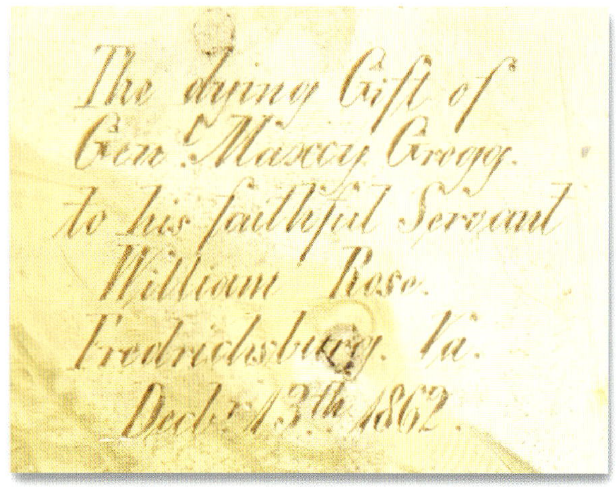

William Rose pocket watch, inscribed "The dying gift of Gen. Maxcy Gregg to his faithful servant William Rose. Fredericksburg, Va. Decb '13, 1862." Courtesy McKissick Museum.

a problem. In 1991 Ernest F. Hollings decided to donate personal and political papers to the university, and George Terry, then vice provost and dean of libraries, created a separate administrative unit to manage post–World War II political collections.[25] Herbert J. Hartsook directed the new unit and moved thirteen modern political collections from the Caroliniana to an off-site warehouse. The initial segment of the Hollings papers arrived in three tractor trailers carrying 1,400 cartons, or approximately 2.8 million pages. Terry envisioned a political collection housed in its own facility, and the acquisition of the Hollings Collection provided the catalyst for the second addition to Cooper Library, the Ernest F. Hollings Special Collections Library, which was completed in 2008.

Library finding aids have evolved from shelf lists to card catalogs to computer-searchable digital files. Today, through websites and an active digital scanning program, the Caroliniana has a significant, worldwide online presence.

The university's Digital Collections Department was established in 2005. It was instrumental — along with Clemson, the College of Charleston, and the South Carolina Department of Archives and History — in founding the South Carolina Digital Library (SCDL). "SCDL now includes over fifty cultural heritage institutions from across the state, bringing hundreds of collections into one searchable, freely accessible website." SCDL joined the Digital Public Library of America (DPLA), a national organization established in 2010 by the Library of Congress, Harvard University, and others to provide "coherent access to our society's digitized cultural heritage." Thousands of institutions across the country — colleges and universities, museums, public libraries, and historical societies — have adopted standards established by DPLA to scan collections and make them available online.[26]

Approximately 80 percent of the material placed online by the university's Digital Collections Department has come from Caroliniana collections. Researchers referred to Caroliniana collections approximately 150,000 times in 2015. Many of them visited the Caroliniana's Sanborn Map collection (fire insurance maps showing the height and material of buildings across the country); it was visited 23,558 times.[27]

Anyone with computer access is able to consult the constantly growing digitized portion of the collection. Funding for digitization comes from a variety of resources. Henry Fulmer, for example, obtained a grant from the National Endowment for the Humanities to digitize the Caroliniana's collection of 120 newspapers spanning the period 1836 through 1923. Depending on the nature of the material, an online collection may be keyword searchable and include images, text, and sound.

Making things digitally available is labor intensive. Each item must be individually examined and described. The description must be entered as metadata to make it accessible by computer, and then everything must be scanned and placed in the appropriate computer file. Patrons using Caroliniana material online benefit from this technology and the invaluable old skill, the page-by-page scrutiny of manuscripts and other historic material.

For half a century, Allen Stokes has participated in processing collections like those Thomas Johnson acquired;

Allen Stokes, circa 2010.

consequently he knows the Caroliniana's resources better than anyone. His knowledge is based on working with Clara Mae Jacobs, his own research, and his tenures as head of the manuscripts division (1972–83) and director (1983–2003, 2005–12).[28] Asked about his insights, Allen modestly quotes one of Les Inabinett's aphorisms: "There are three components in a great library: collections, staff, and patrons."[29]

Scholars acknowledge Allen's help in numerous publications. His *Guide to the Manuscript Collection* and *Kohn-Hennig Library: A Catalogue* are both indispensable for researchers in the library.[30] He fondly recalls working for and with students and authors, including C. Vann Woodward, Carol Bleser, and Drew Gilpin Faust. His gentle, generous guidance is legendary, and his enthusiasm for primary sources is palpable. Stokes becomes animated, for example, recounting a story about the papers of William Ellison.

April Ellison (1790–1861) was an enslaved African American who purchased his freedom and legally changed his name to William. Mechanically gifted and entrepreneurial, he manufactured cotton gins and became wealthy. When he died, he owned forty slaves and approximately one thousand acres. He and his descendants supported the Confederacy.

In the early twentieth century, the Leffelman family owned Ellison's former home, and their children found a box of letters and a cotton gin saw under the house. The family saved the correspondence and gave it to the Caroliniana in 1979. Shortly after the Ellison Papers became available, James L. Roark was in the library working on the career of Wade Hampton III, but, as Allen recalls, "he found Hampton's career less interesting than he anticipated."

Like a fisherman letting bait settle, Allen quietly placed the Ellison Papers on a library table near Roark. Roark, Allen recalls, subsequently "collaborated with Michael P. Johnson, and what began as a project on a free black family led to a broader search in public and private records, newspapers, and other sources that resulted in the publication of two books that opened a window on the lives of free blacks in rural and urban settings: *Black Masters: A Free Family of Color in the Old South* (1984) and *No Chariot Let Down: Charleston's Free People of Color on the Eve of the Civil War* (1986)."[31]

Stokes retired as head of the Caroliniana in 2003 but agreed to serve again (2005–12) when Herbert Hartsook was appointed director of the newly organized South Carolina Political Collections. Although ostensibly retired, he has reimmersed himself in the Caroliniana's manuscript collections.[32]

Recently, working on the Senator John Ewing Colhoun Papers, Stokes discovered a letter, written April 17, 1802, by the famous architect Benjamin Henry Latrobe. The letter explains Latrobe's reasons for not participating in the design competition for South Carolina College. Internal evidence suggests Colhoun had contacted Latrobe after seeing the trustees' advertisement seeking designs. Robert Mills, who would join Latrobe's office in 1803, independently responded to the same advertisement.[33]

A typed copy of the Latrobe letter has been known since 1976. Now, having the original available, archivists know the typescript is a facsimile of the manuscript—including words Latrobe deleted or struck through, others underlined for emphasis, and still others inserted above and below the lines. The scrupulous accuracy of the typescript suggests that it was produced by an historical editor, someone trained as a scientific historian, and the Caroliniana accession number, 184, indicates it came into the library in the late 1930s or early 1940s. Robert L. Meriwether probably transcribed the letter and returned it to the then-unprocessed Colhoun Papers.

Stokes's discovery of the Latrobe manuscript demonstrates how rewarding working with Caroliniana collections can be, for this manuscript conveys the concerns of a famous early American architect who was Thomas Jefferson's friend and Robert Mills's mentor. As a bonus the Latrobe letter is also a "new" primary document concerning the creation of the South Carolina College.

When Stokes retired the second time, Henry G. Fulmer was appointed director of the South Caroliniana Library in 2013. Thomas F. McNally, dean of the university's libraries, noted that Fulmer was an ideal candidate, for he had worked in the library as a graduate student, joined the staff in 1981, and served as curator of manuscripts under Stokes. Beyond his knowledge of the collections, Fulmer knew the building, and he was not surprised when the university determined that obsolete wiring and the lack of a fire suppression system made it imperative to remove the collections and thoroughly renovate the historic building.

The early years of Fulmer's tenure as director will no doubt be remembered for the acquisition of several major collections, including the Gen. William Westmoreland papers and the Mary Boykin Chestnut Civil War photograph albums. Equally notable, however, is the fact that when faced with the renovation, Fulmer and his staff, aided by a team of professional movers, relocated the entire collection to archival storage. They moved and reshelved hundreds of thousands of items so precisely that anything can be retrieved at any time. They have secured the collections and managed to keep the library in continuous operation, open and accessible.

Beyond the historic Mills building, the staff currently works in two locations — the Graniteville suite on the mezzanine of the Thomas Cooper Library, and the former South Carolina Department of Archives and History building at the corner of Bull and Senate Streets. Work on the collections continues. Materials are ferried back and forth. In the reading room, however, everything is tranquil.

In the Caroliniana's archives, thousands of manuscripts lie dormant like desert seeds. Inquisitive researchers can make them flower and bear fruit. Orville Vernon Burton, a historian who knows the collection, writes that "without the South Caroliniana Library a factual history of our state would not be possible."[34] Historians such as Burton express gratitude to the staff in their acknowledgements. For example, Carol Bleser, in *The Hammonds of Redcliffe,* expresses her debt to "Allen Stokes, Manuscript Director of the South Caroliniana Library . . . for bringing the Hammond-Bryan-Cumming Family Papers to my attention, and for making my stay at the Library pleasurable as well as fruitful. His sustained interest and valuable assistance cannot be exaggerated, and I owe him more gratitude than can be expressed here." (She also acknowledges the helpful support of Inabinett and the entire staff.)[35]

The library maintains a list of books generated by and based upon its collections. As of this writing (June 2017) there are hundreds of books on this list. Beyond books the Caroliniana makes material available for undergraduate papers, graduate students' theses and dissertations, articles about various aspects of the state, and personal and family histories. By making scientific history possible, the Caroliniana fulfills the vision of its founders every day.

Appendix One

Robert Woodward Barnwell to the Honorable Board of Trustees, November 29, 1837

To the Honorable The Board of Trustees
The committee appointed by your Honorable body in Dec. last, to superintend the erection of new college buildings, and to apply to the several specific objects the sums designated in the appropriation of $60,000 granted to the college by the legislature, beg leave respectfully to report:

That your committee, early in Jany last, advertised in the principal cities from Boston to Charleston, inviting contractors to make proposals for erecting two college wings, giving all the necessary information as to price of materials, mechanics labor, etc. the 15th of March was fixed on, as the time for giving out the contract, when several bids were received from Philadelphia, Baltimore, Virginia, & from persons in this place, varying in amount from $26,000 to $45,000. Believing that the buildings could not be erected for a sum less than the lowest bid, from the information your committee could gain, a contract was made with Messers Wade & [illegible] who entered into bonds for the faithful execution of the work, to be completed within a specified time viz: one of the wings on or before the 1st Dec next, & the other on or before the 1st March 1838. One building is already finished, & now occupied by students, & the other will be completed by 1st Jan. next. The contract for these buildings exceeds the amount of the appropriation by $1000 but it was deemed advisable to proceed in their construction, as they were much needed for the accommodation of students. There will be balances left, under the appropriation for general repairs, & for the Common's Hall, after necessary repairs & alterations have been completed. A transfer of $1000 may be made to meet the [illegible] deficiency should your Honorable Body think it proper to the direction.

The vouchers & contract with Messers Wade & Davis will be found accompanying the exhibit here with transmitted, & marked "No. 1 vouchers for expenditures 'new College buildings.'"

Your committee further beg leave to report, in reference to the new Library Building that it was soon ascertained that the $10,000 could not be obtained from the So. Car. Society, on the faith of which the Legislature made the grant of $15,000. Under these circumstances, your committee entertain the opinion that this same could not be expended till the matter was referred to the Honorable the Legislature for their further action. Your committee, however, in a contract with Col. Brown for brick made early in Feb. last, included the quantity necessary for the new library. The estimate, for the new college & library was 800,000 brick this number has been paid for, and there remains on hand 374,000.

Your committee next proceeded to make a purchase of a house & lot for the accommodation of the steward's family; and also to make such alterations and repairs in the commons

Hall as necessity seemed to require. A balance of this fund remains on hand, the disposal of which is referred to your Honble Body for further direction.

The accompanying vouchers marked No. 2 will show the objects to which this fund has been applied.

In reference to the purchase of books for the library, your committee made a large selection from Mr. Binda's library, & a few from other sources, the particulars of which will be found, on reference to the accompanying vouchers marked No. 3 with the balance of this fund, it was proposed to purchase books in Europe, but, from the high rate of exchange this has not been carried into effect, and the subject is [referred] to your Honorable body for further direction.

In reference to the fund for Repairs and purposes, your committee proceeded to pay off the balance due for the completion of the wall, contract for which was made by the committee repairs under the former appropriation of $20,000, and contracted for the building of out houses & c to new tenement for professors. The particular object to which this fund has been applied will be found in the accompanying vouchers marked No. 4.

A large balance of this fund will remain, after the necessary repairs have been completed, the further disposition of which is referred to your Honble Body.

Respectfully submitted

R W Barnwell Chm[1]

Appendix Two

Construction Contract and Specifications

Know all men by these presents that we, Charles Beck and James Boatwright are held and firmly bound unto the Trustees of the South Carolina College in the sum of Twenty-thousand dollars, to be paid by said Trustees, their successors & assigns, to which payment we bind ourselves and each and every one [illegible] executors and administrators, jointly and severally firmly by these present sealed with our seals and dated this tenth day of October the year of our Lord one thousand eight hundred and thirty eight.

The condition of this obligation is such that if the said Charles Beck shall well truly and faithfully perform this contract with said Trustees contained on this sheet of paper and the one penciled annexed, bearing cover date with these presents, then this obligation to be void and none effect or else to remain in full forces and virtue.

Signed, sealed & delivered in presence of

C. M. Beck

James Boatwright

This indenture made and entered into by and between Charles Beck of the one part and the trustees of the South Carolina College of the other part.

Witnesseth, that the said Charles Beck has agreed and hereby does agree to build for the South Carolina College on such site within the college grounds, as may be designated by the building committee of the said trustees, a college library and deliver the said completely finished in the very best workmanlike manner, on or before the first day of October next, according to the plans and specifications hereunto annexed, for the sum of twenty thousand dollars. Three thousand dollars thereof to be paid him on signing this contract, and the balance in such sums as the work progresses, that not more than three fourths of the work done shall be paid for at any time before the entire building is finished and received, in which payment the said Charles shall receive from G. Brown all the bricks necessary for the said building, at the price of twelve dollars the thousand, delivered at the site of the building, to be included in the [illegible] payment.

Plans and Specifications

The plans of the building contained in the seven drawings accompanying this contract marked Nos 1, 2, 3, 4, 5, 6 & 7 and endorsed by the said Charles and the chairman of the said building committee, are in every respect to constitute a part of this contract, and the library is to be built of the best materials and finished in the very best stile of architecture according thereto, except when in these specifications deviations therefrom are stipulated for.

Nos. 1 & 2 represent the basement story and the front elevation of the building. The columns of the portico are to be of brick rough cast, with granite plint[h]s and free stone capitals, and the cornice above to be of wood, the whole to be painted in imitation of granite or freestone as the committee may direct. The belting course above the basement story in front and all the window sills are to be of freestone, the sills of the front and back doors in the basement are to be of granite. The rest of the building is to be of brick laid in the best mortar, made of stone lime and clean worked sand, filling the entire wall. The walls of the foundation are to be on a foundation dug two feet deep and well rammed, and twenty-seven inches thick; the basement story walls are to be eighteen inches thick and above they are to be fourteen inches thick, except in front, on each side of the recesses of the windows, they are to be eighteen inches thick. The platform under the portico is to be twelve feet wide and curbed with granite, and paved with brick. The passage in the basement story is to be entirely finished, but the two rooms, on each side of it, are to be left unfinished, except that all the doors are to be completed; the shutters made painted and hung with proper fastenings, and two flues are to be carried up in each room.

No. 3 represents the floor and plan of the library in the second story. In this room the two doors on each side of the fire places are to be mere imitations, and two of the stair cases into the galleries are to be omitted, and in place of these, two closets are to be substituted, properly finished within. On the back of the building there are to be two windows in this story to correspond in all respects with those in front and two blanks are to be formed externally in place of windows.

No. 4 represents the alcoves and galleries, which are to be finished precisely in the same manner as the congressional library at Washington of which [illegible] is a drawing. The whole is to be finished in the best stile and all the recesses and galleries to be shelved ready to receive the library. The distances between the shelves are to be settled by the committee.

No. 5 represents the finish of the two ends of the library, in which there is to be no change except that the mantle pieces are to be of wood moulded and painted in imitation of marble.

No. 6 represents the ceiling overhead, which is to be done in plaster in the very best stile, equal to that of the congressional library, with the exception that instead of its being coved, it is to be straight.

No. 7 represents the back projection of the building & stair case. This projection is to be carried up as high as the parapet, to be finished with stucco cornice within, and covered with a tin roof.

The roof of the building is to be covered with tin with such declivities from the center as will make it perfect free from leaks and the water is to be carried off, in gutters and [illegible] tin pipes extending to the ground of proper size and with proper fastenings & heads. The seven windows in the library are to be furnished with inside shutters formed to fold into the jambs of the wall on each side & the circular heads of those windows are to be filled with stationary venetian blinds—glazing of these windows shall be with the best Boston crown glass. The lower sashes to be hung with weights. The whole interior of the library shall be painted dead white except the shelvings, which shall be painted on the edges with green and excepting the doors, which shall be painted in imitation of oak. The stair case is to have a heavy hand railing of mahogany.

Where any of these specifications or plans are imperfect as to the manner in which the work is to be done the work shall be done in a stile corresponding with the design of the rest of the building. Witness our hands this tenth day of October 1838

Sealed & delivered C. Beck
In the presence of R. Barnwell
W. F. DeSaussure building committee
G. Gregg
Blanding[1]

Appendix Three

A Description of the University of South Carolina Library Based on a Report Prepared by Richard T. Greener, 1875. Published by the Federal Bureau of Education, 1877.

University of South Carolina, Columbia, S.C.
The South Carolina College, now the University of South Carolina, was chartered in 1801, and a library was at once begun. The first grant for it was made by the general assembly in 1802, and when the college opened in 1805, about $3,000, it is estimated, had been paid for books. In 1813 the board of trustees voted to apply the surplus of the tuition fund to the increase of the library. During the period from 1813 to 1845 this amounted to $23,757. In 1823 the general assembly made a grant of $5,000 for the benefit of the library, and in 1825 voted an additional $5,000 for the same purpose. In 1836 $15,000 were appropriated for a library building and $5,000 for the purchase of books; and in 1838 an annual grant of $2,000 was voted for the library. During the period 1836 to 1853 the grants for the library by the general assembly amounted to $43,000, and there was realized from the surplus tuition fund the sum of $19,374, making an aggregate of $63,375 in seventeen years. The library has received altogether from State and private sources over $90,000.

Gov. John Drayton, whose message to the general assembly in 1801 is considered the germ of the college, was among the first, if not the first, to give books to the library. In 1807, he presented his own publications and a number of other works. In 1841, the general assembly presented a copy of the American Archives. In 1842, copies of the acts and resolutions of the assembly from 1700 were presented by order of the general assembly, and have since been received annually. In 1844, Gen. James H. Adams and Col. John Lawrence Manning made valuable gifts of books, and the general assembly presented Audubon's *Birds.*

The number of volumes now in the library is about 27,000, besides 1,000 pamphlets. A literary society, the Clariosophic, connected with the college, has a library of 1,250 volumes.

"The college library contains a large number of rare and valuable books, and is especially rich in works on Egypt. The first copy of Rossellini's *Monumenti dell' Egitto e della Nubia,* 10 volumes, octavo, brought to the United States was imported for this library. There are also many very old volumes, a number of them printed during the sixteenth century, and some dating as far back as 1480."

The library was built in 1841, and cost more than $23,000.[1]

Appendix Four

Minutes of Various Committees

Minutes of Committee on New Library, June 29, 1938

The committee appointed by President McKissick to consider the various questions in connection [*sic*] with the planning and construction of the new library building met in Dean Crow's office in the Education building at 8:00 p.m. The entire committee, consisting of Dean Crow, Chairman, Professors Hoy, Green, Kennedy, Meriwether, Morse, Norwood and Sumwalt, was present. Prof. Morse was made Secretary of the meeting.

After considerable discussion, in which every member participated, the following motions were made and voted on as indicated below:

1. The committee was in entire and hearty accord that first and foremost in importance was the selection of an architect who has had considerable recent experience in the building of college libraries. Such an one would not only be familiar with the functions and activities of present-day libraries, with the best arrangements of offices, stack rooms, reading rooms, seminar rooms, cloak rooms, etc., with the best materials and equipment for the different needs of the library, but would also know what costly and irremediable errors to avoid. Upon him, more than upon any other one factor, will depend the success and future satisfaction of the building.

2. The only other item upon which the committee was in entire accord was that the style of architecture should be in harmony with the architecture of the main campus, and especially with the present library.

3. On the question of location of the new library the committee was divided. Messers. Crow, Green, Kennedy, Morse and Sumwalt were in favor of the site occupied by the Extension building. Messrs. Hoy, Meriwether and Norwood were opposed to the tearing down or removing of the old President's house and were in favor of putting the new library on Gibbes' green, either immediately back of the President's house, or on Pickens Street. The arguments in favor of locating the library on the site of the Extension building were that a library is the heart of a college and should therefore be centrally located. Its dominating importance requires that it be given a dominating position on the campus. Furthermore, it was pointed out that the Extension Building has long been in a dilapidated condition and was doomed by the ravages of time. Sooner or later it would have to be removed or dismantled. The arguments in opposition were that the Extension Building fits in ideally with the rest of the campus and that the traditions and sentiments clustering about it forbid its removal or destruction. Furthermore, it was held that the new library could serve its purposes just as well on Gibbes' Green. Professor Norwood was given permission to bring in a minority report.

4. As to the use the present library should be put to. The committee was even more divided. Messrs. Hoy and Sumwalt were in favor of using it as a Student Union building. Mrssers. Kennedy and Morse favored its use as an art gallery and studios for the Fine Arts Department. The ground floor could be used for Administration offices, if necessary. Messrs. Crow, Green, Meriwether, and Norwood favored its use as a Caroliniana library.

The arguments in favor of the Students' Union building were that a Students' Union building is one of the most pressing needs of the University and that the main room was admirably suited for a ballroom. The other rooms could be used for lounge, meeting, and study purposes. Messrs. Kennedy and Morse contended that the University needed an art gallery and the Art Department sorely needed suitable quarters. The present library would meet those needs almost perfectly. Messrs. Crow, Green and Norwood agreed with Mr. Meriwether that it should be used as a Caroliniana library, the arguments being that it would continue the use of the building as a library and thus preserve its distinction as the oldest college library building in the United States, and that the collection of Caroliniana is growing so rapidly it will soon outgrow any space that may be given to it in the new library. Also that much of the newly aroused interest and enthusiasm in and for Caroliniana throughout the state would be lost if the collection were moved to the new library. The opposition argued that the new library should house all the books of the university, that adequate space could easily be provided and that questions of expense for double maintenance would make it impractical to have two library buildings on the campus.

5. Size: The committee agreed that the library should have a stack capacity of 50,000 volumes and a total book capacity of 310,000 volumes, with provisions for ready increase to 1,000,000 volumes. The reading rooms should have accommodations for 600 students. These figures and estimates were based on similar data of the new University of Virginia library.

Meeting adjourned, to meet again the following night at the same hour.

Josiah Morse, Secretary[1]

Trustees' Minutes, President's Report, December 5, 1940

Some time ago I received the following from Dr. R. H. Wienefeld, acting librarian:

> This memorandum has been prepared by myself and Professor Meriwether for your consideration. It is a plan for bringing under single management the South Carolina collection, the work of collecting South Caroliniana, the management of the old Library Building (excepting the portion for the time being reserved for administrative offices), and the integration of such work with that of the General Library.
>
> Two-thirds of the acquisitions of South Caroliniana for the past ten years have been gifts, and it seems obvious that in such gifts lies the future of the Collection. The gifts, especially those of personal papers, are often secured only by signing of agreements by the person soliciting the gift, and the donors tend to hold him responsible rather than the Librarian of the University. The greater part of the South Carolina Collection, in bulk and in value, consists of manuscripts, and the problems involved in handling manuscripts are entirely different from those of libraries of printed

material. These facts seem to make it necessary that funds assigned to purchases and care of Caroliniana, and the actual administration of the South Carolina Collection and the building should be made an autonomous unit within the University, its relations to the University Library being so defined as to assure efficiency of the Caroliniana work and a unified service of both to the University.

We, therefore, propose:

First, that the President appoint a Director of the South Caroliniana Library who shall, in addition to the duties heretofore performed by the Chairman of the Caroliniana Committee, have control of that Library and its staff.

Second, that the Librarian of the University shall exercise such supervision of the South Caroliniana Library as to keep him informed of its work in order that unnecessary duplication of service, equipment or expenses may be avoided, and in order that there may be no popular impression that there is such duplication or rivalry. To facilitate supervision for this particular purpose the Director should be considered as having the rank of an Assistant Librarian.

Third, the Director shall present an annual report to the Librarian setting forth hours, salaries, services and expenditures for the actual administration of the Library which shall form the basis for the Librarian's supervision.

Fourth, this supervision shall not extend to interference in the administration of the South Caroliniana Library, nor appointments to or promotions of its staff. In case of disagreement between the Librarian and Director as to unnecessary duplication of service, equipment or expenses the matter should be referred to the President.

Fifth, when the present Librarian has effected any reorganization of the Library that he may undertake, he and the Director shall agree upon a classification of the staff and duties of the South Caroliniana Library and shall confer on salaries and promotions thereafter in order that inequalities may as far as possible be prevented.

Sixth, when the Director is a member of the University teaching staff he should have an assistant to do most of the routine work of the South Caroliniana Library. This assistant should have the title of Assistant Director to enable her to take over as much of the work and correspondence of the office as possible.

Seventh, the President shall appoint a Caroliniana Committee to meet each semester. Such committee shall aid the Director in the collection of Caroliniana and advise in the administration of the Society and the South Caroliniana Library. We sincerely believe that the plan indicated above will prove feasible as a long term arrangement. In arriving at these recommendations we have borne in mind that neither the present Librarian nor the present chairman of the Caroliniana Committee will be here forever. Accordingly, we have tried to formulate a working agreement that will function without undue friction regardless of what persons occupy these positions. It may well be that experience will dictate some modifications in the future, but as far as we can perceive under this arrangement efficient cooperation and coordination of the two libraries can be secured while, at the same time, granting The Director of the South Caroliniana Library and staff ample latitude in meeting the special problems of their work.

This plan of administration is both practical and desirable, as well as for the best interest of both libraries, in my opinion.[2]

Approval of the Above Memorandum

It was moved and passed that the plan for the administration of the University of South Carolina libraries submitted by R. L. Meriwether, head of the department of History, and R. H. Wienefeld, acting librarian, be approved. Adopted December 11, 1940.

(signed) Frank F. Welbourne, Secretary of the Board of Trustees[3]

The University South Caroliniana Society

Purpose: To aid, by contributions of service, material, or money, in building up the South Carolina Collection of the University library; to cooperate with other organizations and individuals in the work of keeping South Carolina historical material in this State; and to preserve this material in fireproof quarters.

Officers and organization: A president, a vice-president, and a secretary and treasurer, elected annually by those members in good standing who may be present at the annual meeting; these three officers to constitute the executive committee of the society, charged with preparation of programs for the annual meeting and with the business of the society between its meetings.

Membership: Persons or organizations approved by the executive committee and paying its annual dues of five dollars, or contributing South Carolina material accepted by the Caroliniana Committee as the equivalent of that amount.

Obligations of members: Payment of the annual dues and the gift, if practicable, annually, of some piece of South Carolina material or of some other aid to the South Carolina Collection.

Disposition of funds: The entire income of the society pledged to the purchase of South Carolina material for the South Carolina Collection of the University library; and purchases made with these funds and gifts made by the members credited to these members and to the society.[4]

Robert Lee Meriwether to President J. Rion McKissick, University of South Carolina, March 7, 1940

Dear Rion:
Recently I spoke to you about the administration of the South Carolina Collection after the new library is completed and the main library moved. At your suggestion I am writing to you to state the points that I did not have time to go into then.

The trustees have provided that the entire South Carolina Collection shall be left in the old library but the question whether the staff for the South Carolina Collection should be appointed and supervised by the head Librarian or whether it should be in part or entirely separated from the administration of the main library has not been settled. In my letter to you of August 23, 1938 I stated the conviction to which I had arrived, in conference with several persons very much interested in the Caroliniana work, that the Collection could not be administered by the Librarian of the University, but that for effective work it was necessary that the Collection be under the control of the agency in charge of the Caroliniana work. In view of that conviction and because of various difficult problems connected with the South Carolina Collection I asked that you accept my resignation and appoint a new committee to investigate the situation with a view to drastic changes.

You refused to consider letting me drop the work and insisted that I go on with it. I felt it necessary, therefore, to work out an outline for a practicable plan for the administration and care of the South Carolina Collection and lay these before you. I presented that report to you in the form of a letter on October 26, 1938. I am quoting from that letter the points bearing immediately on the present problem.

The second problem, that of administration, has with the rapid growth of the manuscript and newspaper accessions during the past two or three years, become more and more critical. The discussion of the new library plans for the past few months merely emphasized, and did not change the situation. I see no other solution for this problem than to have the South Carolina Collection managed as a unit entirely separate from the main library, and its staff appointed by the President in consultation with a faculty committee supervising that Collection.

The reason for this conclusion is that the problems of the South Carolina Collection and of the main library, however alike they may seem to superficial observation, are so fundamentally different that no one, however capable and earnest, primarily responsible for one, can give proper attention to the other. This statement is based chiefly on the following points:

> First, the growth or decline of the South Carolina Collection depends primarily on the success with which its managers reach the present and future owners of South Carolina manuscripts and newspapers. This problem is so foreign to the problems of the main library that no head librarian, absorbed with the management of the main library, can ever be expected to give adequate thought to it.
>
> Second, the problems of the general library are primarily with books, and library schools of the United States train their students only for handling books.... It is simply too much to expect or to hope that under the administration of the main library the manuscripts of the South Carolina Collection will ever receive proper consideration. Yet a little reflection must show that in the manuscripts lies the future of the Collection. In actual value they are now worth as much as or more than the books and pamphlets.
>
> Third, I have made every effort, in seeking South Caroliniana, to get gifts and not deposits, and to ensure permanent possession of them by the University. It is impossible, however, to build up a collection of this sort without many agreements and obligations, and the careful and tactful observance of these agreements is vital. As long as there is complete division between the collecting and caretaking agencies of the South Carolina Collection, it will be all but impossible to prevent indifference of the staff to these agreements, if not outright impatience with them. We should get an increasing number of the chief leaders of the state to promise the South Carolina Collection all of their papers. This can only be done by building up the most complete confidence in the minds of the public that there is absolute unity in the collecting and administering agencies of the Collection. As long as one agency makes the agreements, and another separate agency carries them out, there will be danger of mistakes and misunderstandings that will be fatal to the program.

The fourth item in the report referred to the plans that I had put into effect for getting gifts of the office files of newspapers in the state. I omit this as the reasons are similar in nature but not as critical as those in the paragraph above.

Fifth, there has always been a feeling on the part of the South Carolina Room staff that the Caroliniana Committee collects and dumps material on that staff without realization of the difficulties of housing and caring for it. As long as there is complete separation between the collecting and caretaking agencies of the Collection this feeling is inevitable and easy to understand, but it is a grave handicap to the work and there is danger that it will ruin it.

At first thought it is likely to seem proper and logical that all the books and papers on the campus should be under the same supervision and control. In actual fact there is much greater difference between the nature and problems of the South Carolina Collection and the main Library than between almost any two departments of the institution. There should, of course, be cordial cooperation and coordination of work between the South Carolina Collection and the main Library. This should be and readily could be provided for. In this connection I wish to suggest, even though it may seem to be intruding a detail in a letter that deals with general policy, that wherever there are duplicate copies in the South Carolina Collection, unless these copies are quite rare and hard to replace, the duplicate or one of the duplicates be placed in the main library, catalogued and shelved without special reference to the fact that it is a South Carolina book or by a South Carolina author. This will eliminate a very great inconvenience that the users of the general library suffer.

Therefore I can see no other solution of the problem than the one suggested above,—provision for complete separation of the administration of the South Carolina Collection from that of the main library, to go into effect when the new library is completed, with appointment of the South Carolina Collection staff by the President in consultation with a new Caroliniana Committee.

This arrangement, I feel, is absolutely essential for effective management of the Caroliniana Collection, and for taking any real advantage of the possibilities of our Society. And since you have remarked that you are looking for someone to succeed the present head Librarian, I feel that I ought to call this situation to your attention now.

I would be very glad, of course, for it to be considered by the Caroliniana Committee, but it would obviously be embarrassing to have a regular committee meeting for that purpose since the Librarian is a member of it.

In an earnest effort to leave you as free of complications and restrictions as possible in your plans for the two libraries, I have come to the following as possible solutions of the problem:

The first alternative—and the only one it seems to me to serve the purpose—is to separate the management of the South Carolina Collection and the old library building entirely from the main University Library, with provision, of course, for cordial cooperation between the two, as indicated above. I should think that the librarian of the South Carolina Collection under these circumstances might have the same rank as the first assistant to the head Librarian. This librarian of the South Carolina Collection should have two assistants, making the proposed staff the size of the present one. This staff with the NYA student assistants at present assigned to the South Carolina Room and my office could take care of the whole building and keep the South Carolina Collection open from 9 a.m. to 10 p.m. This staff should be appointed by the President entirely independent of the head Librarian, the President making his selections and giving his instructions to this librarian on the basis of the special needs of the

South Carolina Collection. In arriving at his conclusions the President would have the advantage of the reports of the individual in charge of the collecting of the Caroliniana and the advice, if he should ask it, of the Caroliniana Committee. This librarian should be subject to the general direction and supervision of the person in charge of the collection of Caroliniana. The Caroliniana Committee should meet at least annually and supervise the work of the Collection in general and make recommendations.

The second alternative — a poor substitute for the first so far as effective work is concerned — would be to divide the South Carolina Collection into two parts (keeping both, however, in the old library) — manuscripts and printed materials. The management of the books, pamphlets and newspapers has not been a critical problem and the person in charge of this printed material could be appointed by the head Librarian of the main library. Under this arrangement two persons could be appointed by the head Librarian for the printed material and another person with an assistant appointed directly by the President as provided in the First Alternative, for care of the manuscripts. This would provide for unity of the collecting agency and the library management of the manuscripts proper. This arrangement would be cumbersome and somewhat inefficient, requiring for one thing a larger staff but would make proper provision for management of the manuscripts and would secure the absolute essential unity and management between the collecting and caretaking agencies.

The third alternative, the appointment by the head Librarian of the entire staff of the South Carolina Collection, would put the entire management and responsibility for the books, papers and manuscripts in the hands of the head Librarian and persons appointed by him. This would mean complete separation of responsibility of the collecting agency from the library staff, and would, I am convinced, be fatal to the best interests of the Collection. If you should feel that desirable and necessary, I beg that you will see to it that the assistant librarian put in charge of the South Carolina Collection will be able to take entire charge of the seeking and collecting of South Carolina material hereafter, because I would be utterly unwilling to take any responsibility for collecting material under these circumstances. If you appoint a librarian for the South Carolina Collection who will undertake this work and care for the affairs of the Society, I shall be delighted to turn it all over to him. It would be a vast relief to me.

I do not wish to appear to be trying to determine the details of the arrangement you may make, but merely to point out some apparently practical plans which may serve as suggestions. I hope, however, that you can decide the matter in the near future, for it would put an end to a deal of misunderstanding and prevent what will be, I fear, an increasing friction.

Cordially yours, R. L. Meriwether
RLM tr[5]

Appendix Five

Remarks on the Occasion of the Publication of Volume I of The Papers of John C. Calhoun, *by Philip M. Hamer, in Columbia, S.C., October 18, 1959*

Madam President, Ladies and gentlemen:

This is a moment of great pride as well as of sadness for all of us. We are meeting today to honor two men—John C. Calhoun and his editor and interpreter, Robert L. Meriwether. The latter has erected a monument to the former—a monument which he conceived and the foundations of which he laid. That he did not live to see the final shape is a matter of the keenest regret to all of us. But in building a monument to Calhoun, Bob Meriwether has erected a lasting one to himself, and in a form, I am sure, that would have pleased him most—scholarly achievement of the highest order.

Publication of *The Papers of John C. Calhoun* had its inception at a conference, the memory of which I shall always cherish. It was the summer of 1950. Only a few weeks earlier the first volume of a boldly conceived and magnificently executed enterprise, Julian P. Boyd's scholarly edition of *The Papers of Thomas Jefferson,* had been published, and the first copy had been ceremoniously presented to the President of the United States. In accepting the volume, the President not only praised the enterprise and stressed the value of such work for an understanding of your nation's development but he also expressed the hope that the papers of other American leaders would also be published. He asked the National Historical Publications Commission to survey the situation and report a plan for making available the "writings of men whose contributions to our history are now inadequately represented by published works."

It was my pleasant task, on behalf of the Commission, to confer with leading historians and other scholars throughout the country in formulating this program. My steps turned early to South Carolina, for there was one man there with whom I knew I had to confer. This was my former classmate at Wofford, my longtime friend, respected colleague, and distinguished member of the faculty of the University of South Carolina—Bob Meriwether.

As a native South Carolinian, there was to me a towering figure among the State's many great men—John C. Calhoun, the outstanding political theorist of his time, a compelling leader as well as a great intellect. No edition of his papers had appeared since 1899, when J. Franklin Jameson edited selected letters for publication by the American Historical Association. Although Jameson was a fine scholar, much was omitted from his edition. (Later, after Bob Meriwether had struggled long and mightily with Calhoun's erratic handwriting, he facetiously observed that it was his belief that Jameson had published only those letters that he had been able to read!) At any rate, a complete edition of the papers of the apostle of the concurrent minority would certainly be a great contribution. Emulating that well-known South Carolinian, Barney Baruch, Bob and I—with my wife as an interested but characteristically far-from-silent observer—held a conference on a park bench. It was under the tall trees of the University of South Carolina campus, just in front of the South Caroliniana Library. There on that summer day of 1950, the Calhoun papers project was really conceived, although it was many conferences and some two years later before it came officially into being.

Meanwhile, the National Historical Publications Commission had in 1951 recommended a national program for the publication of historical documents. This program has since been endorsed by two Presidents of the United States, the Congress of the United States, the American Historical Association, and many other organizations and individuals. The Commission did not recommend that an extensive publication program be undertaken by the Federal Government. Instead, it recommended that collecting, editing, and publishing be undertaken chiefly by State and local organizations. The Commission has encouraged the establishment of such projects and has cooperated with them. One by one a number of them, modeling themselves after the Thomas Jefferson project, have been established and are now in operation. Among these are projects for the comprehensive publication of the papers of John and John Quincy Adams, sponsored by the Massachusetts Historical Society; Benjamin Franklin, sponsored by Yale University and the American Philosophical Society; Alexander Hamilton, sponsored by Columbia University; James Madison, sponsored by the University of Chicago and the University of Virginia; Henry Clay, sponsored by the University of Kentucky; James K. Polk, sponsored by Vanderbilt University and the Tennessee Historical Commission; Woodrow Wilson, sponsored by the Woodrow Wilson Foundation; and several others.

The Calhoun papers project was the first of these enterprises to be established, and, as the first-born, I confess that it has always had a special place in my heart. It now has the distinction of being the first of these projects to have a volume published.

The Calhoun project is also unusual in that it is financed solely by organizations and institutions in the State, chiefly through funds made available by the South Carolina legislature. (I believe that all other projects I have mentioned have had some foundation support or a grant from a corporation.)

In his preface, Dr. Meriwether makes it clear that the production of a modern scholarly edition of the papers of one of our great leaders is essentially a cooperative enterprise, and he gratefully and generously acknowledges his indebtedness. The University South Caroliniana Society, our host this afternoon, has given of its funds and has encouraged the project in many other ways. The University of South Carolina, represented here by President Robert L. Sumwalt and Dean Robert H. Wienefeld, has assisted with housing and staffing, and the University's Press has produced, in Volume I, a book of excellent typography and design. Clemson College generously made available the core collection of Calhoun's personal papers, without which this undertaking would not have been possible; the late President of Clemson, R. F. Poole, the late Professor A. C. Holmes, and Professor Carl L. Epting have been of special help. The interest and support of Calhoun A. Mays, Chairman, and the other members of the South Carolina Archives Commission, were, I know, indispensable to the project. J. Harold Esterby [*sic*], the able Director of the South Carolina Archives Department was as Dr. Meriwether declared, "the editor's chief reliance" on matters of editorial procedure and "in the general problems of the work." The State Budget and Control Board, headed by James M. Smith, in full recognition of the significance of Calhoun's papers, has given invaluable assistance in handling budgetary problems. And last, but far from least, the members of the State legislature have been generous in their appropriations for this work.

Many organizations, in other parts of the country, played an important part in the collection of copies of Calhoun's papers. Dr. Meriwether singled out for recognition Miss F. Helen Beach, Archivist on the Commission's staff, who, in Bob's words, gave "indispensable aid through her skill and enthusiasm in finding Calhoun papers in the National Archives and the Library of Congress." He mentions many others — more than I can repeat this afternoon, however much I would like to — but to his colleagues on the project, Mrs. Clara M. Jacobs and E. L. Inabinett, Bob expresses a "special debt of gratitude." The staff of the South Caroliniana Library — itself one of Bob Meriwether's enduring achievements — rendered unique service. His daughter, Miss Margaret W. Meriwether, was, he said, his "inspired" proof reader, and as a labor of love, she prepared the excellent index, without which no scholarly volume is complete. The book is dedicated to "M. B. M.," his wife Margaret B. Meriwether, whose understanding, encouragement, and assistance were far more profound than we can gauge.

Large-scale editorial enterprises are obviously and necessarily cooperative, but it is the editor himself who plays the leading role, who adds the creative touch. It is his imagination that gives scope to the work, and, finally, his scholarship by which it will stand or fall. That the first volume of *The Papers of John C. Calhoun* measures up to the best of them is already evident, and Bob Meriwether's mind and hands will have their imprint on volumes yet to come.

Margaret L. Coit, Pulitzer-prize biographer of John C. Calhoun (*John C. Calhoun: American Portrait*), has already lauded Volume I in a long review in the *New York Times* of October 11. "Where Meriwether really broke new ground," she wrote, "was in his copious and comprehensive historical notes, which illuminate obscure points in the letters, and in his 'resurrection' of the stateman's early speeches — It is only to be hoped," she said, "that future editors of this massive series will uphold the standards set in this first volume."

Wayne C. Grover, Archivist of the United States, and Chairman of the National Historical Publications Commission, welcomed the volume as an important contribution not only to an understanding of Calhoun but of the history of the nation, which he served as Congressman, Cabinet officer, and Vice President.

Felix Frankfurter, Associate Justice of the Supreme Court of the United States, who represents the Court on the National Historical Publications Commission, has on several occasions said that he considers John C. Calhoun to have been one of the nation's profoundest political thinkers, and he has often asked me about the progress of the Calhoun papers project. Justice Frankfurter wishes me, on this occasion, to express to the State of South Carolina and to all the organizations and persons who have contributed to this volume, and to the other volumes that will follow, his congratulations for making better known, through publication, the letters, speeches, and other writings of South Carolina's and the Nation's great statesman.

Julian Boyd, whose *Papers of Thomas Jefferson* has served as the prototype for all other modern comprehensive editions, has told me how impressed he is with volume I and has characterized it as a first-rate job of scholarly editing. He considers *The Papers of John C. Calhoun* a contribution of great national importance.

Thus I think we may be satisfied that the project to publish the papers of one of the State's and the Nation's most distinguished sons has been launched with distinction.

If my remarks this afternoon have been personal — and they have been — I hope you will forgive me. My association with the Calhoun papers project has been close, and I cannot regard it entirely with the detachment that is supposed to characterize the scholarly view. As a native South Carolinian, and one who has always been interested in her history and well-being, I am proud that South Carolina is among the leading States of the Union in preserving and making known the records of her history. The publication of *The Papers of John C. Calhoun* is certainly a major contribution to a knowledge of our Nation's history; it just as certainly illuminates and adds luster to the history of our State.[1]

Appendix Six

Benjamin Henry Latrobe to John Ewing Colhoun, April 17, 1802

Sir,
I am highly flattered by your polite letter of the 14th currt and if anything could induce one to enter into such a competition as is proposed by the Advertisement of the trustees of the S. Carolina College, it would be the letter you have written to me. But there are reasons,— which your politeness renders it proper for me to state to you,—which have long prevented men who have a reputation to lose, and who do not absolutely depend upon a chance of business for support, from encountering the sort of rivalry which a public notice calls forth.—The merit of the design of a professional man of experience and integrity is, that nothing is proposed but what is practicable;—permanent;—and economical,—with a view to ultimate expenditure;—& in point of taste,—capable of encountering the severest criticism. But these are merits, of which it is not easy for unprofessional men to judge in a plan; drawing- & on that account the ~~trial~~ decision is not always according to the merits.—I have now before me a most seductive design in point of drawing & coloring, & which has also some excellent points of arrangement,—which has been submitted to me,—to decide, whether it shall be executed or not. It is drawn by a most ingenious Amateur. But the chimnies cannot be carried up: the staircase has not head way enough by two feet, & lands so that the doors are inaccessible, & some of the upper walls have no support. These errors appear on scrupulous examination, & no one was more surprised on discovery of them, that the designer.—Elegant, but impracticable designs,—which in their execution bring discredit on the art, are however not the only unpleasant rivals of those of professional men. Workmen,—who are supposed to know more of expense & construction, than mere tasteful amateurs,—are always deficient, in arrangement. In private building their ~~only~~ own wants & habits govern their plans of dwellings for gentlemen of quite different wants & habits;—and in public buildings they generally have recourse to books.—Excepting when books describe & delineate works of merit, actually executed,—they generally have been published by men, whose want of business, & of course, of experience, has given them leisure to speculate, & to build castles in the Air. Of this kind are almost all the books of Architecture with which I am acquainted, as Thomas's, Paine,—Noan's, &c &c &c.—out of all which a judge of architural merit, can gather valuable materials; but in distinguishing beauties from defects.—

Having determined never to submit a plan to any public body which should not be so digested in its minutest arrangements as to satisfy my own mind of its practicability, & eligibility; & which, in case of my death or absence, should not be sufficient to guide my successor to its perfect completion,—I find it extremely inconvenient & humiliating to devote a month's time to making a complete set of drawings & calculations, & to collecting such information respecting the materials to be had, the contracts to be procured, & the expense attending them — as would authorize a risk of reputation, — and this only for the chance of being preferred to the Amateur, & workman who many enter the lists against me. — It is the misfortune of our country, that in most instances men of natural genius, who have had little instruction, and less opportunity of improvement are preferred to men, who have expended the best part of their lives in endeavoring to acquire that knowledge which a good Architect & Engineer ought to possess. I have in all those instances, in which I have taken my chance with others, been thrown out by some such genius, & I have an habitual dread of them. They have, either as possessing the confidence of building committees, or holding a seat in the committee often made me repent that I have cultivated my profession in preference to my farm. And it is Because I have no means of preventing the inroads of these gentlemen upon the steadiness, the consistency, & energy of my system of operations, unless I were on the spot, that I feel particularly reluctant to offer a plan for a work to be erected at so great a distance.

But should even my plan be adopted, the sum of 350 Dollars (which is the reward offered by the S. Carolina Trustees) is a very inadequate reward only for the labor it would cost me, deducting the actual expense of my office. For before the fair & decisive drawings can leave the office a voluminous map of drawings of the whole detail must be made, first in the rough, and then in two fair copies, one for myself, the other for my employer.

In one late instance, however, similar to the present the flattering request of a gentleman high in the public, as well as in my private respect has induced me to give a design for the City hall in New York. I have done so under the express stipulation, that I shall not be considered as a Candidate, if even ~~should~~ my design shall be preferred, ~~it shall not~~ unless I have the sole direction of the work, appointing my own superintendant, — and at the same time rendering myself fully responsible for the success of my plans, & for conduct of the Superintendant. On these terms I have executed the two great works which have been committed to my care here. They have secured to the public a consistency, an uniformity & a promptness of operation, which cannot be expected from the measures of any Committee; & to myself, — the satisfaction of perfect success. —

After taking up so much of your time, — for which I hope you will pardon me, — I beg leave to say, that I will send to you a design for the S. Carolina College; — not laboriously elaborated, but fairly sketched, — & leave it you to do with it as you please, — provided, — if it should be thought worthy of worthy of preference, — I shall be permitted to send a person to superintend the work. — I will then send also the detailed drawings & instructions, & if possible visit the spot myself once, which will be sufficient. — As to compensation, — there will be no difficulty in arranging it with me. I shall be very easy on the subject, if the terms of contract over the erection are liberal, & I can assure myself, that my character will not, — (as it does most disgracefully at Richmond in Virginia) desend [*sic*] upon the improvements & embellishments of another. — I must however solicit, that you will please to inform me what number of Professors & Students it is intended to accommodate in the house, & whether Stone or Brick is to be employed. — Great accuracy is not required; — your ideas, if you have not perfect information, will be sufficient. —

I hardly know how to apologize for having taken up so much of your time & patience in answering your polite letter.—I beg you will however consider my readiness to transmit to you a design,—as it sincerely is intended,—as a proof of my wish to prove to you how respectfully I am,

Your obliged faithful humble Servt.,

B. Henry Latrobe.

The many marks of haste in the above arise from my wish to answer by return of post, & I must beg you to excuse them.[1]

Notes

Chapter 1
The College Library before the Library Building

1. Dorothy Gail Griffen, "The Eighteenth Century Draytons of Drayton Hall," Ph.D. diss., Emory University, 1985, 343, 389n96. *John Drayton for himself, & as next friend of his sister Mary Drayton, an infant, vs. Charles Drayton & others, Executors of John Drayton, deceased,* case 84, March 1793, cited in Henry William DeSaussure, *Reports of Cases Argued and Determined in the Court of Chancery of the State of South Carolina, from the Revolution to December, 1813, Inclusive* (Columbia: Cline & Hines, 1817), 1:324–31.
2. Hamlin, *University Library in the United States,* 16, 148. See also Louis Shores, *Origins of the American College Library, 1638–1800* (New York: Barnes & Noble, 1935), 30, 166.
3. Shores, *Origins of the American College Library,* 162.
4. Edward Hooker, *Diary of Edward Hooker, 1805–1808* (Washington, D.C.: Government Printing Office, 1897), 852. Hooker mentioned that the college had ordered 5,000 books; he said there were 3,000 when he visited. Subsequent historians have reiterated his description of the collection. The 1807 catalog of the library lists 2,671 volumes.
5. Bryan, *Architectural History of the South Carolina College,* 42–43.
6. Shores, *Origins of the American College Library,* 15, 18, 167; Hamlin, *University Library in the United States,* 12, 13.
7. *By-Laws of the South Carolina College as Revised and Enacted by the Trustees in December, 1847* (Columbia: A. S. Johnston, 1847), 16.
8. *By-Laws of the South Carolina College, as Revised and Adopted by the Board of Trustees . . . 1853* (Columbia: R. W. Gibbs, 1853), 66.
9. Terms designating books by size are imprecise. By tradition a folio is approximately 12 × 19 inches. A quarto is traditionally approximately 9½ × 12 inches. An octavo is traditionally approximately 6 × 9 inches, and a duodecimo is about 5 × 7⅜ inches.
10. J. A. C. Chandler, *The South in the Building of the Nation* (Richmond: L. H. Jenkins, 1909), 11:435. Elisha Hammond was the father of James Henry Hammond, governor of South Carolina from 1842 until 1844.
11. Everhart, "South Carolina College Library," 225, 227, 231.
12. Patrick Scott, "Two Hundred Years of Rare Books and Literary Collections at the University of South Carolina," in Matthew J. Bruccoli, ed., *Dictionary of Literary Biography Yearbook: 2000* (Detroit: Gale Group, 2000), 281–92.
13. Margaret Babcock Meriwether, ed., *The Carolinian Florist of Governor John Drayton of South Carolina, 1766–1822* (Chicago: R. R. Donnelley, 1943), 1. See also Allen H. Stokes Jr., "Governor John Drayton: USC Founder and Benefactor." *Ex Libris* (1996): 19–20.
14. Patrick Scott, *Heart of a Great University,* 2. This catalog provides a concise overview of highlights of the library collections.
15. *Laws of the South-Carolina College, Provisionally Adopted by the Trustees at Their Annual Meeting in December, A.D. 1806* (Columbia: D. & J. J. Faust), 9–11.
16. Arthur T. Hamlin, *The University Library in the United States* (Philadelphia: University of Pennsylvania Press, 1981), 32.

17. *Amendments of the By-Laws of the South Carolina College Adopted December 4, 1849* (Columbia: A. S. Johnston, 1851), 4.
18. *Norton's Literary Gazette and Publishers' Circular,* December 13, 1853.
19. *Laws of the South-Carolina College . . . 1806,* 7.
20. Ibid., 11.
21. Hamlin, *University Library in the United States,* 36.
22. Edwin L. Green, *A History of the University of South Carolina* (Columbia: State Co., 1916), 294.
23. John Belton O'Neall, *The Annals of Newberry* (Charleston: Courtenay, 1859), 107–8. For a partial list of the antebellum librarians, see Green, *History of the University,* 459–60.
24. Minutes of the Board of Trustees, December 10, 1835, 2:387.
25. Minutes of the Board of Trustees, December 17, 1817, vol. 1. Hollis, *University of South Carolina,* 1:45.
26. "The Librarian shall hold his office for one year, and as a compensation for his services shall receive a salary of six hundred dollars." *By-Laws of the South Carolina College,* 35.
27. LaBorde, *History of the South Carolina College,* 160–76.
28. *Catalogue of the Library of the South Carolina College* (Columbia: A. S. Johnston, 1849); Michael Sugrue, "We Desired Our Future Rulers to Be Educated Men: South Carolina College, the Defense of Slavery, and the Development of Secessionist Politics," in Robert Geiger, ed., *The American College in the Nineteenth Century* (Nashville: Vanderbilt University Press, 2000), 105, 109, 114.
29. Hollis, *University of South Carolina,* 1: 99.
30. Ibid., 1:94, 119, 116.
31. E. W. Johnston, comp., *Catalogue of the Library of the South Carolina College: The Books Placed under an Analytical Arrangement, and Their Titles Abridged* (Columbia: Telescope Printers, 1836), i.
32. Ibid., iii–vii.
33. E. W. Johnston to Langdon Cheves Jr., September 25, 1836. West MSS. A.L.S, South Carolinana Library, University of South Carolina.
34. Perhaps Patrick Henry, or Robert Henry, professor of moral philosophy, logic, rhetoric, and belles lettres and president of the college, 1843–45.
35. NEH Project Staff, *An Inventory and Guide to the Archives of the St. Louis Mercantile Library Association* (St. Louis: St. Louis Mercantile Library Association, 1989), ix, 3–10.
36. Hollis, *University of South Carolina,* 1:93. See also Board of Trustees' Minutes, November 30, 1831.
37. Appendix 1, President Barnwell's Report to the Board of Trustees, November 29, 1837, provides a summary of projects undertaken at the outset of his administration.
38. Board of Trustees' Minutes, December 8, 1836, 2:406.
39. Board of Trustees' Minutes, November 28, 1838, 2:31–32.

Chapter 2
Robert Mills and the College Library

1. For a history of the early campus buildings, see my *Architectural History of the South Carolina College.* For Robert Mills's life and work, see Helen Mar Pierce Gallagher, *Robert Mills* (New York: Columbia University Press, 1942); Rhodri Liscombe, *Altogether American: Robert Mills, Architect and Engineer, 1781–1855* (New York: Oxford University Press, 1994); and Bryan, *Robert Mills.*
2. Hamlin, *University Library in the United States,* 29. Hamlin notes, "It was the University of South Carolina that led the way with the first building to be planned for and solely devoted to library purposes (1840). It was in every way a fine building which avoided mistakes made by Harvard (1841), Yale (1846), Williams (1846), Amherst (1853) and others."
3. Robert Mills, *Statistics of South Carolina Including a View of the Natural, Civil, and Military History, General and Particular,* (Charleston, SC: np, 1826), 421–22; David Kohn and Bess Glenn, eds., *Internal Improvement in South Carolina 1817–1828,* (Washington,

DC: Privately printed, 1938), 105, 150–56; Nora M. Davis, "Public Powder Magazines at Charleston," *Yearbook of the City of Charleston, 1942* (Charleston, 1944), 208; Bryan, *Robert Mills,* 189–92.

4. *Laws of the South Carolina College Adopted by the Board of Trustees . . . Various Resolutions of the Legislature, Extracts from Governors' Messages and Other Important Matters Relating to the College* (Columbia: A. S. Johnston, 1848), 60–61.
5. Bryan, *Robert Mills,* 214.
6. Stephen B. Barnwell, *The Story of an American Family* (Marquette, Mich., 1969), 108.
7. Ibid., 111; see also LaBorde, *South Carolina College,* 243–51
8. Barnwell, *Story of an American Family,* 110.
9. Hollis, *University of South Carolina,* 1:126.
10. Ibid., 1:127.
11. Ibid., 1:127–28.
12. Green, *History of the University,* 45, says, "Hon. Robert W. Barnwell of Beaufort was elected president at the annual meeting December 2, 1835. . . . The college regained its old position in the affection of the people as if by magic and grew beyond the capacity of the old buildings so that new dormitories and professors' houses had to be erected."
13. The new dormitories became Elliott and Pinckney. Hollis, *University of South Carolina,* 1:131–33. The faculty residence became Lieber.
14. Board of Trustees' Minutes, December 8, 1836, 2:406.
15. *Washington (D.C.) Daily National Intelligencer,* January 30, 1837. Skip Moskey brought the advertisement to my attention, and I am grateful.
16. Pamela Scott, ed., *Guide and Index to the . . . Microfilm Edition of the Papers of Robert Mills* (Wilmington, N.C.: Scholarly Resources, 1990). Pamela Scott, ed., "Robert Mills' 1836–1840 Journal," in *Guide and Index to the Scholarly Resources Microfilm Edition of the Papers of Robert Mills, 1781–1855* (Wilmington, DE: Scholarly Resources, 1990), 169, microfilm 4006.
17. There is no record of a Mr. Ridgeway, or Ridgway, associated with the college in any capacity, nor was anyone named Ridgeway or Ridgway paid by the state during the period 1838–43. One man, Robert Ridgeway, is listed in the census of 1840, but he lived in the Williamsburg District, and nothing indicates he had anything to do with the college. The 1840 census also lists five small farmers in the Sumter District who spelled their name "Ridgway." The "Mr Ridgway of Columbia" mentioned by Mills remains a mystery.
18. For Latrobe's Baltimore library project, see Talbot Hamlin, *Benjamin Henry Latrobe* (New York: Oxford University Press, 1955), 497–98.
19. Pamela Scott, *Guide and Index,* I/0671; Mills to John Hoffman, July 19, 1817.
20. Financial constraints forced the alteration of a number of Mills's proposals; examples include the Baltimore Washington Monument, the South Carolina Asylum, and the Washington National Monument.
21. Glenn Brown, *History of the United States Capitol* (Washington, D.C.: Government Printing Office, 1900), 1:104.
22. 25th Congress, 3rd Session, Senate, December 4, 1838, 244.
23. For Mills's use of symbolic form, see Pamela Scott, "Robert Mills and American Monuments," in John M. Bryan, ed., *Robert Mills, Architect* (Washington, D.C.: American Institute of Architects Press, 1989), 143–77. For the significance of the dome in Western architecture, see E. Baldwin Smith, *The Dome: A Study in the History of Ideas* (Princeton: Princeton University Press, 1950).
24. The contract is transcribed as Appendix 2.
25. Robert Mills, *Papers of Robert Mills*, 4006, 47.
26. Ibid., 107.
27. Mills, *Journal*, 72.
28. Ibid., 77, 105, 106.
29. Robert Mills, *Guide to the Capitol of the United States Embracing Every Information Useful to the Visitor Whether on Business or Pleasure* (Washington, D.C.: Privately printed, 1834), 29–31.
30. Hamlin, *University Library in the United States,* 147.

31. Nikolaus Pevsner, *A History of Building Types* (Princeton: Princeton University Press, 1976), 94, suggests that the origins of the type date from the thirteenth century.
32. Robert Mills, "The Progress of Architecture in Virginia," unpublished manuscript, qtd. in Gallagher, *Robert Mills,* 155–56. For the social and political implications of the Greek Revival in South Carolina, see McInnis, *Politics of Taste.*
33. *Camden (S.C.) Gazette,* October 19, 1820.
34. *Columbian Centennial,* October 31, 1821.
35. *Southern Agriculturist and Register of Rural Affairs,* September 1835, 8–9.
36. *Edgefield (S.C.) Advertiser,* January 17, 1839.
37. For E. B. White, see Beatrice St. Julien Ravenel, *Architects of Charleston* (Charleston: Carolina Art Association, 1964), 183–202; also see Severens, *Charleston, Antebellum Architecture and Civic Destiny,* 139, 140. Barnwell did not linger in Beaufort. He was a delegate to the secession convention and a senator in the Confederate government during the war. Financially pressed after the war, he returned to the South Carolina College as a faculty member, and from 1877 or 1880 until his death in 1882, he served as the college librarian. Hollis, *University of South Carolina,* 1:141; Green, *History of the University,* 105.
38. Robert Stockton pointed out the Walker connection, and we spent a pleasant morning visiting the College of Charleston library. The entrance to the Bulfinch Library of Congress was through one of the narrow ends of the rectangular room; thus Walker's plan mirrors Mills's rather than the original. For Walker see John M. Bryan, *Creating the South Carolina State House* (Columbia: University of South Carolina Press, 1999), 19–30; also see Severens, *Charleston, Antebellum Architecture and Civic Destiny,* 140.
39. Liollio Architecture, *A Historic Structure Report Architectural Development and Historical Alterations: The Old Beaufort College Building, University of South Carolina Beaufort, Beaufort South Carolina* (Charleston: Liollio Architecture, 1998).

Chapter 3
The College Library, 1840–1932

1. W. N. Chattin Carlton, "College Libraries in the Mid-Nineteenth Century," *Library Journal,* November 1907, 479.
2. Hamlin, *University Library in the United States,* 29.
3. Quoted in Ridge, *Load of Gratitude,* 4.
4. Quoted in ibid., 6.
5. Ibid., 10.
6. Ibid., 68.
7. Ibid., 71.
8. For a full account of the Audubon/Bachman relationship, see Jay Shuler, *Had I the Wings: The Friendship of Bachman and Audubon* (Athens: University of Georgia Press, 1995).
9. Audubon to G. W. Featherstonhaugh, December 7, 1831, qtd. in Ridge, *Load of Gratitude,* 9.
10. Ibid.
11. Alice Ford, ed., *The Bird Biographies of John James Audubon* (New York: Macmillan, 1957), 169–70. The last Carolina parrot died at the Cincinnati Zoo on February 21, 1918.
12. Today illustrations in bird guidebooks, including those endorsed by the Audubon Society, often reflect the pre-Audubon, static silhouette tradition.
13. Audubon, *Audubon and His Journals,* May 1, 1827, 1:297.
14. See Charles Waterton, "Miscellaneous Intelligence," *Magazine of Natural History and Journal of Zoology, Botany, Mineralogy, Geology and Meteorology* 6 (1833): 464–68.
15. Charles Waterton, "On Snakes, Their Fangs and Their Mode of Procuring Food," *Magazine of Natural History and Journal of Zoology, Botany, Mineralogy, Geology and Meteorology* 8 (1835): 663–64.
16. Quoted in Ridge, *Load of Gratitude,* 54.
17. Robert Henry, *The Cultivation of the Fine Arts Favorable to the*

Perfection of Private Character (Columbia: Privately printed, 1840), 6–15. Also see Professor Henry's *Eulogy on the Late Honorable John Caldwell Calhoun* (Columbia: I. C. Morgan, 1850), 48–49.

18. Sugrue, "We Desired Our Future Rulers to Be Educated Men," 114.
19. Gov. James H. Hammond, son of the first South Carolina College librarian, opened the state military academies that had been approved by the legislature on December 20, 1842. See "Origin of the State Military Academies Re-published from Russell's Magazine," pamphlet, South Caroliniana Library, University of South Carolina. For President Thornwell's critique of the academies, see C.C.T., *South Carolina Military Academies* (Charleston: C. Mortimer, 1854), 191–204.
20. Walter L. Fleming, *General W. T. Sherman as College President* (Cleveland: Arthur H. Clark, 1912), 19–37.
21. Patrick Scott, *Heart of a Great University,* 10.
22. Library Records, Bound Volumes, box 6.
23. Library Records, Bound Volumes, box 6, Circulation, 1849–70, 17–24.
24. Charles R. Mack and Henry H. Lesesne, eds., *Francis Lieber and the Culture of the Mind* (Columbia: University of South Carolina Press, 2005). This collection of fifteen scholarly papers presented at a symposium (November 9–10, 2001) in Columbia, South Carolina, demonstrates how one collection of manuscripts may be used to illuminate a variety of topics.
25. John S. Preston wrote Francis Lieber (February 18, 1859) that Baron von Humboldt complimented one of Oscar's publications as "the most satisfactory work . . . met with on American geology." "Calendars of Manuscript Collections in the South Caroliniana Library," Francis Lieber Collection, 1820–1951, unpublished, bound typescript, 175–254. Concerning Oscar, see Graham Duncan, "Oscar Montgomery Lieber and the 1860 Eclipse Expedition," *Caroliniana Columns,* Fall 2009, 8–10.
26. Patrick F. Roughen, "Francis Lieber and the South Carolina College Library: An Examination of a Scholar's Academic Library Use," 2013, ANZLH E-Journal, Refereed Paper No. 3, 1; Roughen quotes Gary D. Solis, *The Law of Armed Conflict: International Humanitarian Law in War* (Cambridge: Cambridge University Press, 2010), 46.
27. Hamlin, *University Library in the United States,* 152.
28. Robert W. Gibbes, *Daily South Carolinian,* July 8, 1857. Quoted by Hollis, *University of South Carolina,* 1:205. The "Guard House Riot," February 17–18, 1856, erupted when one hundred students, armed presumably with their cadet corps rifles, attempted to free a classmate from the city jail. See Hollis, *University of South Carolina,* 1:197.
29. John Hillary Gary Papers, 1859–1937, Manuscripts, South Caroliniana Library, University of South Carolina.
30. Minutes and Rolls of the Clariosophic Literary Society, March 20, 1858, October 30, 1858, January 16, 1858, February 20, 1858, April 24, 1858, and February 26, 1859.
31. Minutes of the Board of Trustees, April 12, 1861: The committee met to consider "the application of Mr. J. Gary, Captain of the College Cadets, to visit the governor of the State, and tender his company for the attack on Fort Sumter." The committee noted their duty was to "maintain the regular exercises of the college" and therefore to discourage any student from entering military service.
32. Mary Boykin Chesnut, *A Diary from Dixie* (Boston: Houghton Mifflin, 1949), 39.
33. Minutes of the Board of Trustees, 1850–1873, May 8, 1861.
34. Chesnut, *Diary from Dixie,* 488, 456–57, 465–66.
35. William T. Sherman, *Memoirs* (Bloomington: Indiana University Press, 1957), 277.
36. Trustees' Minutes, 1850–1873, November 1, 1865.
37. Special Committee, Report Recommending the Senate Use the S.C. University Library as a Meeting Hall for the Remainder of the Session, *Journal of the Senate,* December 17, 1868, 94–95.
38. "Statutes at Large, XIV," in *By-Laws of the University of South Carolina, 1866*, 22, qtd. in Hollis, *University of South Carolina,* 2:45,

and House Journal, Regular Session, 1868–69, 123, qtd. in Hollis, *University of South Carolina,* 2:50. The House moved to the chapel in Rutledge, for the acoustics in Longstreet proved to be unsuitable.

39. For the most complete study of Greener's life, see Michael Robert Mounter, "Richard Theodore Greener: The Idealist, Statesman, Scholar and South Carolinian," Ph.D. diss., University of South Carolina, 2002.

40. Everson's dramatic escape and subsequent testimony may explain his departure from the library and state without giving notice. For his account of his narrow escape, see *Report: 42nd Congress, 1st Session, Senate: no. 1. Condition of Affairs in the Southern States* (Washington, D.C.: Government Printing Office, 1871), 330–49.

41. Michael Robert Mounter, "Richard Theodore Greener and the African American Individual in a Black and White World," in Underwood and Burke, *At Freedom's Door,* 134–35.

42. Trustees' Minutes, October 30, 1875.

43. Ibid. Greener concluded by requesting the board to pay him for "services rendered from May 14, 1875 the time I began to act, until Oct. 31, 1875, in which event I shall be able to pay my assistants." He also "respectfully suggest[ed] that I be, at least allowed the salary which would have been paid to the Librarian." The centennial book Greener mentioned contains a "Table of Public Libraries" and a narrative synopsis of the history and highlights of the South Carolina College collection. The table lists library holdings in each state, and it shows that South Carolina had one library having twenty-seven thousand volumes in 1875. The South Carolina College narrative, the earliest concise history and description of the collection, must be Greener's preface or the work of an editor using his forty-page manuscript. The narrative is transcribed as appendix 3. U.S. Bureau of Education, *Public Libraries in the United States of America* (Washington, D.C.: Government Printing Office, 1877), 79, 221–22.

44. Ibid., vii.

45. An eloquent—albeit silent—echo of the Jim Crow era is found in Green, *History of the University,* 283–85. Neither Everson or Greener appear in this purportedly complete list of librarians, and this despite the fact that writing about the library of the University of South Carolina ten years earlier, Green had quoted at length from Greener's 1875 manuscript. Green attributes the quotation only to "a former librarian." Green's essay, like his *History,* contains a list of librarians, and here too Everson and Greener are conspicuously absent. *Bulletin of the University of South Carolina: Library,* no. 7 (October 1906): 1, 7–9.

46. *A Facsimile of Frank Leslie's Illustrated Historical Register of the Centennial Exposition, 1876* (New York: Paddington, 1974), 67.

47. The organizers of the National Exposition regretted the lack of participation from the South, for the only negative note in their final report is that "in one respect only the Exhibition did not quite come up to our anticipations. We were anxious to see . . . Southern States . . . joining more heartily in the social and semi-political features of the year. . . . The masses of the American people desired to make long strides in the Centennial year toward perfect reconciliation. Divine Providence gave us a splendid opportunity to shake hands. There has been a great deal done, but I wish there had been more."

48. Carol Kammen and Norma Prendergast, *Encyclopedia of Local History* (Walnut Creek, Cal.: AltaMira, 2000), 299.

49. Hugh Hawkins, *Pioneer: A History of the Johns Hopkins University, 1874–1889* (Ithaca: Cornell University Press, 1960), 224–32.

50. Jeremy Belknap to Ebenezer Hazard, February 19, 1791, and August 21, 1795, qtd. in Dunlap, *American Historical Societies,* 65.

51. Daniel Vivian to the author, December 10, 2008, and Daniel Vivian, "The Leisure Plantations of the South Carolina Low Country, 1900–1940," Ph.D. diss., Johns Hopkins University, 2011. Also see Cuthbert and Hoffius, *Northern Money, Southern Land.* Stephen G. Hoffius's introduction, xiii–xxv, provides a concise overview of this phenomenon.

52. Allen Stokes to the author, February 1, 2016. He compiled a list

titled "Collections That Got Away but Are Thankfully Preserved Elsewhere."

53. Roberta Copp, *Caroliniana Columns,* Autumn 1998, 2. At the third annual meeting of the South Caroliniana Society, Charles A. Beard said that McKissick may have been referring to Lyman C. Draper of Wisconsin. Beard quotes "McKissick's felicitous phrase" as "literary carpetbaggers from outlandish parts." University South Caroliniana Society, report of the Secretary and Treasurer for 1941, 21.
54. Hollis, *University of South Carolina,* 2:179.
55. *Proceedings of the Centennial Celebration of South Carolina College, January 8, 9, 10* (Columbia: State Co., 1905), 54–56.
56. Andrew C. Moore, "The Character and Scope of a Museum for the South Carolina College," *Bulletin of the South Carolina College*, no. 4 (January 1906), 8.
57. *Bulletin of the South Carolina College,* no. 4 (1906).The *Bulletin* contains essay by Andrew C. Moore, "The Character and Scope of a Museum for the South Carolina College"; David Strobel Martin, "The Mineralogical and Geological Cabinets of South Carolina College"; J. W. Babcock, "Babcock Collection of Indian Relics"; Edwin L. Green, "The Indians of South Carolina"; Yates Snowden, "A Manuscript Collection"; C. W. Bain, "A Museum of Archaeology"; Patterson Wardlaw, The Need of a Pedagogical Museum"; and George Armstrong Wauchope, "An Educative Collection of Art Reproductions."
58. Snowden, "A Manuscript Collection," 33–34. Three short essays conclude the January *Bulletin;* each demonstrates how various disciplines could use the proposed museum. C. W. Bain, professor of Greek and Latin, contributed a short essay arguing for a museum of archaeology or, better yet, a new department of archaeology. Patterson Wardlaw, dean of the Department of Education, expressed the need for a "Pedagogical Museum." He said that in youth, "a large percentage of impressions that are lasting are received through the eye"; consequently objects are a critical component of education, and a university museum would show teachers how to use objects in their work. South Carolina established a State Museum in 1973. See John M. Bryan, *The South Carolina State Museum* (Columbia: South Carolina Museum Foundation, 2000).
59. Edwin L. Green, "A New Library Building," *Bulletin of the South Carolina College,* no. 7 (1906): 10.
60. Trustees' Minutes, March 8, 1906, 440.
61. Elizabeth D. English, comp., and Robert M. Kennedy, ed., *Author List of Caroliniana in the University of South Carolina Library* (Columbia, 1923), v.
62. "RLM: An Unintentional Librarian," *South Carolina Librarian* vol. 4, no. 1 (1959): 10.
63. Lesser, *Palmetto State's Memory,* 5, n22.
64. Daniel Walker Hollis, "Yates Snowden Cut Colorful Swath through University's Early Years," *Alumni News,* October 1990, 4.
65. Lesser, *Palmetto State's Memory,* 1.
66. Act 559: An Act to Provide for the Appointment of a Historical Commission of the State of South Carolina, for the Purpose of Collecting and Preserving all Matter Relating to the History of the State, Acts and Joint Resolutions of the General Assembly of the State of South Carolina, 1894, 832–33. Also see Act 453, Acts and Joint Resolutions . . . 1905, 906–10, which defines the "duties and powers" of the Historical Commission.

Chapter 4
Collecting Caroliniana

1. M[argaret] H. Rion to Yates Snowden, June 17, 1905. Snowden Collection, South Caroliniana Library. The collection contains ten thousand letters, forty-five scrapbooks, two thousand volumes, and five thousand pamphlets, all assembled by "the most accomplished collector South Caroliniana of his generation." *University South Caroliniana Society Report* (1937), 10–11.

2. H[avilah] Babcock to Yates Snowden, August 2, 1929, Snowden Collection. This Babcock, grandson of the doctor who formed the collection of South Carolina Native American artifacts, became a professor of English at the university. He was known for his hunting stories and his course titled I Want a Word.
3. See *Selected Correspondence of Yates Snowden: Correspondence with Other Colleges, 1896–1933.* South Caroliniana Library.
4. W. E. Dodd, University of Chicago, to Dr. Mitchell, President, University of South Carolina, August 16, 1909. Library Administrative Files, box 7, file 1891–1910, Caroliniana Collection.
5. Hennig, *August Kohn,* 28–29, 50, 198.
6. The Kohn-Hennig Collection, donated to the library in 1999, contains around 4,000 items. A. S. Salley's collection related to the writings of William Gilmore Simms includes 482 titles. See Allen H. Stokes Jr., "The Henry P. Kendall Collection and the Kohn-Hennig Library Find New Homes at the South Caroliniana Library," *Caroliniana Columns,* Spring 2001, 1–3. Also see Allen H. Stokes Jr., *The Kohn-Hennig Library: A Catalogue* (Columbia: South Caroliniana Library, University of South Carolina, 2011).
7. English and Kennedy, *Author List of Caroliniana,* v.
8. "Exhibition Honors Carolina Women," *Gamecock,* March 9, 1978, 3.
9. M. H. Rion Lib to Dr. Mitchell, January 13, 1910. Library Administrative Files, box 7, file 1891–1910.
10. Trustees' Minutes, June 8, 1912, 155, 159, 169. Rion's letter of resignation is dated May 31, 1912.
11. See "Alcove 5. F. Continued. Listed Jany 3, 1898." Library Administrative Files, box 7, file 1891–1910.
12. H. E. Hariman, Atlanta, Ga., to S. C. Mitchell, October 24, 1909, and S. C. Mitchell to H. E. Hariman, November 4, 1909, Records of the President, University Archives, University of South Carolina.
13. Report of Librarian to Lib. Com. (March 1, 1912) for the First Term of 1911–1912, South Caroliniana Library, University of South Carolina.
14. Stone, *American Library Development,* xiii–ix.
15. English and Kennedy, *Author List of Caroliniana,* v. Much of this material must have been shelved elsewhere.
16. Ibid., 329. The manuscripts listed in appendix D are "Autobiography," by William John Grayson; an original draft of the temporary constitution of South Carolina, 1776; and an autobiography by William Campbell Preston.
17. George A. Wauchope was an English professor who published several studies of South Carolina writers.
18. Acknowledging the accession of the "Abney Memorial Library," the trustees noted that "it is probably the most valuable individual donation ever made to the University." Trustees' Minutes, June 1922, 8. The Abney collection consisted of 280 books and 300 pamphlets related to South Carolina and 250 law books. The projected "Abney Library" appendix was never published.
19. Trustees' Minutes, 1910–1925, President's Report, September 1921, 5.
20. Ibid., December 3–4, 1924, 229.
21. Ibid., June 10, 1925, qtd. in Chandler, "Dialogue with the Past," 75.
22. William D. Melton, "Report to the General Assembly of the State of South Carolina," *Bulletin of the University of South Carolina,* no. 137, February 1, 1924, 12.
23. For the most complete study of Johnson's life and work, see Chandler, "Dialogue with the Past."
24. John E. Wells and Robert E. Dalton, *The South Carolina Architects, 1885–1935: A Biographical Dictionary* (Richmond: New South Architectural Press, 1992), 209–19.
25. Chandler, "Dialogue with the Past," 89–94.
26. "Caroliniana is Moved into New Quarters," *Gamecock,* March 9, 1928, 7. This space has been partitioned into a suite of small offices.
27. Snead and Company Iron Works acquired a license to use metal stacks designed by Bernard Richardson Green, an engineer working on the Library of Congress. As a metal fabricator, the Snead Company made the 908 cast-iron steps in the Washington National Monument. See Snead and Company Iron Works, *Library Planning*

Bookstacks and Shelving (Stamford, Conn.: Architecture Press, 1915). See also Baumann, *Influence of Angus Snead Macdonald.*

28. Pevsner, *History of Building Types,* 107; R. S. Smith, "The History of Academic Library Buildings," in J. Thompson, ed., *University Library History: An International Review* (New York: Saur, 1980), 138–41; Bauman, *Influence of Angus Snead Macdonald.*

29. Baumann, *Influence of Angus Snead Macdonald,* 266–77.

30. Leonard T. Baker to J. Carroll Johnson, August 17, 1926. Papers of William D. Melton. Chandler, "Dialogue with the Past," 107–8. While the library wings were being built, Johnson was working on Sloan College (1927) and the field house (1926–27; demolished c. 1965). He subsequently designed the Melton Observatory (1928), an addition to Barnwell College (1929), and Wardlaw College and the adjacent Drayton Hall (1930–31). The Great Depression caused a hiatus, but afterward Johnson was responsible for the design and construction of the J. Marion Sims College (1939), the Caro-Vet (University Terrace) Apartments (1946), the War Surplus Buildings (1946–47), expansion of Carolina Stadium (1948), Petigru College (1949), Sumwalt College (1951), and the Osborne Administrative Building (1951). See Chandler, "Dialogue with the Past," 310.

31. Trustees' Minutes, October 25, 1927, 46; March 17, 1928, 73.

32. Ibid., June 12, 1928, 88.

33. Ibid., June 13, 1928, 91.

34. Ibid., December 9, 1931, 267.

35. Ibid., June 4, 1935, 478–79.

36. Robert Lee Meriwether, *The Expansion of South Carolina, 1729–1765* (Philadelphia: Porcupine, 1974), v.

37. Lesser, *Palmetto State's Memory,* 19–21.

38. Meriwether*, Expansion of South Carolina,* 263–67. For the use of state records in theses directed by Meriwether at this time, see Anne King Gregorie, "Indian Trade of Carolina in the Seventeenth Century," M.A. thesis, University of South Carolina, 1926, 79; Leah Townsend, "Baptists in South Carolina, 1698–1783," M.A. thesis, University of South Carolina, 1926, 77; Robert Woodward Barnwell Jr., "The Beginnings of the Revolution in the Back Country of South Carolina," M.A. thesis, University of South Carolina, 1928, 67–69; Frederick Van Clayton, "The Settlement of Pendleton District, 1777–1800," M.A. thesis, University of South Carolina, 1930, 89–90.; Carla Kathleen Singleton, "The South Carolina Council during the Proprietary Period," M.A. thesis, University of South Carolina, 1931, 80–82; Mary Neel Baker, "The Economic History of Abbeville District, 1860–1876," M.A. thesis, University of South Carolina, 1931, 55–56; Joab Maudlin Lesesne, "The Catawba Indians from Earliest Times to the American Revolution," M.A. thesis, University of South Carolina, 1932, 90–95.

39. *Report of the Historical Commission of South Carolina to the General Assembly of South Carolina at the Regular Session of 1932* (Columbia: Joint Committee on Printing, 1932), 4.

40. Lesser, *Palmetto State's Memory*, provides a vivid account of Salley's whole career. For a concise review of the Meriwether/Salley relationship and its influence on the creation of the South Caroliniana Library, see Kathryn Graham, "Keeping South Caroliniana in South Carolina: The Origins of the South Caroliniana Library," M.A. thesis, University of South Carolina, 2007. Also see Ashley Daniele Stevens, "Becoming an Archivist: Alexander Samuel Salley, Jr. and the South Carolina Historical Commission," M.A. thesis, University of South Carolina, 2001.

41. Report of Special Library Committee (January 1931), 1, Library Administrative Files, Records of the President, University Archives, South Caroliniana Library.

42. Ibid., 8.

43. Ibid., 10–11.

44. *The Proceedings of the South Carolina Historical Association 1931* (Columbia: R. L. Bryan, 1931), 1. Dodd served as American ambassador to Germany from 1933 until 1937; in 1934 he also served as president of the American Historical Association.

45. "Instructions to Contributors," South Carolina Historical Association. Inscribed at the head of this typescript: "[c. 1931] Style Sheet for Proceedings of the S.C. Historical Association when R. L. M. started it," Papers of Robert Lee Meriwether and Margret Babcock Meriwether, South Caroliniana Library, University of South Carolina.
46. Whitehill, *Independent Historical Societies,* 190.
47. "Report for 1937," *Proceedings* (1938), 1. In South Carolina 595 people were employed on WPA library-related projects; another 114 workers inventoried public records. See Lawrence M. Pinckney, "A Statistical Summary of WPA Operations in South Carolina," typescript, Federal Works Agency, 1941, 21; see also Office of the President, Leonard T. Baker, 1933–1934, box 3 (April 27, 1934), Miss Addie H. Hughes, Supervisor Historical Project, to L. T. Baker, President.
48. "Report for 1937," *Proceedings* (1938), 68.
49. "Report for 1939," *Proceedings* (1940), 5.
50. Ibid. Harvey Teal remembers this location as being in the basement of Wardlaw College — the first significant location of off-site storage.
51. Ibid.
52. R. L. Meriwether to McKissick, January 13, 1937; undated leaflet; R. L. Meriwether to President J. Rion McKissick, November 15, 1937. Office of the President, J. Rion McKissick (1937–1938), box 9, folder "University Caroliniana Society," South Caroliniana Library.
53. L. T. Baker, President, to President John C. Hegeman, November 3, 1933 (Office of the President, box 3 [1933–1934]); L. T. Baker to George Bell Timmerman, February 26, 1934 (Office of the President, box 2 [1933–1934]). See also L. T. Baker, President, "to the Committee to supervise and investigate requests of state institutions for loans or grants from the Public Works Commission, September 18, 1933" ["First Request" inscribed at head of typescript], (Office of the President, box 3 [1933–1934], folder "PP: Public Works Administration.")
54. Office of the Present, Box 3 (1933–1934). Letters mentioning additions include J. Rion McKissick to Senator James F. Byrnes, November 27, 1936; J. Rion McKissick to Senator R. M. Jefferies, December 22, 1936; J. Rion McKissick to Senator J. D. Parker, December 22, 1936; D. E. Huger to Senator James F. Byrnes, December 24, 1936; Solomon Blatt to Sen. James F. Byrnes, December 29, 1936; and Harry R. Hughs to Sen. James F. Byrnes, January 5, 1937.
55. Lesser, *Palmetto State's Memory,* 22–25.
56. Statement of J. Rion McKissick, president-elect of the University . . . requesting passage of House Bill No. 2359. President's Office, McKissick, J. Rion (1936–1937), box 2 (n.d.: January–May, 1936). McKissick underlined the words in the quotation.
57. Minutes of Committee on New Library, June 29, 1938, Papers of Robert Lee Meriwether and Margaret Babcock Meriwether. See appendix 4.1. This collection is unprocessed and is cited hereafter as "Meriwether Papers." See appendix 4.1.
58. Ibid. For the location of the new library and the demolition of the President's House, see Trustees' Minutes, Committee on Building and Grounds, August 8, 1938, 310; for funding see ibid., October 26, 1938, 348; for laying the cornerstone, see ibid., November 6, 1939, 163; and for Hibbs see Wells and Dalton, *South Carolina Architects,* 70–71, and Henry F. Withey and Elise Rathburn Withey, *Biographical Dictionary of American Architects (Deceased)* (Los Angeles: Hennessy and Ingalls, 1970), 284–85. Plans for the dedication were announced in the *Gamecock,* May 9, 1941, 1.
59. Trustees' Minutes, June 6, 1939, 70–71.
60. Ibid. For Edwin Seibels's suggestion that the old library be used as "an administrative building," see ibid., July 8, 1938, 283, and December 13, 1939, 208.
61. Meriwether Papers, transcribed as appendix 4.4.
62. Robert Lee Meriwether, "Report," *University South Caroliniana Society Report of the Secretary and Treasurer for 1940,* 1. As the trustees did not vote on his suggestion, Hughs raised the issue again; see ibid., January 6, 1939, 70.

63. Trustees' Minutes, September 3, 1940, 345, and Robert M. Kennedy to J. Rion McKissick, May 14, 1940, Records of the President, University Archives, University of South Carolina.
64. John H. Latane [?] to R. L. Meriwether, April 11, 1931; Robert Greenfield to R. L. Meriwether, May 2, 1931; R. L. Meriwether to R. H. Wienefeld, May 12, 1931. Meriwether Papers.
65. Trustees' Minutes, President's Report, December 5, 1940, 378–79. The memorandum is transcribed as appendix 4.2B. A description of the purpose and organization of "The University South Caroliniana Society" by Meriwether is transcribed as appendix 4.3.
66. Ibid.
67. Trustees' Minutes, Meeting of the Joint Committees on Finance and University Activities, July 23, 1940, 330, 337.
68. I&O, University of South Carolina (S. C. Col.), South Caroliniana Library, receipt of Material Transferred from Main Library, May 19, 1941, parts 1 and 2.
69. *Columbia (S.C.) State,* October 5, 1941.
70. Trustees' Minutes, President's Report, December 14, 1941, 180.

Chapter 5
The South Caroliniana Library

1. Trustees' Minutes, January 1941–November 1943, President's Report, December 8, 1942, 290.
2. Roberta VanHouten Copp, "South Carolina's Historic Records Survey: 1935–1942," M.A. thesis, University of South Carolina, 1988, 2.
3. Talbot Hamlin, *Greek Revival Architecture in America* (New York: Dover, 1964), 55. The first edition was published in 1944.
4. For Eric Gugler see William Seale, *The President's House: A History* (Washington, D.C.: White House Association, 1986), 2: 941–44. For Julian P. Boyd see Charles Moritz, ed., *Current Biography Yearbook, 1976* (New York: Wilson, 1976), 58–61; also see Julian P. Boyd, "Custodians of the Democratic Tradition," *University South Caroliniana Society Report* (1941), 16–25; and for the correspondence, see Julian P. Boyd to R. L. Meriwether, June 22, 1948; Eric Gugler to R. L. Meriwether, June 24, 1948, and R. L. Meriwether to Julian P. Boyd, June 29, 1948. Meriwether Papers.
5. Philip M. Hamer, "Remarks on the Occasion of the Publication of Volume I of *The Papers of John C. Calhoun,*" October 19, 1959, 1. Meriwether Papers, box 16.
6. Ibid., 2–3. See appendix 5.1 for the full text of Hamer's speech praising Meriwether.
7. Ibid, 3–4. *The Papers of Thomas Jefferson* preceded the National Historical Records Publication program. Hamer chaired a session titled "Editing the Papers of Great Men" at the twenty-second annual meeting (1956) of the Southern Historical Association. Meriwether spoke there about the Calhoun project; James F. Hopkins read a paper on the papers of Henry Clay; and William H. Runge made a presentation on the twenty-two-volume series devoted to the writings of James Madison. Holman Hamilton, "The Twenty-Second Annual Meeting," *Journal of Southern History* 23, no. 1 (February 1957): 75. These presentations were not published, and there is no copy of Meriwether's remarks among his papers.
8. Harvey Teal, personal interviews with the author, South Caroliniana Library, March–April 2016.
9. "Harvey S. Teal Oral History Interview," October 30, 2015, Office of Oral History at the South Caroliniana Library (SCLOH), 199, 2.
10. Ibid., 4.
11. Teal, *Partners with the Sun.*
12. See Martha M. Daniels and Barbara E. McCarthy, eds. *Mary Chesnut's Civil War Photograph Album,* vol. 2 of Mary Chesnut's Illustrated Diary Mulberry Edition Boxed Set (Gretna, La.: Pelican, 2011).
13. Courtney Siceloff to "Jack," November 10, 1961; Courtney Siceloff to E. L. Inabinett, January 9, 1962. Erwin Lester Inabinett Papers,

folder "Correspondence 1949–1980." See also oral history interview (SCLOH), William Savage and Les Inabinett, April 9, 1987.

14. Siceloff to Inabinett, February 5, 1962. Erwin Lester Inabinett Papers, folder "Correspondence 1949–1980."
15. SCLOH, William Savage and Les Inabinett, April 9, 1987.
16. Elizabeth Siceloff to Inabinett, April 5, 1962. Erwin Lester Inabinett Papers, folder "Correspondence 1949–1980." James W. Patton (1900–1978) was the director of the Southern Historical Collection from 1948 until 1967. There appears to be no record of the discussion within the university.
17. Columbia Garden Club, *Caroliniana Memorial Garden,* a scrapbook, MP vol. bd., 1960–1961. David E. Abeel, News [Release] from USC, July 26, 1960. See also Hal Brunton, *Renovation and Restoration of the USC Horseshoe: A Memoir* (Columbia: South Caroliniana Library, 2002), 94–95. This first garden lasted little more than a decade, for underground steam pipes and construction on the north facade of the library uprooted everything. In the early 1980s, Mary Taylor, as president of the University South Caroliniana Society, led the redevelopment of the garden as it exists today.
18. Allen Stokes Jr., email to the author, May 4, 2016.
19. Ibid., George C. Rogers, Jr. to Lester Inabinett, November 19, 1971. Erwin Lester Inabinett Papers, folder "Correspondence 1949–1980." Professor Rogers lamented the fact that "Dabbs' papers were going to Chapel Hill . . . they would have come to us if we had gone out and asked for them." He urged Inabinett to try to acquire "the papers of the S. C. Council on Human Relations and those belonging to Alice Spearman."
20. Thomas L. Johnson, interview with the author, South Caroliniana Library, March 2016.
21. SCLOH, William Savage and Les Inabinett, April 9, 1987.
22. Ibid.
23. Terry et al., *Telling the Story,* 10.
24. *Gamecock,* July 6, 1972, and September 9, 1976. William H. Patterson, president of the university from 1974 until 1977, approved the creation of the museum and archives. He was also responsible for the restoration of the nineteenth-century buildings on the Horseshoe in 1974–76 and for placing it on the National Register of Historic Places. Architect John Califf, as a consultant to the university, directed the restoration of the buildings.
25. Terry wore many hats. In addition to serving as the curator of history and the first director of the museum from 1976 until 1988, he was system vice president for administration with statewide responsibilities (1988–91) and vice provost and dean of libraries (1991–2001).
26. Kate Boyd, Heather Gilbert, Chris Vinson, "The South Carolina Digital Library (SCDL): What Is It and Where Is It Going?" *South Carolina Libraries* 2, no. 1 (2016). http://scholarcommons.sc.edu/scl_journal/vol2/iss1/3.
27. Kate Boyd, interview with the author, May 9, 2016; Kate Boyd, email to the author, May 10, 2016.
28. Allen Heath Stokes Jr., "John H. Montgomery: A Pioneer Southern Industrialist," M.A. thesis, University of South Carolina, 1967; and Allen Heath Stokes Jr., "Black and White Labor and the Development of the Southern Textile Industry, 1800–1920," Ph.D. diss., University of South Carolina, 1977. Also see Margaret Belser Hollis and Allen H. Stokes, eds., *Twilight on the South Carolina Rice Fields: Letters of the Heyward Family, 1862–1871* (Columbia: University of South Carolina Press, 2010).
29. Author's interview with Allen Stokes, April 2018
30. Stokes, *Guide to the Manuscript Collection,* and Stokes, *Kohn-Hennig Library.*
31. Allen H. Stokes Jr., interview with the author, April 2016.
32. Herbert J. Hartsook served as director of the Caroliniana from 2003 until 2005.
33. The Latrobe letter is transcribed as appendix 5.2.

34. Burton, "Reconstructing South Carolina's History," 2.
35. Carol Bleser, ed., *The Hammonds of Redcliffe* (Columbia: University of South Carolina Press, 1997), xi.

Appendix 1
Barnwell to the Honorable Board of Trustees . . .

1. Robert Woodward Barnwell Papers, South Caroliniana Library.

Appendix 2
Construction Contract and Specifications

1. *Micellaneous Files.* SCL.

Appendix 3
A Description of the University of South Carolina Library . . ., 1877

1. U.S. Bureau of Education, *Public Libraries in the United State of America* (Washington, D.C.: U.S. Printing Office, 1876), 121–22.

Appendix 4
Minutes of Various Committees

1. Meriwether Papers.
2. Trustees' Minutes, President's Report, December 5, 1940, 378–79.
3. Meriwether Papers.
4. Ibid.
5. Ibid.

Appendix 5
Remarks on the . . . Publication of The Papers of John C. Calhoun

1. Meriwether Papers.

Appendix 6
Benjamin Henry Latrobe to John Ewing Colhoun

1. The Papers of John Ewing Colhoun. No reference to the letter appears in Talbot Hamlin's biography of Latrobe. I found a typescript of it in the South Carolina Department of Archives and History and published it in *An Architectural History of the South Carolina College* (Columbia: University of South Carolina Press, 1976), 123–25. Edward C. Carter, ed., *The Microfiche Edition of the Papers of Benjamin Henry Latrobe* (Clifton, N.J.: Maryland Historical Society, 1976), fiche 165, E6, also contains a typescript. Neither typescript contains a salutation identifying the recipient. The *Latrobe Papers* mistakenly indexed Colhoun as "Calhoun." Allen Stokes found the original letter in March 2016 while working on the Papers of John Ewing Colhoun. The accession number of this collection, no. 184, suggests it was acquired in the late 1930s or 1940s. Colhoun was a U.S. senator from South Carolina in 1802. He apparently contacted Latrobe as an interested citizen, for he was not involved officially with the South Carolina College. See also James L. Green, *Our Honored Relation* (Greenville, S.C.: Southern Historical Press, 2009), 156ff. The "fairly sketched" design Latrobe said he would send Colhoun is unknown.

Bibliography

Audubon, Maria R. *Audubon and His Journals.* Vol. 1. New York: Scribner, 1897.

Barker, Tommie Dora. *Libraries of the South, A Report on Developments, 1930–1935.* Chicago: American Library Association, 1936.

Baumann, Charles H. *The Influence of Angus Snead Macdonald and the Snead Bookstack on Library Architecture.* Metuchen, N.J.: Scarecrow, 1972.

Bryan, John M.. *An Architectural History of the South Carolina College, 1801–1855.* Columbia: University of South Carolina Press, 1976.

———. *Robert Mills: America's First Architect.* New York: Princeton Architectural Press, 2001.

———, ed. *Robert Mills, Architect.* Washington, D.C.: American Institute of Architects, 1989.

Burton, Orville Vernon. "Reconstructing South Carolina's History *Through* the South Caroliniana Library." In *The University South Caroliniana Society Eighty-First Annual Meeting*, 2–25. Columbia: Privately printed, 2017.

Bye Laws of the South-Carolina College, Enacted by the Trustees at Their Annual Meeting, in December, 1804. Columbia: D. & J. Faust, 1805.

Catalogue of Books Belonging to the South-Carolina College Library. Columbia: Printed by Daniel & J. J. Faust, 1807.

Catalogue of the Library of the South Carolina College. Columbia: Printed by A. S. Johnston, 1849.

Catalogue of the Library of the South Carolina College: The Books Placed under an Analytical Arrangement, and Their Titles Abridged. Compiled and Published by the Librarian of the College. By Order of the Hon. the Board of Trustees. Columbia: Telescope Print, 1836.

Chancellor, John. *Audubon, a Biography.* New York: Viking, 1978.

Chandler, Andrew Watson. "Dialogue with the Past—J. Carroll Johnson, Architect, and the University of South Carolina, 1912–1956." M.A. thesis, University of South Carolina, 1993.

Chesnut, Mary Boykin. *A Diary from Dixie.* Edited by Ben Ames Williams. Boston: Houghton Mifflin, 1949.

Copp, Roberta VanHouten. "South Carolina's Historic Records Survey: 1935–1942." M.A. thesis, University of South Carolina, 1988.

Cuthbert, Robert B., and Stephen G. Hoffius, eds. *Northern Money, Southern Land: The Lowcountry Plantation Sketches of Chlotilde R. Martin.* Columbia: University of South Carolina Press, 2009.

Dickson, Paul. *The Library in America.* New York: Facts on File, 1986.

Dunlap, Leslie W. *American Historical Societies, 1790–1860.* Madison: Privately printed, 1944.

Everhart, Frances B. "The South Carolina College Library." *Journal of Library History* 3, no. 3 (1968): 221–41.

Forbes, Janet L. "A Comparison of the Collections of Four Colonial Libraries." M.A. thesis, University of South Carolina, 1990.

Foshay, Ella M. *John James Audubon.* New York: Abrams, 1997.

Graham, Kathryn. "Keeping South Caroliniana in South Carolina: The Origins of the South Caroliniana Library." M.A. thesis, University of South Carolina, 2007.

Green, Edwin L. *History of the Buildings of the University of South Carolina.* Columbia: Bryan, 1909.

Hamlin, Arthur T. *Greek Revival Architecture in America.* New York: Dover, 1964.

———. *The University Library in the United States: Its Origins and Development.* Philadelphia: University of Pennsylvania Press, 1981.

Hennig, Helen Kohn, *August Kohn: Versatile South Carolinian.* Columbia: Vogue, 1949.

Henry, Robert. *The Cultivation of the Fine Arts Favorable to the Perfection of Private Character and the Development of Public Prosperity.* Columbia: Privately printed, 1840.

———. *Eulogy of the Late John Caldwell Calhoun Delivered at Columbia, South Carolina Thursday, May 16, 1850.* Columbia: Morgan, 1850.

Hollis, Daniel Walker. *University of South Carolina: College to University, Volumes I and II.* Columbia: University of South Carolina Press, 1956.

Hosmer, Charles B., Jr. *Presence of the Past: A History of the Preservation Movement in the United States before Williamsburg.* New York: Putnam, 1965.

Johnson, Thomas L. *A Day in May.* Hartsville, S.C.: Coker College Press, 1996.

———. "James McBride Dabbs: A Life Story." 2 vols. Ph.D. diss., University of South Carolina, 1980.

Kammen, Michael. *Mystic Chords of Memory: The Transformation of Tradition in American Culture.* New York: Vintage Books, 1993.

LaBorde, Maximilian. *History of the South Carolina College.* Charleston: Walker, Evans & Cogswell, 1874.

Lesser, Charles H. *The Palmetto State's Memory: A History of the South Carolina Department of Archives and History, 1905–1960.* Columbia: South Carolina Department of Archives and History, 2009.

McInnis, Maurie D. *The Politics of Taste in Antebellum Charleston.* Chapel Hill: University of North Carolina Press, 2005.

Meriwether, Nicholas. "Robert L. Meriwether and the South Caroliniana Library." *Provenance: Journal of the Society of Georgia Archivists* 21, no. (2003): 5–21.

Merrill, James M. *William Tecumseh Sherman.* Chicago: Rand McNally, 1971.

Metcalf, John. *Information Retrieval, British & American, 1876–1976.* Metuchen, N.J.: Scarecrow, 1976.

Pollard, Edward A. *The Lost Cause: A New Southern History of the War of the Confederates.* New York: Treat, 1867.

Rains, Albert, and Laurance G. Henderson, eds. *With Heritage So Rich.* New York: Random House, 1966.

Ridge, Davy-Jo Stribling. *A Load of Gratitude: Audubon and South Carolina.* Columbia: Thomas Cooper Library, 1985.

———, ed. *Rare Book Collection in the McKissick Memorial Library, the University of South Carolina.* Columbia: McKissick Memorial Library, 1966.

Rowland, Lawrence S., Alexander Moore, and George C. Rogers Jr. *The History of Beaufort County, South Carolina,* vol. 1, *1514–1861.* Columbia: University of South Carolina Press, 1996.

Scott, Patrick. *The Heart of a Great University: A Bicentennial Exhibit Charting Two Hundred Years of USC Libraries.* Columbia: Thomas Cooper Library, 2001.

Severens, Kenneth. *Charleston, Antebellum Architecture and Civic Destiny.* Knoxville: University of Tennessee Press, 1988.

Sherman, William T. *Memoirs of General William T. Sherman by Himself.* Bloomington: Indiana University Press, 1957.

Stokes, Allen H., Jr. *A Guide to the Manuscript Collection of the South Caroliniana Collection.* Columbia: South Caroliniana Library, University of South Carolina, 1982.

Stone, Elizabeth W. *American Library Development, 1600–1899.* New York: Wilson, 1977.

Sugrue, Michael. "South Carolina College: The Education of an Antebellum Elite." Ph.D. diss., Columbia University, 1992.

Teal, Harvey S. *Partners with the Sun: South Carolina Photographers, 1840–1940.* Columbia: University of South Carolina Press, 2000.

George D. Terry, et al. *Telling the Story, 1801–2001.* Columbia: McKissick Museum, University of South Carolina, 2004.

Underwood, James Lowell, and W. Lewis Burke, eds. *At Freedom's Door: African American Founding Fathers and Lawyers in Reconstruction South Carolina.* Columbia: University of South Carolina Press, 2000.

Weyeneth, Robert R. *Historic Preservation for a Living City, Historic Charleston Foundation, 1947–1997.* Columbia: University of South Carolina Press, 2000.

Whitehill, Walter Muir. *Independent Historical Societies: An Enquiry in Their Research and Publication Functions and Their Financial Future.* Lunenburg, Ver.: Stinehour, 1962.

Williams, Timothy J. *Intellectual Manhood: University, Self, and Society in the Antebellum South.* Chapel Hill: University of North Carolina Press 2015

Index

Page numbers in italics refer to illustrations.